INTERNATIONAL POLITICAL ECONOMY SERIES

General Editor: Timothy M. Shaw, Professor of Political Science and International Development Studies, and Director of the Centre for Foreign Policy Studies, Dalhousie University, Nova Scotia, Canada

Recent titles include:

Pradeep Agrawal, Subir V. Gokarn, Veena Mishra, Kirit S. Parikh and Kunal Sen
ECONOMIC RESTRUCTURING IN EAST ASIA AND INDIA
Perspectives on Policy Reform

Solon L. Barraclough and Krishna B. Ghimire
FORESTS AND LIVELIHOODS
The Social Dynamics of Deforestation in Developing Countries

Jerker Carlsson, Gunnar Köhlin and Anders Ekbom
THE POLITICAL ECONOMY OF EVALUATION
International Aid Agencies and the Effectiveness of Aid

Edward A. Comor (*editor*)
THE GLOBAL POLITICAL ECONOMY OF COMMUNICATION

O. P. Dwivedi
DEVELOPMENT ADMINISTRATION
From Underdevelopment to Sustainable Development

John Healey and William Tordoff (*editors*)
VOTES AND BUDGETS
Comparative Studies in Accountable Governance in the South

Noeleen Heyzer, James V. Riker and Antonio B. Quizon (*editors*)
GOVERNMENT–NGO RELATIONS IN ASIA
Prospects and Challenges for People-Centred Development

George Kent
CHILDREN IN THE INTERNATIONAL POLITICAL ECONOMY

Laura Macdonald
SUPPORTING CIVIL SOCIETY
The Political Role of Non-Governmental Organizations in Central America

Gary McMahon (*editor*)
LESSONS IN ECONOMIC POLICY FOR EASTERN EUROPE FROM LATIN AMERICA

The Move to the Market?

Trade and Industry Policy Reform in Transitional Economies

Edited by

Paul Cook
Senior Lecturer in Economics
The University of Manchester

and

Frederick Nixson
Reader in Economics
The University of Manchester

St. Martin's Press

First published in Great Britain 1995 by
MACMILLAN PRESS LTD
Houndmills, Basingstoke, Hampshire RG21 2XS
and London
Companies and representatives
throughout the world

A catalogue record for this book is available
from the British Library.

ISBN 0–333–58825–8

10 9 8 7 6 5 4 3 2 1
04 03 02 01 00 99 98 97 96 95

Printed and bound in Great Britain by
Antony Rowe Ltd, Chippenham, Wiltshire

First published in the United States of America 1995 by
Scholarly and Reference Division,
ST. MARTIN'S PRESS, INC.,
175 Fifth Avenue,
New York, N.Y. 10010

ISBN 0–312–12404–X

Library of Congress Cataloging-in-Publication Data
The move to the market? : trade and industry policy reform in
transitional economies / edited by Paul Cook and Frederick Nixson.
p. cm. — (International political economy series)
Includes bibliographical references and index.
ISBN 0–312–12404–X
1. Free enterprise—Developing countries—Congresses.   2. Free
enterprise—Europe, Eastern—Congresses.   3. Post-communism–
–Economic aspects—Congresses.   4. Developing countries—Commercial
policy—Congresses.   5. Europe, Eastern—-Commercial policy–
–Congresses.   6. Industrial policy—Developing countries–
–Congresses.   7. Industrial policy—Europe, Eastern—Congresses.
I. Cook, Paul, 1944- .   II. Nixson, F. I.   III. Series.
HC59.7.M68   1995
338.9'009172'4—dc20
                                                        94–23029
                                                           CIP

Contents

Part IV   Central, East and South-East Asia

Part V   Sub-Saharan Africa

Part VI   Conclusion

List of Figures

List of Tables

List of Abbreviations

ADB	Asian Development Bank
ASEAN	Association of South East Asian Nations
cif	Carriage Insurance and Freight
CIS	Confederation of Independent States
CMEA	Council for Mutual Economic Assistance (Comecon)
CPE	Centrally-planned Economy
DFI	Direct Foreign Investment
DPRK	Democratic Peoples Republic of Korea
EC	European Community
EEC	European Economic Community
EFTA	European Free Trade Association
EPZ	Export Processing Zone
ERP	Effective Rate of Protection
fob	Free on Board
GATT	General Agreement on Tariffs and Trade
GDP	Gross Domestic Product
GDR	German Democratic Republic
GMP	Gross Material Product
GNP	Gross National Product
HDI	Human Development Index
IBRD	International Bank for Reconstruction and Development
ICOR	Incremental Capital Output Ratio
IMF	International Monetary Fund
ITC	International Trade Centre
JV	Joint Venture
LDC	Less Developed Country
MVA	Manufacturing Value Added
NGO	Non-Governmental Organization
NIC	Newly Industrialising Country
OECD	Organization for Economic Cooperation and Development
PTA	Preferential Trading Agreement
R&D	Research and Development
RENAMO	Movement for National Resistance in Mozambique
SADCC	Southern African Development Coordination Conference
SET	Socialist Countries in Transition
SITC	Standard Industrial Trade Classification

SLORC	State Law and Order Restoration Council
SoE	State-owned Enterprises
SSE	Small-Scale Enterprises
UNCTAD	United Nations Conference on Trade and Development
UNCTC	United Nations Centre for Transnational Corporations
UNDP	United Nations Development Programme
UNIDO	United Nations Industrial Development Organisation
USSR	Union of Soviet Socialist Republics

Preface and Acknowledgements

This volume is concerned with the economic issues raised by the move of the socialist and ex-socialist centrally planned economies towards more market-orientated economic systems. In particular, the contributors to the book examine the key role that trade and industrial sector policy reforms are likely to play in the process of transition.

The transitional process itself continues to be a topic of debate, both in terms of the concept itself and in terms of the means by which it is to be achieved. Prior to the 1980s, there was little previous experience either with countries relinquishing 'socialism' or totally abandoning central planning. The People's Republic of China led the way in 1978, followed by other Asian and African economies in the mid-1980s, and Eastern European economies and the former Soviet Union (USSR) towards the latter part of the 1980s. To varying degrees, these economies have undergone major economic reforms, which have lessened the direct control that governments exercised over economic affairs and have led to greater reliance being placed on the market mechanism.

There are differences of opinion concerning the speed with which reforms should be implemented and the relative emphasis to be given to specific reforms, as well as to their sequencing. There is also controversy concerning the extent to which economic reforms should be preceded or accompanied by political changes. Again, the degree to which countries have undertaken political reforms varies widely. Most of all, however, there is disagreement over the relative importance of stabilization and structural adjustment programmes. Proponents of the former tend to minimize the difficulties that may be encountered in establishing the institutions and economic environment necessary for a market-orientated economy. Those that emphasize the need for structural adjustment focus on supply-side issues but are often excessively 'price-ist' and underestimate the problems that constrain the emergence of a dynamic private sector. The relationship between the state and the market rarely features in these controversies.

The contributions to this volume throw some light on these issues through a number of carefully documented case studies which examine the way various countries have approached reform, with particular reference to the industrial and trade sectors. Most of the papers on which the chapters are based were delivered at a Workshop on trade and industry policy reform in transitional economies organised by the Development Studies Association Industry and Trade Study Group held at the University of Manchester.

The manuscript was mainly prepared by Lesley Bernardis of the Institute for Development Policy and Management (IDPM). The efficiency of her work and her patience with the Editors are more than gratefully acknowledged. Thanks go also to Jayne Hindle of IDPM and Sue Hilton, Sue Massey and Ann de Maestri of the School of Economic Studies.

PAUL COOK
FREDERICK NIXSON

Notes on the Contributors

Stephen Batstone is Lecturer in SME Management at the University of Warwick, where he teaches in the area of entrepreneurship and small business. Prior to this he was a lecturer at Leicester Polytechnic and research assistant at Trent Polytechnic. He has published papers on several aspects of entrepreneurship.

Paul Collins is Principal Consultant, RIPA International and Head of Task Force at RIPA's Transitional Economies Centre. He is Editor of *Public Administration and Development* and a member of the IIAS Scientific Committee. He was previously Principal Adviser, UNDP Management Development Programme, New York and has published widely on development management.

Paul Cook is Senior Lecturer in the School of Economic Studies at the University of Manchester. He teaches macroeconomics and development economics. He is currently researching into privatization in developing and transitional economies. He has published *Privatisation in Less Developed Countries* and *Macroeconomics for Developing Countries* (with Colin Kirkpatrick).

Pat Devine is Senior Lecturer in the School of Economic Studies at the University of Manchester where he teaches industrial economics and comparative economic systems. He is joint author of *An Introduction to Industrial Economics* and author of *Democracy and Economic Planning*. He is currently working on models of participatory decision-making and European industrial strategy.

Diane Elson is Reader in Development Economics in the School of Economic Studies at the University of Manchester. Her research and teaching interests include trade, industrialization, structural adjustment and gender analysis. Her recent publications include *Male Bias in the Development Process* (editor) (1991), and 'Uneven development and the textiles and clothing industry', in L. Sklair (ed.) *Capitalism and Development* (1994).

Peter Lawrence is Lecturer in Economics at Keele University. He teaches development, micro and macro economics, and the economics of privatization. He is co-editor of *Rural Cooperation in Tanzania* and editor of *The World Recession and the Food Crisis in Africa*. He is also author of articles on African development, UK unemployment and privatization in Hungary.

Philip F. Leeson, now retired, was Director of Development Studies and Senior Lecturer in Economics at the University of Manchester. His main teaching activity was in courses in development economics for postgraduate students. His most recent publication was as editor (with M.M. Minogue) and contributor to *Perspectives on Development* (1990).

Ian Livingstone is Professor of Development Economics in the School of Development Studies at the University of East Anglia, Norwich. His main publications include *Rural Development, Employment and Incomes in Kenya* (1986); *Irrigation Economics in Poor Countries* (1982); *Development Economics and Policy: Readings* (1981); *Lao PDR: Industrial Transition* (1994); and *Agro-Industry for Rural Employment Generation in Vietnam* (1994).

Alasdair MacBean is Emeritus Professor of Economics at Lancaster University. He is also Visiting Professor, Fudan and Peoples' Universities, China. He teaches international trade and development. He is currently engaged in research on export promotion in East Asia–lessons for East European economies. He is author of *Export Instability and Economic Development* (1966); and *Commodity Policies: Problems and Prospects* (1987, with Tim Nguyen).

Tidings Ndhlovu is Lecturer in Economics at the Manchester Metropolitan University (formerly Lecturer in Economics at the University of Manchester, UMIST and the University of East Anglia and part-time lecturer in Economics at the Universities of Essex, Liverpool and Bradford). His main teaching areas include: development economics, micro/macro economics, principles of economics, policies of the EU (formerly EEC), international trade and development, and economics for health studies. His most recent book is *Development Strategies in Zimbabwe: Rhetoric and Reality*.

Frederick Nixson is Reader in the School of Economic Studies at the University of Manchester. He teaches development economics and has a research interest in transnational corporations and economic reform in transitional economies. He has published *Economics of Change in Less*

Developed Countries (with David Colman), and *Industrial Structure and Policy in Less Developed Countries* (with Norman Lee and Colin Kirkpatrick).

Mehdi Shafaeddin is Officer-in-Charge, Trade Policy Analysis Section, International Trade Division, UNCTAD. He has published widely in the field of international trade and development. He is author of *Fallacies in Trade Policies: Recent Experience of Developing Countries*.

John Thoburn is Reader in Economics at the University of East Anglia, and author or co-author of *Primary Commodity Exports and Economics Development* (1977), *Multinationals, Mining and Development* (1981), *Foreign Investment in China Under the Open Policy* (1990), *Industrial Subcontracting in the UK and Japan* (1992), and *Tin in the World Economy* (1994).

John Weiss is Senior Lecturer in the Development and Project Planning Centre at the University of Bradford. He is an author of *Industry in Developing Countries* (1990) and joint author of *Project Analysis in Developing Countries* (1992).

Mo Yamin is Lecturer in International Business at the Manchester School of Management, UMIST. He has written extensively on the activities of transnational companies and his recent research has focused on institutional aspects of TNC behaviour and the impact of TNCs on the transition process in Eastern Europe.

Le-Yin Zhang was born and educated in China. She received her Ph.D. from University College London, in 1991 and after that studied in Germany. She is currently working as a researcher in the China Regional Development Project in the University of Greenwich, London.

Part I

Introduction

1 The Move to the Market
Paul Cook and Frederick Nixson

INTRODUCTION

The changes in the dominant economic paradigm that occurred in the late 1970s and early 1980s, with most 'mixed' economies in the world adopting more market-orientated economic strategies, was mirrored in the late 1980s by the dramatic collapse of communist states. The relinquishing of communist ideologies has resulted in these countries searching for new relationships between the state and the market. Central planning had failed to achieve the economic and social developments expected of it and the market economy was seen as the answer to the 'failures' of socialism.

Although the ending of political control by communist parties was abrupt, the manner in which economies have reacted and adjusted to the changes has varied significantly. Adjustment to a more market orientated economy has been particularly painful in many of the more highly centralized states in Eastern Europe and the former Soviet Union (USSR), where the state sector had accounted for between 65 and 95 per cent of gross domestic product (GDP) (Schwartz, 1995). In others, such as Poland and Hungary, with less rigid planning systems, adjustment has been easier. In these economies, many of the reforms had already been introduced before the formal ending of Soviet influence, and elements of the private sector had already begun to work alongside the planning system.

In contrast, the process of transition in the socialist developing countries in Asia, including the economies of Myanmar, Laos and Vietnam, has been different from that of their Eastern European counterparts. These differences can largely be explained by the underlying structural and historical conditions. In some cases the command economy was less well entrenched, and they had begun to reform within the centrally-planned system at an earlier stage. In Vietnam, for example, the non-state sector had remained a significant component in GDP throughout the centrally-planned years and it could be argued that this is a feature that has eased the prospects for transition (Cook and Kirkpatrick, 1994). Although many of the changes in the early phase of reform were directed towards improving the functioning of the state apparatus, many of the

The Move to the Market

later changes were designed to develop the private sector. These types of reform had already been introduced in Laos, for example, in the late 1970s (Cook, 1993).

The balance between adopting market orientated reforms and formally relinquishing socialism has been uneven and, in some cases, paradoxical. Vietnam has not formally abandoned socialism and has not moved to a multiparty democracy but has carried out significant economic reforms (Nixson, 1995). By contrast, Laos and Myanmar (and the states of Eastern Europe) have formally dropped socialism and undertaken econ-omic reforms. The formal relinquishing of socialism, however, does not neces-sarily correspond to the introduction of more democratic political institu-tions. This is illustrated vividly by Myanmar, where political power has become centralized in the hands of the military while some semblance of economic reform has been introduced (Cook and Minogue, 1993).

Table 1.1 provides a highly subjective interpretation of the extent and pace of economic and political reform in a number of transitional

Table 1.1 Economic and political change in transitional economies

	Economic change		Political change	
	Strong	Weak	Strong	Weak
Eastern Europe				
Hungary	X (1968)		X	
Poland	X (1986–7)		X	
Russia	X (1991)		X	
Central Asia				
Mongolia	X (1989–90)		X	
Asia				
Vietnam	X (1986)			X
Laos	X (1986)			X
Myanmar		X (1987–8)		X
Cambodia		X (early	X	
China	X (1978)	1990s)		X
North Korea		X (1990)		X
Africa				
Mozambique	X (1987)			X
Angola		X (late 1980s)		X
Zimbabwe		X (1988-9)		X

Source: Authors' assessment.
Note: The dates indicate when economic reforms were consolidated and strengthened.

economies. In general, in Eastern Europe, political change has preceded economic change, although as time has passed the economic reforms have been gaining pace. By contrast, the general picture in Asia is one of little political change, alongside significant economic reforms. Indeed, China provides a puzzling illustration of an economy that has undertaken economic reforms progressively since the late 1970s, including the substantial liberalization of the agricultural sector, but with comparatively little power change (White, 1991).

This study deals with a range of countries. Some were formally and directly under the influence of the Soviet Union and were members of the Council for Mutual Economic Assistance (CMEA). Other countries called themselves socialist but had weaker formal ties with the Eastern bloc. The ex-socialist economies, whether relinquishing socialism formally or not, can be grouped into four main geographical areas: the socialist countries of Eastern Europe; Russia and the ex-Soviet Republics; the previously developing socialist countries of South-East Asia; and those in Africa. Cuba still stands alone as an economy politically committed to socialism while embracing some (limited) market principles (Zimbalist and Eckstein, 1987).

A distinctive feature of the treatment of the issues of transformation from socialism to market orientation has been the strong segmentation of the literature along these geographical lines. The bulk of the literature has concentrated on the transitional problems facing Eastern Europe (see, for example; Knell and Rider, 1992; Clague and Rausser, 1992; Peck and Richardson, 1991). In part, this separation is linked to the differences in the objectives that underlie transition in each of the regions, and in part to differences in their historical experiences. However, all share the aim of moving from a centrally-planned to a more market-orientated economic system. Equally there is a common desire to become more integrated into the world economy and, in particular, to achieve this through closer regional associations: Eastern Europe with Western Europe, and the Asian socialist economies with the Association of South East Asian Nations (ASEAN). The Eastern European economies desire greater integration with the European Community (EC) and with the General Agreement on Tariffs and Trade (GATT). The former Soviet republics of Central Asia and Mongolia, along with pursuing independence from Russia, wish to cultivate trading opportunities with neighbours in the Middle East and Central Asia.

There are useful lessons for each economy that arise out of the experiences of transition. Along with the geographical divisions that characterize the literature, commentators have tended to discuss the problems facing the Asian socialist economies in a developmental context and those in Eastern Europe from a Eurocentric viewpoint. While the adoption of such perspectives is understandable, we believe the subject would benefit from a more integrated approach that links the processes of transition and development.

A preliminary step towards furthering this type of analysis is attempted in Table 1.1 by comparing the extent of the economic and political changes that have been introduced in each region. In some cases the changes have been extensive and rapid, and in others they have been few but substantial. Table 1.1 can only offer a stylized picture since the situation is continually evolving. Yet even from this crude assessment, we can see different geographical patterns emerging regarding the degree of economic and political reform that has been undertaken. The dates for the commencement of reforms, shown in Table 1.1, do not represent the date the earliest reforms were recorded, but rather refer to periods when the reform process was most intense and where there was little evidence of policy reversal. The distinction between strong and weak cases of reform in the political and economic spheres is based on our subjective assessment of the literature.

Despite the diversity of experience, a common feature of all countries introducing reforms has been the attention given to the trade and industry sectors. The reasons for this have varied between countries. With some exceptions, however, these were the sectors where the state was predominant and they were, therefore, obvious candidates for reform in the initial stages. The agricultural sector in much of Eastern Europe, Africa and Asia had already been transferred into private hands during the earlier periods of reform under central planning, or had remained in the private sector under communism. This was certainly the case for small-scale production. China (and to a lesser extent Russia) is probably the most vivid exception, since most of agriculture had been collectivized and put under state control soon after the coming to power of communist parties. In the Chinese and Russian economies, therefore, reforms to the agricultural sector are important elements of the process of transforming the economy.

The remainder of this chapter is organised into four parts. The second outlines the situation in the pre-reform period and highlights the main econ-omic problems faced by the centrally-planned economics. The third part reviews the different types of reform measure that have been introduced in each of the country groups and comments on post-reform economic performance. The final part draws some conclusions on transition and development.

CENTRALLY-PLANNED ECONOMICS IN THE PRE-REFORM PERIOD

The Face of Central Planning

The common feature of all the ex-socialist economics was the central role accorded to the Soviet model of planning. Most aspects of supply and distribution were subject to compulsory allocation (Ellman, 1989). In these economies all activities, including large-scale manufacturing, mining, communications, services and banking, were in the state sector. Agriculture was largely collectivized and domestic trade was organized by state-controlled marketing and distribution agencies. Among these economies the predominant mode of planning was based on a system of material balances. The allocation of materials, labour and financial resources was related to anticipated requirements for achieving predetermined supply objectives. Under this scheme, the production and consumption of products was co-ordinated. Resources, whether produced locally or imported, were balanced against the distribution of products for individual consumption and those which were used as inputs for further production and exports. Labour balances were used to co-ordinate human resources with output requirements. Financial balances were concerned with the creation and distribution of money income. Finally, demand elasticities were estimated and used to balance supply and demand. In principle, where imbalances were found, adjustments were made either to supply (through increasing output, technological improvements or substitution of inputs) or demand (curtailing wants or requirements).

Within the planning system, budgetary revenues were mainly of the non-fiscal type. These were largely generated from the public enterprises that dominated production and which contributed between 60–70 per cent of government revenue. In effect, all savings derived from the agricultural and public enterprise sectors were transferred to the government budget. In turn, these revenues were used to finance investment in infrastructure and the social sectors. In addition, some social services were provided under the auspices of public enterprises, and their social role was often quite extensive, including the provision of health, education and leisure facilities.

Another feature shared by those countries influenced by the Soviet model was the concentration within the industrial sector on heavy industry which emphasized extensive (as opposed to intensive) growth, leading to high incremental capital output ratios (ICORs). This resulted in the relative neglect of light and consumer goods sector (Meyanathan, 1989). This, as will be discussed later, was a feature more commonly found in the former socialist economies in Eastern Europe than in Asia and Africa (although Mongolia, North Korea and the former North Vietnam were exceptions in this respect). Under central planning, both capital and labour were relatively immobile. Labour was not free to move in response to market-determined supply and demand factors. Instead, human resources were often allocated to various projects and could be moved from one region to another once these projects were completed.

Performance under Central Planning

It is difficult to make direct comparisons between the performance of these economies before and after the reforms. Apart from the acute methodological difficulties of undertaking before–after analysis, the underlying database for comparison is weak. These shortcomings apply to the ways in which indicators of performance under central planning were assembled and can be interpreted. A major problem hindering a before–after comparison is the predominant use of quantitative indices of output and input use in the pre-reform era. It is also difficult to find means of judging performance when information has been based on targeted levels and expressed in terms of whether or not targets have been achieved. Besides the problem of knowing whether targets were ever established realistically in the first place, there are difficulties in interpreting results of under-fulfilled or over-fulfilled targets. Finally, estimates of performance may suffer because information is both incomplete and unreliable.

Despite these difficulties it is possible to discuss differences in the experiences of the countries under central planning both within and between the main regional groupings.

Eastern and Central Europe

The experience of the central planning period of the Eastern European economies under Soviet influence and the outcome of reform has been mixed. Romania, for example, adopted a Stalinist strategy of industrialization and the Soviet model of central planning from 1948 onwards. During that time, however, it received little help from the Soviet Union in implementing plans. Romania had to pay war reparations to the Soviet Union and lost control of most of its oil, mineral and timber resources through joint venture arrangements that favoured the Soviet Union (Ben-Ner and Montias, 1991). As with many other Eastern European countries, the bulk of investment resources were directed to heavy industry. Low-quality machinery and arms were exported to non-Soviet block countries (including Western and developing countries) in exchange for oil imports and raw materials.

In contrast, Hungary was more reformist at an earlier stage. In 1968, transition began with the adoption of the New Economic Mechanism, when detailed central planning was dropped and replaced by a system of financial and economic controls to regulate the economy (Hare, Radice and Swain, 1981).

The Bulgarian economy was less industrialized than the other main Eastern European economies of Poland, Hungary and Romania. It was virtually a peasant agricultural economy in the 1950s that urbanized and industrialized rapidly under the centrally-planned system. By the 1960s, however, it was still a predominantly agricultural-based economy. Nevertheless, it traded its growing share of industrialized goods predominantly with the Soviet Union in exchange for raw materials. Its problems, as Jackson (1991) has noted, differed from those of Hungary and Romania in that economic planners early 'faced the challenges of generating growth through improvements in total factor productivity rather than from capital accumulation combined with shifting labour from agriculture to manufacturing industry'. This led to the introduction of reforms in the 1960s in an attempt to increase the share of industry. The results of the initial reforms were disappointing and they were eventually replaced by further reforms in the 1970s and 1980s aiming to create larger-scale 'agro-based' industries. Unfortunately, the move to larger-scale had adverse effects on smaller-scale agriculture, which culminated in the decline of agricultural output and exports.

The Yugoslav economic system represented the middle ground in being not fully capitalistic nor centrally planned. The reforms introduced in this economy between 1952 and 1974 have been described as a shift from central planning to the market and represented a contrast to the reforms which followed immediately afterwards. These recentralized power in some form of bureaucratic bargaining process for allocating resources (Estrin, 1983; Estrin, 1991a). The end-product was that the Yugoslav economy, despite the earlier moves to the market, had in the mid-1980s an economic system similar to the decentralized planning systems of Poland and Hungary.

Despite the diversity of economic systems that existed within the Soviet-influenced economic planning model, all the Eastern European economies were experiencing deteriorating economic conditions during the latter part of the 1980s (Lawrence, Chapter 5 of this volume).

Asian Economies

The performance of the Asian economies and their experience with reforms varied under central planning. Reforms were introduced at different times and emanated from a variety of sources. Despite the differences, however, there have been similarities in the outcome.

The Vietnamese government, following reunification in 1975, severely curtailed the activities of the private sector in the south. It failed in its attempt to abolish all private business, however, and increasingly the policy was relaxed. Changes were made in the early 1980s that gradually permitted greater scope to the private sector and lessened the hold that rigid planning had over it (Beresford, 1989). The impatience with policy outcomes frustrated decision-makers, and appears to have accounted for the considerable uncertainty in the policy environment during the initial years of unification and central planning.

The policy of partial liberalization pursued in Vietnam during the 1980s, without relinquishing centralised control, led to what many observers described as excessive bureaucratic centralism which resulted in significant levels of inefficiency. As a consequence, economic performance declined during the 1980s, resulting in attempts to eliminate some of the more restrictive controls via the radical reforms that were introduced after 1986 (Nixson, 1992; Booth and Vo Nhan Tri, 1992).

The Laotian centrally-planned system that was introduced in 1975 also changed significantly during socialism. The strong emphasis on Soviet-style planning was later modified to incorporate elements of an indicative approach to planning, in which the government played a less directive role in determining how the objectives established by the planning process were to be met. Nevertheless, despite these changes in planning style, real GDP growth declined during the first half of the 1980s and subsequently became negative. In similar fashion to Vietnam, substantial reforms under the new economic mechanism (NEM) were introduced in 1986.

The situation in Cambodia was more complex because of the chaos left by years of civil war which had destroyed most of the infrastructure and the industrial base of the economy. It had less of the continuity with respect to political regimes under socialism than had the other Asian economies. Reliable and useful information on economic performance prior to the 1990s is not available.

In both North Korea and Myanmar economic crises have precipitated the introduction of major economic reforms and they have been labelled 'reluctant reformers' (Nixson, 1995 (for North Korea); Cook and Minogue, 1993 (for Myanmar)). In the case of Myanmar economic performance indicators had deteriorated in the 1980s under the centrally-planned regime and this was the case in spite of attempts to introduce reforms in some parts of the economy, most notably towards public enterprises (see Cook, Chapter 11 in this volume). Economic decline was particularly evident in the export sector, with the exports of rice and timber, once significant in world terms, falling to extremely low levels.

Africa

The economic performance of the economies of Ethiopia, Angola, Mozambique and Tanzania under socialist central planning has been mixed. Civil war and external intervention have led to massive destruction in the first three economies and have made the objective evaluation of economic performance impossible. Unlike the Asian transitional economies, the African economies were less isolated from the international economy and as a consequence their performance has been affected by external, as well as internal, economic factors. They were also not fully integrated into the Soviet trading system although capital goods imports from the communist bloc were a decisive element in their import structures (in Ethiopia, for example).

ECONOMIC REFORMS AND PERFORMANCE IN THE POST-COMMUNIST PERIOD

The new orthodoxy that underlines the economic reforms being introduced in the ex-socialist economies places a much greater emphasis on the role of the market mechanism in the allocation of resources. It also calls for a reduction in the size of the public sector and a withdrawal of substantial elements of public-sector intervention. Accompanying these changes is an emphasis on trade and industrial sector liberalization and deregulation.

Within the broad literature on economies in transition there are various ways of describing the reforms. First, they maybe characterized as being partial or comprehensive. Comprehensive reforms refer to the introduction of more widespread reforms covering the domestic and external trade sectors. In some cases they also refer to the reforms that have led to the broader changes between the rural and urban sectors, such as those introduced in China. Reference is also made to reforms along institutional lines, where distinctions are made between varying degrees of centralization and decentralization.

Other treatments of the issues of transition have viewed the subject primarily in terms of macroeconomic stabilization and the liberalization of various markets. This type of analysis includes the separate treatment of monetary, fiscal and external policies. The issue of structural transformation, particularly in the case of the Eastern European economies, has been confined largely to the issues of enterprise reform and privatization. The weakness of this limited view of structural change can be seen in Rybczynski's (1991) comment that 'macro stabilisation programmes do not work successfully because of the inadequate response of the supply side'. The relationship between the financial and enterprise side is usually discussed in terms of which models of corporate control and regulatory styles are the most appropriate for the transitional economies.

The reforms have also been categorized in a strategic sense on the basis of intensity and sequencing, ranging from gradualist to shock therapy approaches. The shock therapy approach, sometimes termed the 'big bang' approach, emphasizes the positive effects of rapid market liberalization, and was adopted in most of Eastern Europe (and Mongolia) in the early 1990s. This approach embraces macro reforms, liberalization and privatization. It is argued that the rapid implementation of these policies combines to improve productivity, efficiency and, in particular, investment growth rates. Exponents of this view stress that the inefficiencies and costs imposed on the economy by not acting quickly may outweigh the benefits that result from shock therapy (Shirley and Nellis, 1991) but they play down the detrimental effects for the economy that may result in the short run (Solimano, 1993).

The alternative approach argues for a more gradual introduction of the reforms and argues that shock therapy risks the adoption of suboptimal policies. This approach has been adopted in Hungary and in most of Asia. Examples of this strategy can be found in China and more recently in Laos, Vietnam and Myanmar. The gradualists argue that the rapid approach to reform can result in inflation, falling output and employment as well as harmful effects on public and private investment and consumption. They also emphasize the need to consider the order and sequencing of the reforms. In this respect, Fry and Nuti (1992) highlight the institutional issues that need to be addressed in the reform process in Eastern Europe. They suggest that the first institutional change required for transition is the transformation of the monolithic monetary and banking structure of the communist system into a multilevel, competing and pluralistic system. The second is the development of an effective tax system and the third is the development of asset markets, accompanied by substantial privatization of state property.

In contrast to the institutional and macro stabilizing approaches that have been advocated in the Eastern European economies, structural adjustment has been in the forefront of the debate over the transition of the socialist developing countries. In these economies, although elements of stabilization and policy sequencing have been important, it is the adjustment process that has been emphasized.

Regional approaches to reform have thus varied considerably. The transitional economies of Eastern Europe have adopted the 'big bang' approach to economic reform, with rapid and extensive deregulation and liberalization of various markets. This has generally been accompanied by intensive restraint on aggregate demand and monetary contraction. This contrasts with the gradualist approach to market liberalization adopted in the Asian and, to some extent, the African transitional economies. The choice of approaches has, however, been determined to a large extent by political rather than economic circumstances. It is likely that the political environment and institutional structures that have been inherited from the pre-transition period have in large part determined the speed and direction of economic changes. In Eastern Europe, as noted above, political change preceded economic changes, and the collapse of the centrally-planned system created an economic void, with only a limited market system in existence to replace the centrally-planned system of economic organization and regulations. In Asia, the economic reforms have been introduced in a context of substantial continuity in their political systems, with the changes in economic policy being introduced and managed by the ongoing regime (Myanmar: Cook and Minogue, 1993; Vietnam: Nixson, 1995; Laos: Livingstone, Chapter 12 in this volume).

Economic Performance of Transitional Economies

The macroeconomic performance of the transitional economies following reform has varied significantly. This is particularly the case when comparisons are made on a regional basis (see Tables 1.2 and 1.3). In the Asian economies, output has grown during the reform period, in contrast to the fall in output experienced by both the Eastern European economies and the ex-Soviet republics. Output has fallen significantly in Hungary, Bulgaria, Czechoslovakia and Russia, and most notably in a number of former republics. Economic performance in the African transitional economies has been constrained by the pressures of adjustment and, while not achieving the significant growth levels experienced by the Asian economies, has not suffered the dramatic collapse characteristic of the Eastern European economies and the ex-Soviet republics.

Table 1.2 Inflation in transitional economies (per cent)

	1989	1990	1991	1992
Asia				
Myanmar	27.2	17.6	32.3	30.0
Vietnam	95.8	36.4	68.1	37.7
Laos	59.5	35.7	13.4	9.8
East/Central Europe				
Hungary	17.0	28.9	36.4	23.0
Poland	251.1	585.8	70.3	43.0
Former Czechoslovakia	1.4	10.8	59.0	11.0
Bulgaria	6.4	21.6	333.5	82.6

Source: Asian Development Bank (ADB) (1993) and International Monetary Fund (IMF) (1992a).

Within the European experience, the reforms implemented in Hungary have been relatively gradual and the experience of shock therapy in Poland has led to a re-evaluation of that approach. Similarly, the European transitional economies are only just beginning to comprehend the difficulties that more structurally-orientated reforms may entail. While the options facing policy-makers, once socialism had collapsed, were limited by the economic crisis facing their economies (high inflation in Poland and Yugoslavia, for example), the initial concentration on stabilization was nevertheless one-sided, as can be seen in Table 1.4. The heavy emphasis on macroeconomic stabilization has masked the need for policies that are required at a microeconomic level and aimed at the longer term. In these economies, demand management policies and monetary constraint associated with high real interest rates were adopted. These policies, aimed at short-run stabilization, had implications for longer-term development. Indeed, the design of fiscal policy, and in particular budgetary control, is complicated for economies in transition. During the transformation process it is likely that as expenditure in one area is reduced, demand for an increase in expenditure arises in another area. Similarly, the revenue base that is important for sustaining expenditure may be eroded as a result of structural transformation. Public enterprise that had previously formed a significant element of the budgetary revenue will contribute less during structural transformation and stabilization, the effects of which tend to lower the tax base (Kaser and Allsopp, 1992). At the same time, during transition the pressure to extend the system of social 'safety nets' puts upward pressure on budgetary expenditure (McAuley,

Table 1.3 Growth of real GDP in transitional economies (per cent)

	1989	1990	1991	1992
Asia				
Myanmar	3.7	2.7	1.3	1.2
Vietnam	8.0	5.1	6.0	8.3
Laos	11.5	5.9	4.3	7.3
Cambodia	–	–	–	–
Africa				
Ethiopia	2.4	–2.5	–	–
Mozambique	5.5	1.9	–	–
Tanzania	4.8	3.6	–	–
East/Central Europe				
Albania	–27.7	–7.8	3.5	–
Bulgaria	–11.7	–5.6	–2.0	–
Former Czechoslovakia	–15.9	–8.5	–	–
Slovak Republic	–	–	–9.3	–
Hungary	–11.9	–4.4	–	–
Poland	–7.6	1.0	4.0	–
Romania	–15.1	–15.4	–2.5	–
Former USSR				
Armenia	–11.8	–40.0	–	–
Azerbaijan	–0.7	–26.3	–10.0	–
Belarus	–1.9	–10.0	–14.4	–
Estonia	–11.9	–23.3	–2.3	–
Georgia	–20.6	–45.6	–5.0	–
Kazakhstan	–13.0	–14.0	–7.5	–
Kyrgyz Republic	–5.0	–26.0	–11.8	–
Latvia	–8.3	–32.9	–10.0	–
Lithuania	–13.4	–35.0	–9.4	–
Moldova	–18.0	–21.3	–15.0	–
Russia Fed	–12.9	–18.5	–14.9	–
Tajikstan	–	–	–	–
Turkmenistan	–4.7	–5.3	3.9	–
Ukraine	–13.4	–14.0	–18.0	–
Uzbekistan	–0.9	–9.5	–5.3	–
Central Asia				
Mongolia	–9.9	–7.6	–1.3	–

Source: ADB (1993) and IMF (1992a).

1991). There is, then, a need to consider longer-term reforms of the revenue system, in particular, to ensure that as the private sector develops to complement or even replace the state-owned enterprises, it contributes to tax revenues.

Table 1.4 Stabilization and reform in Eastern Europe

	Yugoslavia	*Poland*	*Romania*	*CSFR*	*Bulgaria*
Date commenced	1989	1990	1990	1991	1991
Monetary/fiscal policy	Tight but temporary	Restraint	No restraint	Restraint	Little restraint
Devaluation	Yes	Yes	Yes	Yes	Yes
Trade liberalization	Extensive	Extensive	Little	Extensive	Little
Privatization	Some	Some	Mainly land	Slow	Slow

Source: Compiled by authors from referenced material.

The clash between stabilization and the need for longer-term structural reform is also evident in monetary policy. One of the main concerns is with the financing of the budget deficit when financial markets are under-developed. In this case, monetary policy is difficult to manage. Monetary targets are difficult to formulate since it is likely that the demand for money will vary during transition. Increases in the supply of money are used to finance deficits that domestic and foreign borrowing cannot cover. Domestic borrowing is constrained because the main source of capturing private savings is through the use of banking sector deposits which, although rising, are limited because incomes and savings are still low and the 'banking habit' might not be well developed. It is also likely that the institutional changes that are undertaken in the short run – for example, in establishing central banks and commercial banks to widen savings outlets and improve the workings of monetary policy – will initially tend to be largely cosmetic. There is a danger that institutions will be set up which operate in a vacuum because the corresponding authority to operate effectively has not been provided. It will take considerable time and reforms of a more structural nature to instil the competitive forces needed to make a previously monolithic banking structure work. This will require reforms that go beyond organizational changes. Institutional changes need to be reinforced by extensive managerial reform which, in turn, may require extensive longer-term investment in human resources.

The 'shock therapy' approach adopted by the Eastern European economies has emphasized deregulation and the merits of the private sector. Under this approach, public enterprises have been encouraged to undertake schemes of privatization. This process has proved extremely difficult and generally the pace of privatization has been slower than anticipated. Despite the enormous variety of schemes that have been used to implement privatization in the European transitional economies, ranging from self-privatization in Hungary and Poland and the establishment of investment funds for privatization in Poland, to the mass privatization programmes in the former Czechoslovakia and Russia using a voucher scheme and direct sales, progress remains slow.

In part the slow progress can be explained by the inability of the governments to undertake prior reforms that would make privatization more successful (Cook and Kirkpatrick, 1994). There have been financial and managerial resource constraints which have inhibited the scope for undertaking comprehensive programmes of enterprise restructuring and rehabilitation prior to ownership transfer. In part it is because, under shock therapy, measures to reform enterprises before privatization have been discouraged because these types of intervention have been viewed as being counter-productive (Shirley and Nellis, 1991). It is argued that the costs of delay in moving to a more market-orientated system can be quite considerable and that the private sector is more able than the public sector to undertake any necessary enterprise restructuring. This view is also concerned that intervention to restructure and rehabilitate will revert to '*ad hoc*ism' and lead to distortionary interference. Nevertheless, privatization of large-scale activities has not in general taken place in all countries and, indeed, this might give weight to a counter view that emphasizes the need for greater policy guidelines from government, particularly in relation to industrial policy.

Russia and the Ex-Soviet Republics

The republics of the former Soviet Union, and Mongolia, have experienced negative real rates of growth in GDP, as was shown in Table 1.3. These economies have also had significant levels of unemployment, inflation and, with few exceptions, budget deficits. The high rate of inflation following price liberalization has impeded the ability of the price system to allocate resources effectively and has undermined the strength of national currencies in the region. As a consequence of poor economic performance these economies have suffered substantial capital flight. The inflationary pressures have largely resulted from credit creation required to support the extensive network of subsidies, particularly to public enterprises. Subsidies continue to remain high and in Russia amounted to nearly 25 per cent of GDP in the early 1990s (World Bank, 1993).

The policy approach in these economies has emphasized price liberalization and the elimination of subsidies, fiscal stabilization, monetary restraint and trade liberalization. In general, attention to structural reform has been slower and has proved politically to be more difficult to implement. Overall though, even progress with macroeconomic stabilization has been acknowledged to be slow.

With the break-up of a single monetary authority for the former Soviet Union, the rouble area was thrown in disarray. Some countries have decided to rely on their own independent currencies rather than be tied to the monetary policy established by the Central Bank of Russia, while others are deciding whether or not to enter into bilateral relations with Russia. Although there are disadvantages, creating an independent currency has allowed countries to impose a tighter independent monetary constraint to fight inflation and to eliminate inflationary pressures by restricting credit subsidies to public enterprises. The Baltic countries of Latvia, Estonia, Lithuania and the Ukraine initially insulated themselves from the other states in the former Soviet Union, and particularly from the inflationary pressures, by introducing their own currencies (Spencer and Cheasty, 1993). Other former Soviet republics, including Kyrgyzstan and Turkmenistan, have followed this example.

Inflationary pressures also continue to remain a feature of the transition process, however, and opting for independent currency has not solved this problem. The Ukraine, with an independent currency, has an inflation rate fuelled by credit expansion for public sector expenditure that exceeds that of Russia (IMF, 1992a).

A common characteristic of all economies, whether or not in the rouble currency area, has been the shortfall in revenue and the consequent budget deficit. The withdrawal of subsidies by Russia, even those that were not explicitly in the budget, has resulted in substantial losses in government revenue. Despite reforms to the tax systems, including the introduction of value added taxes and increases in direct tax rates for businesses and personal incomes, fiscal deficits remain prevalent.

In partial recognition of these problems, the International Monetary Fund (IMF) established in 1993 a temporary structural transformation facility (STF) to support macroeconomic stabilization. Several economies have drawn on this facility, sometimes in conjunction with IMF standby credit.

The experience with privatization in the former economies of the Soviet Union has been relatively limited. Although a large number of enterprises have been privatized by one means or another, privatization has mainly been confined to small enterprises. The Baltic States, Russia and Mongolia have experienced more extensive privatization than the economies of the Ukraine, Kazakhstan, Belarus and the Kyrgyz republic, where numerous obstacles to implementation remain. In the case of Russia, Ukraine and Belarus, privatization of larger enterprises is complicated because enterprises have an important regional significance and are often in military hands. Under the former system there would have been the politics of large regional unemployment to consider, and in the current period there is resistance to privatization from the powerful military interests. The Mongolian proposals for privatization are viewed as ambitious, and have already raised questions as to their practicality and longer-term impact on the development process in that country (see Nixson, Chapter 10 this volume).

Asian Transitional Economies

In the Asian transitional economies the reasons for reform, the timing of the reform process and the emphasis given to specific measures in the reform programme have varied between countries. Nevertheless, there has been some common ground in their approaches to reform. They have all been preoccupied with legislative changes necessary for the development of an institutional framework that would facilitate the implementation of the intended policy reforms. They have all, except for Mongolia introduced economic reforms with little change in their political environments. Myanmar has witnessed the recentralization of power in the hands of the ruling party (Cook and Minogue, 1993). They all introduced reforms in a gradual manner before the collapse of the Soviet system. Major market-orientated reforms were introduced in Laos in 1985 with the New Economic Mechanism (see Livingstone, Chapter 12 this volume; Cook, 1993). Market-orientated reforms were strengthened in 1986 with the programme of restructuring ('Doi Moi') in Vietnam, and a more limited reform programme was embarked upon in North Korea in 1990 (Nixson, 1995). In the case of Vietnam, by 1989 it was argued that the allocation of resources no longer depended on the direct administrative mechanisms of the Soviet style of central planning (Fforde, 1989).

With differing degrees, the initial emphasis of the economic reforms in the Asian transitional economies has been to expose the economies to greater market forces, to open up trade and foreign investment opportunities and to strengthen the role of the private sector (Laos: Livingstone, Chapter 12, this volume; Myanmar: Cook, Chapter 11 this volume; and Vietnam and North Korea: Nixson, 1995). Sometimes the more structural reforms have been accompanied by bouts of stabilization. This was the case in Laos when the results of the initial reforms were disappointing, and policies aimed at reducing inflation and restoring equilibrium to the balance of payments had to be introduced.

Although the move to market-orientated reforms in the Asian economies began as a result of internal factors, rather than from external pressure from international financial institutions, the stabilization elements have been at the forefront of IMF's support for transition. However, Myanmar has no policy-based lending from the IMF or the World Bank, and neither has North Korea. Vietnam has only limited World Bank programmes at present, although World Bank involvement can be expected to increase with the lifting of the US embargo. It is Laos which has the most extensive support from both the IMF and the World Bank, with structural adjustment facilities and credits extending between 1989 and 1995 (Cook, 1993). However, conditionality in the Asian transitional economies appears to be less stringent than that implemented in the low-income countries of Sub-Saharan Africa.

Common to all the transitional Asian economies, including China, is the growing importance of aid from OECD members, and increasing inflows of foreign investment. There have been significant inflows of investment from Taiwan, Singapore, South Korea and Japan, and investment flows between the transitional economies themselves are already beginning to take place.

The interest in foreign investment is partially linked to the need to replace the large depleted capital stock that these economies face, much of it with vintages exceeding twenty years and made worse by the withdrawal of Soviet aid both to support new acquisitions and for the maintenance of existing equipment and machinery. The policy approach to foreign investment in these economies, as shown particularly in the case of China, is to regard investment as part of trade policy by switching from imports to foreign direct investment which brings with it new technology (see MacBean, Chapter 8 in this volume). As Zhang and Thoburn (Chapter 9 in this volume) emphasize, trade is being used as a tool of investment and not, primarily, as a means of exploiting comparative advantage. The Asian transitional economies are suitably placed geographically to benefit from the gains made in neighbouring newly-emerging technological innovators (for example, South Korea) and, in the case of China, to benefit from inward direct investment flows from overseas Chinese communities.

All the developing transitional economies of Asia face the problem of mobilizing resources for investment from the domestic economy. Both absolute levels of saving and savings ratios are low in relation to other low-income developing countries such as India (Cook, 1993). They are, however, higher in China, where household savings form a high proportion of total domestic savings. The low levels of private savings have been attributed to the reliance of socialist policy on public savings and on external support from the former Soviet Union. Both have diminished with the move to market-orientated reforms, and although taxation systems to improve the performance of public-sector savings have been undergoing structural reforms, they have not yet been adequately supplemented by commensurate increases in private-sector savings. Developments in this area will depend on the important role played by the strengthening of the institutional framework and the intermediary functions they perform, which will support the working and efficiency of financial markets (see Yamin and Batstone, Chapter 4 in this volume).

However, as in the case of the Eastern European economies, besides the low levels of income that constrain savings, potential savings do not reach market-orientated financial outlets because of the degree of uncertainty that still prevails in these economies. The source of this uncertainty, however, does appear to be different within European and Asian economies. In the former it is linked to fears of further resurgence of state control. In Asia this aspect is of less importance as there appears to be a greater acceptance of the role that the state will play in the transition process, given their greater awareness of the role that the state has played in the development of South Korea and Taiwan (Amsden, 1989).

As in the case of the European transitional economies, the Asian transitional economies have had difficulties with the implementation of programmes of privatization and public enterprise reform (Cook and Kirkpatrick, 1994). Progress with privatization has been slow (Mongolia is an exception in this respect, however) and in most instances it has been in the form of leasing arrangements, contracting out and joint ventures, particularly with foreign investors. Similarly, public enterprise reform has met with difficulties. The policy focus has largely been to provide state-owned enterprises with a greater degree of autonomy and to introduce incentive packages for management. The initial results, however, have indicated that in the case of Vietnam and Laos, the new opportunities have been exploited by enterprises that have gained new freedom, and enterprise managers (and, to some extent, workers), have rewarded themselves excessively (Cook and Kirkpatrick, 1994).

Nevertheless, the privatization and public enterprise reform programmes have been undertaken in Asia with less urgency than have their European counterparts. In part this reflects the different perspective attached to the role of privatization, which is viewed in Asia as a means to an end rather than, as in the European transitional economies, an end in itself. In the European economies, programmes of mass privatization have been attempted because the old public sector is viewed as the main source of new entrepreneurship and private-sector development. In contrast, the options for developing the private sector appear to be wider in the Asian transitional countries, since even under socialism, large segments of the economy remained in private or non-state-sector hands and a lower proportion of the public sector is in heavy capital intensive industries that will be difficult to transfer to private ownership. However, even the experience of the Eastern European countries indicates that the pursuit of privatization may not be the best policy for private-sector development and indeed, private-sector development is taking place separately from privatization (Frydman and Rapaczynski, 1993).

TRANSITION AND DEVELOPMENT

The experiences of countries undergoing changes following the break-up of communist regimes, and in the process of transition from planned to more market-orientated economies, have shown that it is difficult, if not impossible, to describe these developments with reference to a single model or ideal path to be followed. The processes of economic, political, social and institutional change that these economies are experiencing at the present time do not display enough common characteristics to allow us to describe a common process of change (Nixson, 1995). Differences with respect to historical background, contemporary economic and political structures, levels of development, degrees of industrialization, and the extent and patterns of trade, are significant. The same is true of the process of reform being undertaken by the more mixed-economy developing countries that are moving to minimalist state involvement and seeking a greater degree of market orientation.

The differing experiences of the transitional economies in Eastern Europe and Central Asia, South-East Asia and Africa have raised a number of issues for which answers have not yet been found. Indeed, it is unlikely that explanations will be very convincing until more comparative research has been undertaken. This research will need to incorporate the experiences of all countries in the process of transition and those undergoing structural change. As Leeson (see Chapter 15 in this volume) points out, development economics can most usefully be applied to the analysis of present-day transitions since it is this approach to economics that has sought to grapple with the issues of structural rigidities and structural change.

Leeson also argues that the lack of a development approach to transitional problems, particularly in Eastern Europe, has been in part because of the failure to incorporate a robust enough role for the state in the development process. This point is reiterated by Weiss (Chapter 13 in this volume) who asks why development economics was unable to provide any guidelines for the low-income socialist countries. Clearly, the Soviet centrally-planned model was not the answer. The neo-classical argument of minimalist government, however, may prove to be as equally fallible if the longer-term institutional and structural aspects of the transition process are ignored. Little is yet known of the process of structural change during transition and, in particular, of the part that the market can usefully play in the process (see Devine, Chapter 2 in this volume). We have yet to discover whether forms or intervention similar to those of South Korea and Japan are needed to ensure that the new forms of capitalism survive. As Pat Devine reminds us, we know little about the role of planning in the context of political and economic democracy because it has yet to be tried.

The explanations that have been provided for the transition process in Eastern Europe do not necessarily explain the process elsewhere. Nor are they necessarily correct when the investigation is broadened to incorporate the comparative experiences of all economies undergoing some process of transition. The decline in economic performance indicators, after the adoption of economic reforms in Eastern Europe, for instance, has been explained in a number of ways (Solimano, 1993). But the explanations proposed might have contradictory meanings if applied to the Asian economies, which have experienced faster growth but yet may have been subjected to similar external shocks.

The poor performance of the Eastern European economies and those of Central Asia has been linked to the severity with which the contraction of demand, as part of the policy of stabilization, has been applied. As such, it is viewed as only a temporary phenomenon. Similarly, the reduced emphasis on central planning and the changes in organizational structures following the break-up of communist regimes are viewed as having affected supply capabilities adversely and disrupted production processes. This occurs because the way in which vital decisions are made concerning output are conducted differently. The new reforms have been rushed and new regulations and laws are not well understood nor easily interpreted. While some restrictions have been removed they have often been replaced by other forms of regulation.

Finally, the breakup of the CMEA imposed severe external shocks to the transitional economies of Eastern Europe and Central Asia. The widespread removal of subsidies, particularly by Russia for energy exports to the republics, have had adverse income effects through terms-of-trade shocks for these countries. It has also been suggested that a too-rapid rate of liberalization has highlighted the underlying weaknesses, in terms of technological competitiveness, of the previously centrally-planned economies, which has resulted in poor export performance.

Yet the Asian transitional economies have faced similar external shocks with the breaking of trade links with the former Soviet Union and Eastern Europe, with the decline in Soviet aid and the organisational and administrative turmoil caused by the demise of central planning. Their experience has been different, however, with rapid export growth, lower inflation and high output growth.

The reasons for the differences between these two groups are complex and will be the subject of future research. They may, however, reflect differences in the range of policy options that have been available to the transitional economies. The options may be greater in the case of the Asian economies because of their shorter periods under socialism or central planning and, for some of them, their limited isolation from the international economy.

The Asian economies have been able to adjust more gradually without the application of shock therapies. They have been able to adopt this gradual approach because of the ability of the private sector to develop independently of the dismantling of the state; that is, private sector development has not been dependent on the process of privatization. The existence of small-scale entrepreneurs and significant levels of foreign investment, together with remittances from previously exiled citizens, have aided the adjustment process. The Asian economies have also been fortunate in having large public-sector concentrations of light industry relative to heavy industry, as the former are easier to privatize. As a result, the scope for more immediate private-sector development is enhanced (Cook and Kirkpatrick, 1994).

The Asian economies have also maintained extensive trading links with fast-growing neighbouring economies. It is this regional context that distinguishes the Asian transitional economies from those of the old Soviet Union and Eastern Europe whose markets were within the CMEA, and with the socialist developing countries themselves.

Finally, the potential for an easier transition must be linked to the regional prospects for growth. The Asian transitional economies are extending trade and investment relationships rapidly with neighbouring successful economies and may eventually be pulled into the new 'growth pole' that has emerged in the Pacific Rim region (World Bank, 1993).

However, as the title of this volume implies, it cannot be assumed that, even in the longer run, the transition to a fully-fledged market economy will be successful. The very notion of 'a market economy' is often abstract and ahistorical, although perhaps less so in the case of the Asian transitional economies who have the Korean and Taiwanese ' models' on their doorsteps.

For most transitional economies (although most notably at the time of writing, not China or Vietnam, and certainly not Cuba or North Korea), the move to the market is a euphemism for the establishment of the capitalist mode of production. But for years development economists have debated the possibilities for the development of capitalism in the Third World (quite apart from its observability) without yet reaching anything that could be described as a consensus.

Although most transitional economies are 'joining' the Third World (whether they like it or not) and although we have agreed that a 'development perspective' is necessary for both an understanding of the transitional process and policy prescription for transition, these economies are not always classic 'Third-World, less-developed countries' (even though they are often very poor: for example, Vietnam). The transition they are undergoing is a new experience historically; there are no examples from which lessons can be drawn and, if the 'move to the market' is likened to a journey, it could be argued that it is one for which no maps are available. The neo-classical economics textbook (which so many countries are taking as their guide) is seriously deficient in this respect and it is to be hoped that development economists will in future play a more active role, through research, training and policy advice. Without the development perspective, the objectives of reform and development can easily be lost sight of. As Singh (1993) argues, the final objectives are not marketization and privatization *per se*, but industrialization, employment and rising standards of living. Development economics brings historical, institutional and structural dimensions of transition to the forefront. It is our hope that this volume will prove to be a useful contribution to the continuing debate.

Part II

The Transition to the Market: Some Theoretical Issues

2 Alternative Possibilities for Post-Communist Economies
Pat Devine

INTRODUCTION

All modern economies combine planning and markets; they differ in the relative weights attached to each element. All hitherto centrally-planned command economies are now seeking to introduce a greater role for markets. The questions that face them are how to make the transition to a 'market economy', and what role should be played by the state in the new system they are seeking to create.

In the initial stages of the reform process, discussion focused around how to introduce a greater role for markets without allowing market forces to dominate the process of resource allocation. However, none of the attempts at reform in the period up to 1989 succeeded in combining planning and markets in a way that satisfied the requirements of both socialist values and efficiency.

Since the political revolutions of 1989–91, such attempts at finding a 'third way' have been largely abandoned. Poland, Czechoslovakia, Hungary and Russia have all in turn adopted the objective of a 'fully-fledged market economy', a euphemism now generally accepted as meaning capitalism in one form or another.

The question, of course, is, in what form: the *laissez faire* 'casino capitalism' of the USA and the UK; or the social-market capitalism of Western Europe? Whatever form it turns out to be, there is bound to be a continuing role for the state and even for some sort of economic planning.

PLANNING

The essential case for planning is that it enables *ex ante* co-ordination of interdependent decisions. Market forces operate to allocate and reallocate resources by repelling them from lower-profit activities and attracting them to higher-profit activities through the separate, atomistic decisions of enterprises acting independently of one another. The argument is that this process results in waste and human misery. In growing industries the lack

29

of co-ordination in advance results in too many resources being committed. In declining industries, resources leave through a slow process of attrition-redundancies, closures, low wages and depressed communities. At the level of the economy as a whole, market forces give rise to the familiar cycle of boom and slump, inflation and recession, acute labour shortage and mass unemployment.

Karl Marx looked forward to the ending of private ownership of the means of production as a necessary condition for ending both exploitation and the anarchy of production. He argued that if society's productive resources were owned socially, society could decide how they, as an integrated whole, should be used. The allocation and reallocation of resources could be planned in advance, before the resources were committed, on the basis of the use society wished to make of them. So private production for profit, co-ordinated anarchically by market forces, would be replaced by social production for use, co-ordinated by planning.

Soviet Administrative Command-Planning and Market-Socialism

The Soviet planning system was developed in the 1930s in order to carry through a process of rapid industrialization. It was able to mobilize resources for investment in heavy industry as the overriding priority. The repressive monolithic political system created by Josef Stalin enabled opposition to the social and human costs involved to be suppressed. A comparable system of central planning was developed in Britain during the Second World War, to concentrate resources on the war effort as the overriding priority. However, the crucial difference was that the democratic political system in Britain provided broad consensual support for the sacrifices involved.

The Soviet system was relatively successful, albeit at enormous human cost, when the task was to concentrate resources on a very limited number of overriding priorities. However, as the Soviet economy developed, the task changed to the efficient use of resources in all lines of production and the promotion of innovation, with increasing expectations by the Soviet people of living standards comparable to those in the West. The Soviet model of planning, despite attempts at reform from the mid-1960s onwards, proved incapable of meeting these expectations and has now effectively collapsed. In Eastern Europe essentially the same system, imposed after 1945, has also failed.

Why has the Soviet model proved to be historically exhausted? There are basically two reasons, to do with *information* and *motivation*. Administrative command-planning is a system in which enterprises supply information to the planners about their productive capacity, the planners decide what each enterprise should do with its productive capacity and express this in output targets, and enterprises are rewarded on the basis of the extent to which they fulfil their targets.

As the economy becomes more complex, the planners cannot handle all the information, and cannot mesh it together in a way that efficiently co-ordinates the productive activities of all the enterprises before they start production. At the same time, since enterprises are rewarded on the basis of output-target fulfilment, they have an incentive to provide the planners with biased information, in the hope of obtaining easy targets. Furthermore, since enterprises are bound by their targets, they have no incentive to respond flexibly to unforeseen changes. The result is that planners are swamped by biased information which they cannot use effect-ively, and enterprises are not motivated to make effective use of the pro-ductive resources entrusted to them.

Market socialism has been one response to this situation. It is a system in which planners set the economic environment within which enterprises operate, and enterprises compete with one another, seeking to maximize their profit and hence the rewards of those working in them. The idea is that the economic environment can be shaped to reflect overall social con-siderations, and enterprises can then be left to pursue their self-interest, which will encourage efficiency and so contribute to the social interest. Adam Smith's invisible hand becomes market socialism's consciously guided hand.

A major problem with this system arises in relation to what happens when some enterprises are more successful than others. The purpose of the system is to motivate enterprises to use productive resources efficiently by rewarding those that do so successfully, and penalizing those that do not. The result is that some enterprises will enjoy high wages and security of employment, while others will suffer low wages, redundancies and ulti-mately bankruptcy and closure. The attempt to use market forces as an instrument of planning is an attempt to find a way of disciplining produc-ers (managers and workers) to be efficient and will only work if there is an effective system of rewards and penalties.

Experience in Eastern Europe before the revolutions of 1989, especially in Hungary, confirms this analysis. Initially, market socialism was seen as a system in which major investment continued to be decided centrally by the planners, while enterprises themselves decided on the use of their existing capacity. However, enterprises were not allowed to benefit fully from high profits, partly because they sometimes arose from monopoly power; nor to suffer unduly from low profits, partly because they sometimes arose from circumstances beyond the enterprise's control. The result was continued dependence on the state and continued inefficiency.

The conclusion drawn from this experience was that enterprises would only be forced to become efficient if they were fully independent of the state, expanding or declining according to their profitability. This could only happen if investment decisions were taken by the enterprises themselves and not by the planners. It followed that the next step should be the establishment of a capital market and stock exchange to enable enterprises to raise finance for investment and to provide an institutional means for changes in the ownership and control of unprofitable enterprises.

In such a system, the allocation of resources would take place predominantly through the operation of market forces. Planners would no longer plan but would seek at most to manage the economy using fiscal and monetary policy, competition and industrial policy, prices and incomes policy, and other policy instruments designed to influence the behaviour of independent enterprises. While the ownership status of enterprises might differ, in all other respects the system would be effectively the same as managed capitalism.

State Intervention and Planning in Capitalist Economies

No capitalist economy operates solely on the basis of market forces. The state has always played a crucial role, with the degree and form of state intervention varying significantly from one historical period to another and from country to country. The role of the state has been shaped by the changing conditions that have had to be met for capitalism to continue to function effectively, including the requirements of international competitiveness, and by the pressure generated by class and social conflict.

In nineteenth century Britain the state played a minimalist but vital role in establishing and safeguarding private property rights, the laws of contract and sound money. In most other countries, notably in recent years Japan and the successful newly-industrializing countries (NICs), the state has had a much more prominent interventionist role in organizing the development of capitalism and promoting its international competitive position. In Britain during the Second World War, as has already been noted, the state operated a system of central planning to mobilize resources for the war effort.

Following the experience of the inter-war years, when world capitalism appeared close to terminal collapse, and under the influence of the perceived achievements of Soviet planning and the theories of J. M. Keynes, most advanced capitalist countries in the post-Second World War period adopted demand-management policies in order to achieve and maintain full employment. In many countries these were accompanied by interventionist policies at the level of industries and enterprises to promote restructuring and international competitiveness. At the same time, the post-war period saw the establishment, under US domination, of a system for managing the capitalist world economy, particularly international trade and payments.

By the 1970s this post-war system was beginning to unravel. The long boom ended, unemployment and inflation started to rise, and international economic instability set in, with the emergence of Germany and Japan as major economic powers, and the end of US economic supremacy. Different capitalist countries reacted differently to this new situation. Britain and the United States adopted the most extreme form of market-orientated monetarism, seeking a major reversal in the role of state intervention in the economy. Most countries changed the balance between state and market in favour of the latter, but they by no means abandoned a pivotal role for the state in orchestrating economic change. A few smaller countries, most notably Sweden, managed to adapt to intensifying international competition while preserving a social consensus and maintaining full employment.

At the same time, a new international economic order was painfully being put together. Co-operation between the central banks of the major capitalist countries is still fragile, but it is real. The European Community (EC) is moving towards greater economic and political union, with Eastern Europe now seeking to be included. Tensions remain, of course: between the major economic-power blocs centred on the United States, Europe, and Japan; within the EC; and between the advanced capitalist world and the Third World, exemplified by the debt crisis. Nevertheless, resource allocation and reallocation, nationally and internationally, although primarily determined by the operation of impersonal market forces, are also shaped by conscious political decisions implemented by states subject to domestic democratic influence.

MARKETS AND THE STATE

The general case for markets is that they enable decentralized decision-making to be co-ordinated without the involvement of any central agency. Individuals respond to changing relative prices and perceived opportunities for profit-making on the basis of their self-interest and, in the absence of monopoly power, competition ensures that they do so in a way that benefits the social interest. The two main modern theoretical traditions emphasizing the beneficial role of markets are the neo-classical and the Austrian schools, although their arguments differ significantly.

The neo-classical school focuses on the analysis of an economy consisting of a set of interlocking 'perfectly competitive' markets. Its principal theorem is that, if certain very restrictive assumptions are met, such an economy will settle down into a state of general equilibrium in which it will not be possible to improve the welfare of any individual in the society without reducing the welfare of another individual. Such a 'Pareto optimum' implies that resources are being used as efficiently as possible to contribute to the welfare of the individuals in the society, given the existing distribution of the ownership of productive assets and the consequential distribution of income.

If the assumptions underlying this theorem are not met, the neo-classical school recognizes that 'market failure' may exist, in which case the state may need to intervene to correct for such failure. Four causes of market failure are generally recognized: *monopoly power*, which enables sellers to exploit buyers; *externalities*, which exist when the consequences of individual decisions affect other individuals with no say in the decision; *public goods*, which are said to exist when individual decision-making gives rise to an outcome that the individuals involved do not want and collective decision-making is the only way to achieve their desired outcome; and *considerations of equity*, which arise when society decides that the existing distribution of wealth and income is incompatible with its values.

The Austrian school rejects the neo-classical focus on the general equilibrium *state* resulting from market competition and instead emphasizes the competitive *process*, stressing the crucial role of the entrepreneur. The entrepreneur is the person who interprets changing relative prices and profit opportunities, takes risks, receives the rewards if successful, and bears the costs if unsuccessful. Austrian analysis argues that the market is the only institution which can co-ordinate and promote the effective use of dispersed information, enables entrepreneurs to respond quickly to new information, and provides them with the incentive to do so. For Austrian theorists the principal advantage of the market is not that it results in a Pareto-efficient allocation of resources but that it encourages innovation.

While the neo-classical school sees a positive role for state intervention to correct for market failure, the Austrian school regards state intervention as the principal source of inefficiency, promoting behaviour that seeks state protection from competition and inhibits the resource-reallocating role of market forces. Thus, while the neo-classical school favours competition policy to combat monopoly power, with regulation and sometimes public ownership when this is not possible, the Austrian school provides the main theoretical rationalization for the currently dominant trend towards deregulation and privatization.

At the macroeconomic level a similar controversy exists over the role of the state. As already noted, Keynesian macroeconomic management was adopted in most capitalist countries after 1945 to maintain full employment, control inflation and influence the balance of payments. Macroeconomic management was intended to alter the level of effective demand in the economy through fiscal and monetary policy, and policy to control prices and money incomes. It involved active state intervention in response to continuously changing conditions in the private sector of the economy, as individuals altered their behaviour in pursuit of their self-interest.

The 1970s, characterized by a combination of simultaneously rising inflation and unemployment in the capitalist world economy, saw the eclipse of Keynesianism and the emergence of monetarism as the dominant influence on macroeconomic policy. At the level of political economy, monetarism consisted of the adoption of the control of inflation as the primary policy objective, abandonment of any commitment to full employment, and the use of market forces and unemployment as a means of disciplining enterprises and workers. At the technical level, active state intervention to manage demand was replaced by the announcement of 'monetary targets' – targets for the rate of growth of the supply of money in the economy.

Monetarism was adopted most fully in the least-successful capitalist countries: Britain and the United States. In continental Western Europe, by contrast, although the balance shifted towards the market, a social-market economy based on broad consensus, with the state seeking to combine competitiveness, citizenship and welfare, was maintained. In the context of a growing internationalization of economic activity, the international co-operation needed to sustain the social-market economy in Western Europe has increasingly taken place within the framework of the EC as it has moved towards closer monetary and economic union.

The contrast between Britain and the United States, and the rest of the advanced capitalist world has also been evident in the sphere of industrial policy. In the most successful capitalist countries, even those apparently most private-enterprise and market-orientated, the long-run development of the economy has not been left to the impersonal operations of market forces. Some degree of forward co-ordination has been attempted, both within and between industries and sectors. In Japan, this has taken place in the sectoral bureaux within the Ministry of International Trade and Industry, and through a system of informally negotiated consensus and guidance. In (West) Germany the system of industrial banking has enabled some co-ordination to be undertaken with the encouragement of but without the direct involvement of the state. In France there has been a system of state-organized sectoral commissions and again guidance based on a network of informal contacts.

The crucial point, the significance of which appears to be unrecognized by many 'marketeers' in the countries of the ex-Soviet Union and Eastern Europe (whose experience of state bureaucracy has led them to insist on the *independence* of enterprises) is that in modern economies *interdependence* within and between sectors is such that some degree of negotiation and consensus on long-run development is generally necessary for effective investment. Whether this co-ordination has been organized by the state, by financial institutions, or by associations of enterprises, has depended on the particular history and circumstances of each country. Where it has not occurred in one way or another, the result has been the UK/US syndrome of relative decline.

AN ASSESSMENT: ALTERNATIVE POSSIBILITIES FOR POST-COMMUNIST ECONOMIES

Given the evolution of planning in the Soviet Union and Eastern Europe, the history of state intervention and planning in capitalist countries and the discussion of the market and state intervention that were outlined earlier in this chapter, what can be said about current thinking on the relationship between planning and the market? The advantages of planning are, first, that it enables the long-run objectives of society to predominate in the process of resource allocation and, second, it makes possible the co-ordination in advance of major investment decisions. The advantages of the market are that it allows decentralized decision-making on the basis of local information and provides an incentive for enterprises to make efficient use of the information available to them.

The failure of centralized administrative command-planning has led most commentators to conclude that responsibility for economic decision-making needs to be clearly located with an identifiable and not too large group of people, who bear the associated gains or losses and therefore have an incentive to make efficient use of the resources involved. This is what accounts for the new conventional wisdom, held equally by market socialists and advocates of capitalism, that there is no alternative to market forces as the principal mechanism for allocating resources. A minority view is that planning in the context of political and economic democracy has yet to be tried and offers the best prospect for combining efficiency and socialist values.

Against this background, four broad alternatives can be identified for the evolution of the post-communist economies of the ex-Soviet Union and Eastern Europe – casino capitalism (*laissez-faire*, minimal state); social market capitalism (corporatist consensus, social solidarity); regulated market socialism (worker self-management, indicative planning); and democratic planning (social ownership, negotiated co-ordination).

Casino capitalism is a real danger. The unrealistic view of the way in which markets work that seems to be so prevalent in the East has been accentuated by the New Right ideologues who have dominated the advice coming from the West. The social reality underlying this trend is the urgent need to break the hold of the old state bureaucracy and it may be that 'big bang' privatization is the only way to do this in 1990s conditions. On the other hand, the problems of transition have almost certainly been underestimated, market forces on their own are particularly inappropriate in circumstances where rapid structural change is needed, and opposition to the social consequences of fully fledged marketization is bound to grow rapidly if this alternative is followed.

Social market capitalism is the most desirable and probably the most likely alternative in the short-to-medium term. However, the social consensus on which it is based and the institutions through which it operates are the result of decades of organization, struggle, social learning and compromise. Social market capitalism has evolved historically in the particular circumstances of each country and cannot easily be transplanted. Nevertheless, the experience of countries in which a developmental and welfare state has been evolved as a result of democratic pressure has much to offer those in the East. Democratic pressure is the only way to prevent these countries from being turned into free enterprise zones for capital to exploit, unencumbered by the constraints operating in their more prosperous Western neighbours. For the East European countries, the relationship they are able to arrive at with the EC will be of great importance in their future development.

Regulated market socialism appears to be a non-starter for the foreseeable future, given the absence of any important social forces committed to some form of socialism. The problem, however, is not just whether the social forces exist; it is also theoretical. Market socialism involves regulating the behaviour of enterprises that are independent, but not privately owned, so that in pursuing their own self-interest they contribute to society's objectives. Such regulation would need to achieve two outcomes. First, a price structure that reflects both existing relative costs and society's social and developmental objectives. The primary inputs into the production process are labour and natural resources. The prices of these primary inputs need to reflect society's priorities. This would involve an incomes policy and a rental on the use of scarce natural resources over and above the cost of making use of them. On the basis of these socially determined primary-input prices, enterprises would set the prices of the goods and services they produce. Exceptions to this would arise when society wished to support, through subsidies, the use of certain products, such as basic consumption goods or environmentally friendly products; and discourage through taxes the use of other products, such as tobacco and alcohol, or environmentally damaging products. A further exception would be when monopoly power exists and prices would have to be controlled to prevent enterprises from obtaining monopoly profits.

Second, a structure of investment that also reflects society's social and developmental objectives. For this to be achieved there has to be some institutional process for reaching a broad strategic consensus which is then backed up by a system of incentives for enterprises to undertake investment that is consistent with the agreed priorities. Such an incentive system might include tax concessions, credit policy, preferential trading arrangements, government grants and informal guidance. It is important to note that investment decisions cannot be made rationally on the basis of the existing set of relative prices. Investment, by changing the balance between supply and demand, typically changes relative prices, and the relevant prices for guiding investment decisions are therefore expected future relative prices rather than existing relative prices. This is the theoretical reason why interdependent investments can only be decided upon rationally if they are co-ordinated in advance. Hence the need for negotiation and strategic consensus.

These two objectives of regulation, a price structure and an investment structure, both reflecting society's priorities, correspond to the two different dimensions of what is normally just referred to as 'the market', namely market *exchange* and market *forces*. Market exchange is concerned with the use of *existing capacity* – what enterprises sell, and what customers buy. The operation of market forces is one way of bringing about *changes in capacity* – investment and disinvestment.

There is widespread agreement that market exchange is the appropriate way to decide on the use of existing capacity. It is in relation to changes in the allocation of resources, to investment and disinvestment, that controversy over the relative roles of planning and market forces arises. The dominant view among socialist reformers is that regulation of the structure of investment is not only desirable but also possible. In this view, while market forces should be the principal means for co-ordinating investment decisions they should not be allowed to operate without regulation. The invisible hand can and must be guided by state and other collective forms of intervention. This is essentially the same argument as that for an active industrial policy to enable some forward co-ordination of investment in managed social market capitalism.

A minority view, based on the experience of the new economic mechanism (NEM) introduced in Hungary in 1968 and now in the process of being dismantled, questions the possibility of effective regulation of investment. J. Kornai has concluded that the pioneers of market socialism, who believed in the harmonious, mutually-correcting duality of 'plan' and 'market', were naïve (Kornai, 1986, p. 1729). He maintains that regulation in practice always requires the regulators to negotiate with enterprises over the terms of the regulations. Enterprises pursuing their self-interest will therefore be able to use their local knowledge to outwit or capture the regulators, with the result that regulation will be largely an illusion. The argument is similar to the case for deregulation in capitalist countries.

Democratic planning through negotiated co-ordination is in my view the most desirable alternative in the longer term. The argument is that the experience of statism, East and West, need not cause a retreat to effective *private* ownership, whether capitalist or worker self-managed, with economic activity co-ordinated by market forces. Rather, it should stimulate the exploration of ways of moving beyond *state* ownership to democratically controlled *social* ownership. This would enable information, about what people want, to be generated by market exchange, while the allocation and reallocation of resources in response to that information and longer-term social objectives would be planned consciously through negotiation among those affected, and not left to the impersonal operation of market forces, whether regulated or not.

The fundamental principle of democratic self-government is that those affected by decisions should be involved in taking those decisions. People are only likely to co-operate in achieving social objectives if they participate in the formation of those objectives. Participatory democracy – economic as well as political – is the only sure foundation for the continuous negotiation and renegotiation of the consensus that is required for effective – co-operative as opposed to adversarial – social action.

The principle of participatory economic democracy can be illustrated in terms of the ownership status of enterprises, and the process for negotiating the co-ordination of investment decisions. For enterprises to be socially owned, the right to decide on the use of their existing capacity must be exercised by those affected by that use. The interests involved clearly include an enterprise's workers. However, other interests are also affected, such as customers, the community in which the enterprise is located, competing enterprises, environmental groups and so on. All should be represented on the governing body of enterprises. Thus social ownership must be distinguished from ownership by an enterprise's workers, which is effectively a form of private ownership, albeit one that does not involve exploitation.

When it comes to the co-ordination of investment decisions, the same principle – that all those affected should be represented in the decision-making process – applies. This would involve all the enterprises in the relevant branch of production, the communities in which they are located, major customers and suppliers, representatives of regional, national and international planning bodies, environmental groups and so on. The institutions within which the negotiated co-ordination of investment decisions would take place might be developed from the various ways in which negotiation and consensus already occur. However, for the process to be democratic it must be opened up to all affected interests, and the privileged position of private capital or the old *nomenklatura* must be ended.

This is one way of thinking about what a self-governing society might look like. Self-government in the economic sphere requires democratic control over the use of society's assets by the people who are affected by that use. The planning of major investment decisions through a process of negotiated co-ordination, combined with self-government at the level of the enterprise, would enable production to take place within a framework that had been shaped consciously in accordance with socially agreed priorities.

The movement towards political democracy in the countries of the former Soviet Union and Eastern Europe has so far been associated with the belief that market forces and privatization are necessary for socially acceptable economic performance. That belief is unlikely to survive as the realities of capitalism make themselves felt. Economic democracy and participatory planning offer an alternative perspective, in the East as much as in the West.

3 Transition to the Market: Some Implications for Human Resource Development

Diane Elson

INTRODUCTION

The transition from central planning to market forms of co-ordination can be expected to have some positive implications for human development.[1] In particular, it can be expected to liberate individual initiative and to foster entrepreneurship through the provision of new incentives and the opening up of new opportunities. It also promises more flexibility in the allocation and reallocation of human resources to the most productive uses; and more regard for efficiency and quality in production. This obviously has positive implications for international competitiveness. The transition is also widely expected to provide a good foundation for democratic rights by promoting decentralization of decision-making, and reducing the role of the state.[2]

However, markets also have some deep-seated inadequacies with respect to human development, stemming from the fact that human resources are not exactly like other resources, although in some ways there are similarities. Failure to recognize these inadequacies and to devise policies to address them is likely to undermine the gains which may be derived from market co-ordination. Moreover, instead of democratization, the outcome may be what has been called 'market Stalinism', based on the continuing repression of autonomous organizations. Or democratization may stop at the door of the household, and the economy may rely on what might be called 'market patriarchy': an increase in the salience of author-itarian family forms. Instead of further development of human capacities through improvements in health and skills, there may be deterioration, as public expenditure on health, education and training services is run down, and social services are encouraged to focus on monetary rather than human indicators.

This chapter provides a brief discussion of some relevant considerations. It is divided into three sections. The first deals with some of the inadequa-

41

cies of markets in the development of human capacities; the second discusses some illustrative empirical evidence, drawing on studies of China and Vietnam; and the third section considers some policy implications.

INADEQUACIES OF MARKETS IN THE DEVELOPMENT OF HUMAN CAPACITIES

Markets have inadequacies both with respect to the formation of human capacities and with respect to the utilization of human capacities in production.[3] The role that markets play in the co-ordination of the formation of human capacities is limited, in even the most market-orientated economies in the contemporary world, by the fact that children are not generally produced for sale; and the work of looking after them and keeping them, and adults, in good working order is mainly undertaken without pay by women in their roles as mothers, wives and daughters. Families rather than markets are the key social institution. Nevertheless there is an influential line of argument, still known as the 'new household economics' even though by now it is rather middle-aged, which suggests that the formation of human capacities can be treated as if it were co-ordinated by markets; and as if children were produced for sale, treating them as akin to investment goods or consumption goods. Different patterns of expenditure of time and income on different types of children (male and female; older and younger) can be explained by the differential returns from different types of children. If girls get less health care, less education and less food, this is because the returns from investing in girls are less than the returns from investing in boys. If women spend more time than men on unpaid work of human resource maintenance this is because of differences in aptitudes and opportunity costs. If there are not any real markets co-ordinating fertility and child-care decisions, then there are well-functioning quasi-markets.[4]

The useful contribution made by this approach is to stress the salience of economic incentives in the determination of fertility and child-rearing practices within families. But the particular way in which the new household economics theorizes the role of economic incentives is open to question; as is its complacency about the social adequacy of its quasi-markets, not just from the point of view of equity between women and men but also from the point of view of efficiency. The choice-theoretic utility-maximizing framework of the new household economics has been criticized extensively by N. Folbre (1986), who advocates the use of bargaining models which recognize imbalances in power between different agents involved in having and rearing children; and by A. K. Sen (1984 and 1990), who proposes a 'co-operative conflicts' model which goes beyond bargaining to discuss perception issues that call into question the very notion of the choosing subject as an appropriate characterization of all agents. Limitations upon choice are stressed by authors who point to the weight of social expectations and obligation – I. Palmer (1991), for instance, suggests a quasi-tax model rather than a quasi-market model. She suggests that social obligations to have and rear children operate on women with the force of a tax, which they pay with the time spent on child-care. Others point to the role of overt coercion (including patriarchal authority and domestic violence) in the process of human capacity formation (Kabeer, 1991).

Besides gender equity issues, there are also externalities, indivisibilities and irreversibilities. It is not possible for parents to capture all the costs and benefits associated with their children. Hence the case for a population policy. But there is a feedback between population and gender equity issues, since there is a great deal of evidence to suggest that more educational and *independent* income-earning opportunities for women both increase their bargaining position in the family and reduce birth-rates (UN, 1991). As we shall see, there is reason to fear that in some cases transition to the market may have an adverse impact upon these opportunities, and this may tend to lead to a slow down in the rates of decline of population growth. This result would be particularly likely if there is an emphasis on the 'family economy', that is, on small-scale enterprises that are run by male household heads using the unpaid labour of other family members, since these tend not to afford women an independent income and at the same time put a premium on increasing the pool of family labour; they thus provide an incentive to have more children. In many countries transition to the market does involve an emphasis on the 'family economy' as a form of production likely to be very responsive to market incentives. Thus transition to the market may have unwelcome demographic implications.[5]

There are also inadequacies in markets as co-ordinators of decisions about expenditures that enhance human resources. For it is not possible for individuals to capture all the costs and benefits associated with their health and educational status. Hence the universally recognized case for some degree of public provision of health and education services. However, since some of the costs and benefits may be captured individually or on a family basis, there is inevitably some degree of tension between public and private provision. Whatever its other faults, central planning has proved to be capable in some centrally-planned economies of dealing with these externalities in a more effective way than in many market economies at comparable levels of development.

Table 3.1 shows how selected economies ranked in the mid to late 1980s in terms of GNP per capita and the UNDP Human Development Index (based on achievement of targets for life expectancy at birth, adult literacy rates, and average per capita income). In all the centrally-planned economies shown in the table, the HDI ranking was higher than GNP per capita ranking, with China and Vietnam doing exceptionally well. Among market economies only Sri Lanka has a comparable record. As can be

Table 3.1 GNP and human development, 1985–7

Country	GNP per capita rank	Human development index	HDI rank minus GNP rank
Centrally planned			
China	22	0.716	44
Cuba	66	0.877	26
Lao PDR	9	0.506	37
Mongolia	57	0.737	13
North Korea	67	0.789	15
Mozambique	10	0.239	3
Vietnam	16	0.608	40
Czechoslovakia	102	0.931	4
Hungary	87	0.915	14
Poland	83	0.910	15
USSR	101	0.920	4
Market			
Botswana	69	0.646	−11
Brazil	85	0.784	−5
Chile	73	0.931	34
Costa Rica	77	0.916	26
Cote d'Ivoire	52	0.393	−20
Hong Kong	111	0.936	−3
India	25	0.439	12
Indonesia	41	0.591	13
Malaysia	80	0.800	5
Mexico	81	0.876	10
Singapore	110	0.899	−14
South Korea	92	0.903	5
Sri Lanka	38	0.789	45
Sweden	125	0.987	4
USA	129	0.961	−17

Source: UNDP, 1990, table 1, pp. 128–9.

seen from the table, China does considerably better than the Asian NICs, as does Laos. The record of North Korea compares favourably with Singapore, Hong Kong and South Korea. Cuba does better than many comparable Latin-American and Caribbean economies, although Chile has a better record, while Costa Rica has a comparable record. Mozambique does better than some of the so-called success stories in Africa, such as Côte d'Ivoire and Botswana. The four Eastern European countries do notably better than the USA and, in the case of Hungary and Poland, even do better than Sweden.

As the data in Tables 3.2 and 3.3 show, centrally-planned developing countries have tended to out-perform the average for developing countries as a whole on health and education indicators, with China and Cuba having particularly good records. Czechoslovakia, Hungary and Poland have also done well in achieving standards better than or comparable to the average for industrial countries, despite having a per capita GNP considerably lower than the average.

Table 3.2 Health profile, selected centrally planned economies

Country	Per capita GNP (US$ 1987)	Maternal mortality rate (per 100 000 live births, 1980–7)	Under-55 mortality rate (per 1000 live births, 1988)	Life expectancy (years, 1987)	Health expenditure percentage of GNP (1986)
All developing countries	650	290	121	62	1.4
China	290	44	43	70	1.4
Cuba	–	34	18	74	3.2
Lao PDR	170	–	159	49	–
Mongolia	–	100	59	64	1.3
North Korea	–	41	33	70	1.0
Mozambique	170	–	298	47	1.8
Vietnam	109[1]	140	88	62	–
All industrial countries	10 760	24	18	74	4.7
Czechoslovakia	5 820	10	15	72	4.2
Hungary	2 240	26	19	71	3.2
Poland	2 070	11	18	72	4.0
USSR	4 550	48	32	70	3.2

Note: [1]Leipziger 1992, table 3.
Source: Unless otherwise indicated, Human Development Indicators, table 10 and 11, UNDP, 1990.

Table 3.3 Education profile; selected centrally-planned economies

Country	Education expenditure (as percentage of GNP, 1986)	Combined primary and secondary enrolment ratio (1986–8)	Scientists and technicians (per 1000 people, 1970–87)
All developing countries	3.9	75	9.7
China	2.7	82	7.0
Cuba	6.2	95	52.0
Lao PDR	1.2	67	–
Mongolia	–	95	1.6
North Korea	–	73	–
Mozambique	–	34	–
Vietnam	–	69	–
All industrial countries	5.2	97	140.5
Czechoslovakia	3.6	78	130.0
Hungary	3.8	88	251.0
Poland	4.5	95	168.0
USSR	5.2	100	128.0

Source: Human Development Indicators, table 5 and 14, UNDP, 1990.

The question is whether transition to market co-ordination will be compatible with maintaining an adequate resource base for public provision. Will a more individualized and family-based economy erode mechanisms formerly used to channel resources to health and education? A particular problem that may arise is the potential erosion of the public revenue base. As a recent World Bank discussion paper notes:

> Although there can be substantial gains in expenditure savings as direct subsidies to state owned enterprises are eliminated, the reverse flow of transfers normally expected as mandatory payments to the central government in the socialist framework (be they labelled depreciation payments for capital assets, dividends from enterprises, or the equivalent of taxes) will also fall. (Leipziger, 1992, p. 8).

Markets also have inadequacies in co-ordinating the use of human resources in paid production because of the necessary incompleteness of labour contracts; a point which, as F. Green (1988) has argued, was made in the Marxian distinction between labour power and labour, and has been rediscovered in the new institutional economics based on the recognition of imperfect information and of principal–agent problems. Thus the enterprise is the key social institution in co-ordinating the use of labour in paid production; but the way that it does this depends on the way that it is integrated in to the economy as a whole. If the form of integration is solely through unregulated markets, then there will certainly be competitive pressures to get as much work as possible from the labour power that has been hired even though this may be detrimental to health and safety. Moreover, since capital markets are necessarily imperfect because of information asymmetries, and because there are indivisibilities and irreversibilities in the technologies of production, those who are selling their labour power will be limited in their ability to counteract this pressure by setting up businesses of their own. Up to a point, the competitive pressure to get as much work as possible from the labour power that has been hired (through increasing actual working time and the intensity of work during that time) will produce genuine improvements in productivity by utilizing spare human capacity. But beyond a certain point extra output is won only at the cost of depletion and degradation of human capacity, and productivity increases are illusory (as they are in the parallel cases of natural resources).

This is not only a humanitarian issue; depleted and degraded human capacities do not make a good base for long-run maintenance of competitive advantage, which depends not so much on provision of low-cost standardized products but on ability to learn and innovate. The question is whether transition to the market will push beyond this point. An enterprise subject only to market co-ordination is likely to press beyond that point so long as it is able to replenish its stock of human capacities at no additional cost, because of the problems of capturing all the returns associated with a strategy of enhancing rather than depleting human capacities.[6]

A further problem arises in the reallocation of human resources between enterprises. Market co-ordination certainly provides an incentive to shed labour, but it is uncertain in its ability to redirect the unemployed towards employment. The incompleteness of contracts, and asymmetries in information, means that there is an in-built tendency for labour markets not to clear, irrespective of 'interventions' of governments or trade unions.[7] Non-convexities in consumption sets means that even if they do clear, the wages may be too low to sustain life – there is always the risk of entitlement failure.[8] These are problems that cannot be overcome by trying to make markets more perfect through the removal of external distortions; they are inherent in the nature of markets.

A rapid rate of capital accumulation will tend to reduce these problems in so far as it reduces surplus labour, but it requires holding back the growth of consumption, which may be difficult if transition to the market has raised expectations of rapid improvements in the standard of living.

Transition to the market may also have adverse effects on the rate of accumulation if the transition process increases uncertainties and/or takes place in conjunction with a deflationary stabilization programme. Markets are subject to inherent co-ordination failures and need to be embedded in networks of social co-ordination if these failures are to be overcome (Elson, 1988).

EMERGING CAUSES FOR CONCERN IN ECONOMIES IN TRANSITION: CHINA AND VIETNAM

Evidence is now emerging which does suggest that transition to the market may be taking place in a way that may not preserve all the human development achievements of the centrally-planned system. No attempt will be made here to give an overall review of the situation with respect to all the issues discussed in the previous section. Rather, attention will be focused on some of the issues emerging in Vietnam and China, which had outstanding records of achievement in comparison to other countries in the late 1980s as measured by the UNDP Human Development Index, but which may in the 1990s be in danger of experiencing a disruption in their progress.[9]

Both countries have taken steps to recreate a system of household-based farming producing for the market. This is agreed to have had a very positive impact on the growth of agricultural output. Vietnam has been transformed from an importer of rice to the third-largest rice exporter world-wide, and agriculture has been the source of much of the dynamism of the economy (Leipziger, 1992). In China, the gross value of agricultural output doubled between 1979 and 1986 (a growth rate of more than 10 per cent per year) (Drèze and Sen, 1989).

But the recreation of market-orientated family farming systems has wider implications for human development. While it may increase food availability and rural per capita incomes, it also has demographic implications, and implications for gender equity, which are far from being wholly positive. Success in family farming is critically dependent on the ability of a family to mobilize a labour force. This gives an impetus to the development of rural labour markets, but also gives a pro-natalist impetus to decisions about family size. In so far as control over family resources and inheritance of family resources is vested (formally or informally) in men, it also reinforces preference for sons, and disadvantages women, whose economic and social contacts with the community beyond the family may well be reduced. One of the leading researchers on gender inequality in

China concludes that, 'Generally speaking though, because the household responsibility system has restored the peasant family – an institution within which women are still very much disadvantaged – as the basic unit of agricultural production, the reforms seem likely to reinforce many aspects of sexual inequality' (Davin, 1991, p. 39).[10]

The pro-natalist impetus is checked in China by an extremely strict population control policy: the one-child family policy. However, the enforcement of this policy in the conditions of an agricultural policy which puts a very high premium on families having sons has led in a substantial number of instances to a response which was perhaps predictable but was far from an enhancement of human development: female infanticide (Davin, 1991).

Not surprisingly, it is difficult to put figures on the incidence of female infanticide: one leading expert on Chinese demography has concluded that there was an increase in female infant mortality rates in China from about 36 to 67 per thousand live births from the beginning of the reforms in 1978 to 1984, but cautions that there is no independent proof that this was caused to a significant extent by female infanticide (Banister, 1987, table 4.18 and p. 116). Official Chinese data give indications that there were large decreases in male infant mortality rates in the period 1974/75 to 1983/85 in five provinces, while at the same time female infant mortality rates rose substantially (in two of the provinces), stayed more or less the same (in one of the provinces), or fell somewhat (in two of the provinces) (Nolan and Sender, 1992).

These divergences in male and female infant mortality rates are certainly consistent with an intensification of preference for sons, though this may be expressed more in terms of bias in the provision of food and health care rather than outright infanticide.[11] They are *prima facie* evidence for development of 'market patriarchy', though full substantiation of this hypothesis clearly requires more investigation.

A further cause for concern relates to health issues.[12] Access to the health care system in China may well have suffered in the transition to the market. Sen (1992) argues that there has emerged a 'general problem of financing rural health care and health insurance in a new regime of privatised agriculture . . . With the privatisation of agriculture the availability of communal funds for health care became more problematic, and the coverage of rural health insurance went rapidly down – from 89% in the late 1970s to 10% in 1987' (p. 1309). Nolan and Sender (1992) suggest there is no cause for concern because, despite falls in the general level of 'collective retentions' for financing welfare expenditures as a proportion of total rural income, there has been an impressive increase in collective retentions per capita in real terms in the period 1980–88 (p. 1287). There have also been increases in hospital beds per 1000 people, and numbers of professional health personnel per 1000 people (though more so in the urban than in the rural areas) (p. 1288). In response, Sen (1992) raises the issue of entitlements versus availability of resources, pointing out that although the per capita availability may have increased, the uninsured rural poor may be unable to get access to these resources, particularly since the charges for medical care doubled between 1980 and 1985 (Henderson, 1990). Sen (1992) notes that a survey by the Chinese Ministry of Health in 1988 found that 20 per cent of rural households were unable to seek health care when they were ill; and 16 per cent reported that members of the household failed to receive needed in-patient medical care because they could not afford the cost. One study (Knight and Song, 1991) has found that co-operative health insurance does affect mortality rates. A 1987 comparison of 52 villages containing 62 000 people in co-operative medical schemes, with 52 villages containing 48 000 people in private payment schemes, found that in this situation, 'Health insurance reduces the crude death rate by 14 percent' (Knight and Song, 1991, p. 18). In addition, there was clear evidence of an increase in some infectious diseases in rural China in the early 1980s (Henderson, 1990).

In addition to these problems, changes in the labour market and the organization of industrial production appear to be having a negative effect on health and safety at work. The Safety Bureau of China's Ministry of Labour released figures in April 1993 showing a rising rate of fatalities in industrial accidents, which was attributed to 'Negligence at some enterprises which tried to gain higher output at the expense of worker safety' (*Financial Times*, 24.4.93).

Problems such as female infanticide, entitlement failures in health care, and intensification of changes in industrial workplaces are among the factors that appear to have kept China's death rates (per thousand of the population) in the 1980s above the levels achieved in 1978 and 1979 (before the transition to the market really took hold) (Nolan and Sender, 1992; Sen, 1992).

There is also concern that transition to the market in Vietnam may undermine the mobilization of resources for health and education, and limit the access of poorer groups to these resources, and to other such services. As a recent World Bank paper on Vietnam points out:

> The major social sector difficulty facing transitional socialist economies is that the social sectors will progressively be starved of budgetary funds. . . The risk then is that social development will suffer

during the reform period. Indeed, as enterprises are given incentives to maximise profits and seek market-tests for their performance, they will perforce be fulfilling less of a social function. Given this trend, the state will need to redefine its role. Unfortunately, given the budget constraints on both firms and governments, the outcome is likely to be less coverage of health, pension, and unemployment benefits. The distribution of income will probably become more skewed as greater wage differentiation occurs, and returns to capital are increasingly captured by private entrepreneurs. (Leipziger, 1992, p. 28)

Certainly, the transition to the market in Vietnam has seen an erosion of fiscal revenue, which is reported to have fallen from 12.2 per cent of GDP in 1987 to 7.6 per cent in 1991, largely as a result of a fall in transfers from state enterprises to the central government, from 9.2 per cent of GDP in 1987 to 2.6 per cent in 1991 (Leipziger, 1992). The budgets of the health and education services have been under considerable pressure and user charges have been introduced. One estimate suggests that the costs of school fees and books in 1990 was 64 000 dong per student at primary level and 93 000 dong at secondary level, more than 10 per cent of the average wage of workers in state enterprises (Thanh-Dam, 1990). In Quanh Ninh province, it has been estimated that 1300 teachers have been made redundant since 1986, partly because user fees are linked to an increasing drop-out rate, especially among female students (Thanh-Dam, 1990).

Another factor pushing up the drop-out rate is the growth of family farms. A study conducted by the Hanoi Women's Studies Centre in a number of provinces (though not in Quanh Ninh province) found that the growth of family-based production has been accompanied by a reallocation of children's time from school to household economic activities (Thanh-Dam, 1990).

An assessment for UNDP of the situation in the formal education system in Quanh Ninh province found 'a general situation of crisis' which 'may eventually threaten the deeply-seated value in Vietnamese culture about knowledge and education' (Thanh-Dam, 1990, p. 13).

PUBLIC ACTION FOR HUMAN DEVELOPMENT IN TRANSITION TO THE MARKET

The introduction of markets can mobilize private initiative in ways that can lead to a quick pay-off in terms of increases in output, as the experience of China and Vietnam has shown. But it can also jeopardize achievements in human development.

Clearly, new means must be found of channelling resources to public provision of health and education services in ways that safeguard the access of the poorer groups and guard against any tendency to deplete human resources. At the same time, new means must be found to empower women to improve their bargaining position in the family economy, and to diminish the strength of son preference.

One possible way forward is through 'public action', action which involves associations of citizens acting together to shape the activities of the government at national and local levels. The concept had been popularized in relation to freedom from hunger by Drèze and Sen (1989), who explain that public action 'is neither just a matter of state activity, nor an issue of charity, nor even one of kindly redistribution. The activism of the public, the unity and solidarity of the concerned population, and the participation of all those who are involved are important features of public action'.

Participation can be both 'collaborative' and 'adversarial' in relation to government policy:

> The collaboration of the public is an indispensable ingredient of public health campaigns, literacy drives, land reforms, famine relief operations, and other endeavours that call for co-operative efforts for their successful completion. On the other hand, for the initiation of these endeavours and for the government to act appropriately, adversarial pressures from the public *demanding* such action can be quite crucial. For this adversarial function, major contributions can be made by political activism, journalistic pressures and informed public criticism. (Drèze and Sen, 1989, p. 259)

Furthermore,

> Incentives are, in fact, central to the logic of public action. But the incentives that must be considered are not only those that offer profits in the market, but also those that motivate governments to implement well-planned public policies, induce families to reject intra-household discrimination, encourage political parties and the news media to make reasoned demands, and inspire the public at large to co-operate, criticize and co-ordinate. (Drèze and Sen, 1989, p. 259)

Effective public action, involving a range of associations of citizens (organized on a variety of bases – for example, locality, class, ethnicity,

gender, and shared values) could be the key to raising additional
resources and reordering national budgetary priorities so as to safeguard
state expenditure on health and education, and safeguard the entitlements
of the poor. It could be the key to ensuring that women, as well as men,
see their rights as individuals enhanced in the transition to the market;[13]
and that human resources are not depleted in the pursuit of short-term
monetary gains.

In thinking about the effectiveness of public action, it may be helpful to
consider the case of Kerala,[14] a small state in India, where the per capita
income is lower than for India as a whole, but where achievements in
health, education, and fertility reduction are higher than for India as a
whole, and indeed compare very well with China and with the average for

Table 3.4 Social development in Kerala, 1989

	Kerala	India	China	Upper middle-income developing countries[1]
Indicator				
GNP per capita (U$)	200	290[1]	290[2]	1890
Crude birth rate	22.4	33.6	20.0[3]	27.0
Crude death rate	6.2	11.9	7.0[3]	8.0
Total fertility rate	2.1	4.4	2.4[3]	3.5
Infant mortality rate	27	96	43[3]	50
Maternal mortality rate	1.3	3.5	4.4[3]	1.2
Life expectancy at birth				
(male)	67	55	70.1[4]	64
(female)	70	54	71.8[4]	70
Literacy rate[5]	70	36	69	–
(male)	75	47	82	–
(female)	66	25	56	

Notes: [1]1986 data.
[2]1987 data.
[3]1988 data.
[4]1990 data.
[5]1981 data for India and Kerala; 1985 data for China.

Source: Sen, 1992, p. 262 (based on data published by Government of Kerala,
Government of India and World Bank); UNDP, 1990; 1992 (data on
China).

the 'upper-middle-income' group of developing countries, as is shown in Table 3.4.

In terms of the total fertility rate, infant and maternal mortality rates and female literacy, Kerala does noticeably better than China, reflecting the less patriarchal structure of society in Kerala.[15]

Kerala has had the unusual experience of being part of a capitalist market economy, but having had, at state level, the world's first elected communist government (in 1957). This was preceded by several decades of social and political ferment, including political organization, social reform movements, caste organization, and trade union activity. As Gita Sen puts it:

> The reform movements brought about a democratization of society through which many of the hitherto unheard groups in the population could articulate their demands and legitimize their needs. In so doing they completely transformed the meaning of the public space and beliefs about the proper role of government. They ensured also that the benefits of social development percolated down the social hierarchy to include much of the population. (Sen, G., 1992, p. 263)

An important aspect of this success lies in systems of accountability, which went far beyond occasional voting in parliamentary elections, and ensured that public expenditure was effective. Officials were held account-able not just for making adequate budgetary allocations to health and edu-cation expenditure, but also for ensuring health and education services functioned as planned.

There are no simple remedies for creating the kind of public action that is conducive to human development, as is made plain in a recent compre-hensive consideration of these issues (Wuyts *et al.*, 1992). But one can draw some conclusions about the kind of enabling environment that is required. The spread of market relations tends to encourage the pursuit of private gain and can erode or distort forms of mutuality that are crucial for human development. This tendency can be counteracted if new forms of mutuality are permitted to emerge in the form of organizations of citizens that will develop the power to make demands on and discipline both the state and private enterprise.

There is a particular danger in transitions to the market which are not accompanied by political democratization ('market Stalinism'): the danger that existing forms of mutuality conducive to human develop-ment will be decomposed while the recomposition of new forms of mutuality, appropriate to and based in a market economy, are outlawed. In so far as this is the case, whatever the gains that transition to the market beings in terms of accelerating growth of GNP, there may be losses in terms of the broader objectives of human development.

Notes

1. Human development is defined by the United Nations Development Programme (UNDP) as development that promotes the formation of human capabilities *and* enlarges the scope for using these capabilities (UNDP, 1990; 1). It denotes 'both the *process* of widening people's choices and the *level* of their achieved well being', (UNDP, 1990; 10, emphasis in the original).

2. As the first Human Development Report emphasizes, political freedom, guaranteed human rights and personal self-respect are important aspects of overall human development (UNDP, 1990; p. 1), though they are not currently measured by the Human Development Index.

3. It is fashionable to refer to any human resources beyond the most basic capacities for purposive expenditure of human energy as 'human capital'. This concept is deliberately not used here because it is a misleading analogy, suggesting that human capacities should be treated as being separable from the human beings that possess them, as if they were the same as machines or sums of money. This is both morally undesirable, leading to the treatment of humans beings as purely instrumental means rather than as ends in themselves; and analytically undesirable, since it hinders an adequate understanding of how labour markets and labour processes work.

4. The founding father of this analysis is Becker, 1981.

5. This point has been argued at some length with respect to structural adjustment programmes in sub-Saharan Africa, in Palmer, 1991. Such programmes emphasize market liberalization, privatization and reductions in the role of the state, and thus have a number of features in common with transition to the market in former centrally-planned economies.

6. Unregulated private enterprises co-ordinated only by markets will tend to underinvest in human capacities because they cannot prevent other firms poaching the workers they have trained. In some circumstances this tendency will be counteracted by the operation of social norms which promote lifetime employment in the same enterprise.

7. For further discussion, see Green, 1988

8. Non-convexities in consumption sets are discussed by Das Gupta, 1991. Entitlement failure is explained in Dréze and Sen, 1989, ch.2.

9. UNDP (1990) classifies China as a case of 'disrupted human development' along with Chile, Jamaica, Colombia, Kenya and Zimbabwe. These countries are described as having achieved success in human development but having been unable to maintain this (p. 51). It must be noted that *in comparison with other countries*, China and Vietnam continued to have outstanding records, as revealed by calculations of the Human Development Index and GNP per capita based on 1990 data (UNDP, 1992, table 1, pp. 127–9). The issue we are discussing is, however, their record in comparison with their own past achievements. Some light would be shed on this by looking at movements in HDI overtime, comparing the pre-market period and the

period of marketization. Unfortunately the UNDP Human Development Reports to date do not provide this kind of comparison.

10. A gender-sensitive HDI, which adjusts the HDI for male–female disparities, was introduced in the second Human Development Report (UNDP, 1991) but only for a limited range of countries which, as yet, does not include China.

11. For a discussion of the complexities of mothers' 'male bias' in the provision of resources to their children, see Elson, 1991, p. 8.

12. This is a controversial issue, recently debated in *World Development* between Sen, A. K. (1992) and Nolan and Sender (1992). On balance, Sen's case seems to be the more convincing.

13. For further discussion of this point see Elson (1992).

14. The discussion of Kerala draws extensively on Sen, G. (1992).

15. For more details about the social position of woman in Kerala, see Sen, G. (1992).

4 Institutional Obstacles to Marketization in Post-Socialist Economies
Mo Yamin and Stephen Batstone

Ex-communist countries are advised to move to a market economy, and their leaders wish to do so, but without the appropriate institutions no market economy of any significance is possible. If we knew more about our own economy, we would be in a better position to advise them. (Coase, 1992, p. 714).

INTRODUCTION

The ideological, historical and theoretical contexts within which systemic changes towards a market economy are taking place are likely to mitigate against a realistic perspective on marketization: the nature of marketization is likely to be misunderstood and the problems faced are likely to be underestimated or even mis-specified.

At the ideological level, the transition to the market is taking place in the aftermath of the victory of the 'New Right'. The New Right tends to favour or even glorify an extreme form of individualism and argue that 'markets can do no wrong'. Market solutions are proposed for every allocation problem, even in those areas of the economy where the 'old' Right may have seen a role for regulation or public provision (externalities such as pollution, or the provision of health, education and local services).

The historical experience of socialist countries is such that it makes the ideas of the New Right attractive to some influential thinkers and policy-makers in these economies. Thus the association between central planning and political repression, and the extreme inflexibility of the economies and the need for massive restructuring, add apparent credence to those who advocate a total break with the past. J. Kornai, for example, has declared that 'following a number of decades in which a maximal state prevailed, it is now time to take great steps in the direction of a minimal state. Perhaps later generations will be able to envisage a more moderate mid-way' (cited by Nove, 1991, p. 258). Thus Kornai even rejects the need for progressive taxation.

Finally, these transformations are taking place in a theoretical void. The experiment with marketization is without precedent and no coherent body of theory or conceptualization of the nature or problems of this process exists. In fact, economists are much more likely to *learn* from the unfolding process of marketization about how markets come into being than to be able to provide any help or advice for those who are trying to affect the transformations. The lack of an adequate theoretical framework has had the following consequence.

It is assumed, implicitly, that markets come into being in much the same way that they are supposed to function. The essence of marketization is thus seen to be the removal or absence of state control. By contrast, we see marketization as a process that creates essentially new institutions[1], by which we mean patterns and regularities in behaviour and not merely formal legal and contractual structures (for example, the creation of a legal code or the setting up of a stock exchange).

In the former perspective, markets are, apparently, viewed as (the aggregation of) spontaneous exchange; as a product or manifestation of the supposedly natural propensity of agents to 'truck, barter and exchange one thing for another'. Thus M. Nuti has remarked that '[only] total marketization is a simple, effectively *self implementing* move with the total abolition of central controls' (Nuti, 1986, p. 98, our emphasis).

We shall argue that exchange is, on the contrary, always in part a 'leap into the unknown' (Hodgson, 1988, p. 167) and that it requires a whole set of institutional supports to enable it to spread. Some recent analysis has stressed the role of opportunism and lack of trust, in situations characterized by information asymmetry, as an important source of market failure and has, by implication, highlighted the development of institutional solutions for such failure (for example, the provision of guarantees, investment in reputation and so on). Note that these proposals are institutional in two related senses. First, they imply some sort of regularity or predictability in patterns of behaviour. Second, they are instruments or supports that help the functioning of existing markets rather than the creation of additional markets themselves. Neo-classical theory, by contrast, sees the solution to market failure as the creation of absent markets.

Our contribution is to argue that in addition to information asymmetries and lack of trust, there are more fundamental obstacles to exchange and to the emergence of a market economy. Basically, we wish to emphasize that in a monetary economy, in an economy where exchange is monetized, there is an asymmetry that is embedded in the exchange itself, quite apart from (or in addition to) the asymmetries that may arise from information possessed by different agents or by their behavioural characteristics. Our asymmetry stems from the fact that money is by definition a perfectly homogeneous commodity and has a constant and invariant 'quality'. On the other hand, virtually all artefacts and services that may be exchanged for money are subject, with some positive probability, to 'performance failure'. As a consequence of this asymmetry in monetized exchange, the buyer incurs a greater risk than the seller. Monetized exchange is thus characterized by 'buyer's risk' and, without some institutional features that either shift some of this risk away from buyers or otherwise support exchange, markets are unlikely to develop deep roots in an economy.

The Soviet Union and other centrally-planned economies were, of course, also monetary economies: however, the nature of exchange and the risks involved are fundamentally different in centrally-planned economies as compared to market economies. The fact that centrally-planned economies have a tendency towards persistent shortages means that the main risk faced by agents is whether they can affect exchange at all. The efforts of agents will be concentrated in trying to avoid being too liquid. By contrast, in market economies, *given* that agents have an income and can undertake some exchange, the problem of buyer's risk will undermine their willingness to do so. A functioning market economy thus develops a variety of mechanisms and institutions that reduce (at least the perception of) buyer's risk to manageable levels.

Marketization, by which we mean the creation of a market economy, is thus fundamentally a *process* whereby patterns of social relationships, based on conventions and regularities of behaviour by individuals that are appropriate to the growth of exchange, are created and sustained. An important aspect of our argument is that, contrary to what may be expected, these patterns of behaviour imply some departure from pure and unadulterated individualism.

The origins of, or the initial catalysts for, market-generating (or market-sustaining) patterns of behaviour may be viewed essentially as *entrepreneurial* action. More precisely, the catalyst is likely to be the kind of action that performs dynamic or 'institutional' arbitrage by proposing, innovating or investing in the reduction or removal of the buyer's risk problem in particular parts of the economy. By comparison, the Austrian entrepreneur performs only static arbitrage in as much as, *within a given institutional setting*, they fill the gap between demand and supply in particular markets.

A major problem of the transitional phase is precisely how to frame the initial measures or marketization policies so as to encourage entrepreneurship in the above sense. In the context of the debate over socialist reforms, two types of privatization have been outlined. These are referred to as 'top-down' and 'bottom-up' privatization (Winiecki, 1990; Herrman-Pillath, 1991). In top-down privatization, an economy of private enterprise is created by selling existing organizations into private ownership. Bottom-up privatization means the creation of a private-enterprise economy by relaxing the conditions under which production is carried out, so that people who so wish are better placed to act on their own initiative.

PRIVATIZATION VERSUS MARKETIZATION

Although it would seem that a programme of bottom-up privatization is probably more of an effective vehicle for institutional entrepreneurship than the privatization in the more normal sense of selling off state assets, the energies of the reformer are nevertheless likely to be taken up by the latter. This is because of the belief that a major step in the transition to the market is the destruction of the existing institutions of the command economy and that selling off of existing state businesses is the quickest short-run solution.

Top-Down Privatization

The main issue in the literature on (top-down) privatization in the centrally-planned economies is how to effect the privatization of state-owned assets in an economy where a significant private sector is not already in existence. Thus one of the points that is stressed in this litera-ture is both the quantitative and qualitative contrasts between the British privatization programme and the proposed programmes in the Eastern European economies and other centrally-planned economies (CPEs) (Estrin, 1991b; Frydman and Rapaczynski, 1990). The rationale for priva-tization, in a predominantly market- or capitalist economy, is that the particular enterprises will face the full rigours of market discipline, particularly in the market for corporate control. In the CPEs too, it is hoped that privatization will produce a similar outcome. Thus privatiza-tion is expected to achieve more than the mere transfer of ownership of enterprises from the state to individuals: it is regarded as a process by which 'the very institution of property, in the sense that lawyers and economists are used to employ this term, is reintroduced into Eastern European societies' (Frydman and Rapaczynski, 1990, p. 2). Similarly, D. Lipton and J. Sachs (1990, p. 294) argue that 'privatisation means creating anew the basic institutions of a market financial system'.

It is thus argued that significant structural reform of these economies cannot simply proceed at the macroeconomic level. 'Liberalization' measures such as wage restraint, reductions in subsidies and credits or even a more radical programme of 'price reforms' can only have a short-lived effect. It is further stressed that such reforms are not even adequate (contrary to the initial expectation in Poland, for example) for the creation of the *initial* basic conditions for a transformation to a market-based system: privatization must not be seen as the 'final step' in a process started by macro-liberalization and price reforms. The emerging dominant view seems to be that this sequence of reform puts the measures in the wrong order: 'It is a relatively safe proposition that without some fairly dramatic steps on the microeconomic level, the hopes for a structural adjustment for the Polish economy associated with the macro economic programme, could not be fulfilled' (Frydman and Rapaczynski, 1990, p. 6).

However, in our opinion, the failure of the macroeconomic liberalization and price reforms, in generating the desired structural reforms, may not have been totally, or even mainly, due to the absence of accompanying privatization measures. It may also have been partly a consequence of the fact that human behaviour is 'habitual' and that certain patterns of behaviour may persist or outlast the rules and institutional/organisational structures that originally determined or encouraged them. In other words, macro-liberalization measures may have proved to be ineffective partly because managers and workers adopted a 'wait and see' attitude towards the reforms. This tactic seems to have been adopted and subsequently regarded as correct during earlier reform phases. In general, only if changes in the macro environment are believed to be permanent and irreversible will the expected 'efficient' response actually take place (surplus workers be laid off, unprofitable businesses shut down and so on). The recent experience of Poland provides some supporting evidence for this view. Kolarska-Bobinska (1990) explains the ineffectiveness of the stabilization programme in the following terms:

That programme was intended to stop state subsidies to enterprises, and thus to enforce a change in their behaviour, to enforce innovativeness and entrepreneurship behaviour, and also to enforce dismissal of superfluous employees and to bring about bankruptcies of inefficient enterprises. To the surprise of economists the financial restrictions did not bring about the expected behaviour. Enterprises started neither to go bankrupt nor to modify their policies...Enterprises resorted to the tactics which had proved very successful during the many years of communist endeavour to reform the economy: it was the tactics of wait and see...Both managers and employees hoped that the change would be neutralized and the system would return to its 'normal' state. (p. 280)

Of course, it may be argued that 'efficient' outcomes can, even if only temporarily, be avoided, because in the CPEs no market discipline exists, so that even enterprises with negative profits are not forced to go bankrupt.

However, very similar problems will also confront a more 'radical' reform programme with the pivotal role for privatization. In the absence of an effectively functioning capital or control market, privatized businesses will face no real market discipline either. Expectations to the contrary notwithstanding, privatization *per se* can do no more than create private ownership of businesses. It does not automatically create a market for these privatized assets. It is the existence of a market for these assets that guarantees 'efficiency' by forcing firms to maximize the value of the assets under their ownership.

The development of a market for privatized assets is closely bound up with the issue of governance. This refers to the mechanisms through which the managers of a privatized business are controlled and forced to run the business in the interests of the shareholders rather than in their own interests. 'Efficient' governance implies some concentration in shareholdings as this avoids or reduces the free-riding problem implied if a very large number of shareholders collectively share the costs involved in the monitoring of managers. In the context of privatization in the CPEs, the governance issue appears to be particularly acute. This is because, in order to make the privatization of state businesses socially acceptable,[2] it may be necessary to give an equal share in these businesses to every member of the population. In this situation managers cannot be controlled effectively and their behaviour need not be any more efficient or responsive than under the previous command economy regime.

Governance can thus be treated as fundamentally, though perhaps not exclusively,[3] a distributional issue. It is primarily a device to prevent the consumption of profits by the managers of the firm, an instrument in the struggle over who appropriates profits rather than over the generation of the profits themselves. In *capitalist* economies, it can, normally if not always, be taken for granted that the firm is making *some* profit, irrespective of the structure of governance. This is guaranteed by the institutional structure of the system and the associated patterns of behaviour. Most people simply expect, as a way of life, to have to work for others and to have to conform to certain standards of productivity enforced by their employers. Because appropriate institutional conditions already exist in a capitalist economy, the governance issue is thus, more or less automatically, resolved. Competition among shareholders results in those shareholders who put a greater premium on control and/or those with greater financial power winning control.

But the requisite institutions and patterns of behaviour or attitudes are not prevalent in the CPEs. Profit-seeking is not generally regarded as legitimate or normal behaviour.[4] Thus, ruling out repression, workers may choose to adopt a 'wait and see' attitude, particularly in the absence of reliable signals indicating that the new system is likely to develop strong roots. In this case, they will persist in their traditional work patterns and attitudes. The consequence of this, in turn, is that few people will attach a premium to the *ownership of control-bestowing shareholdings*. Thus there seems to be a 'Catch 22' situation: there is no real incentive to control businesses for the purpose of monitoring and disciplining inefficiency and managerial consumption because the underlying behavioural/institutional prerequisite for profit-making is absent. But on the other hand, because the governance issue is unresolved, no one has any real incentive to attempt a change in the underlying patterns of behaviour. As long as the traditional patterns of behaviour are not broken down, the process of systemic change gets trapped in some kind of short-term, 'wait and see' equilibrium.

The upshot of the above argument is that privatized assets are unlikely to become *commodities*. In other words, a *capital* market cannot develop – even if the authorities establish a stock exchange.[5] Thus we are simply echoing the Marxist dictum that capital is not only the privately-owned means of production but is fundamentally a particular *social* relationship. Marketization is essentially a process of social transformation, and the simple transfer of ownership from the state to individuals is unlikely to be an effective agency in this transformation (Herrman-Pillath, 1990).

The limitations of privatization can also be seen from a somewhat different theoretical perspective. The emphasis on privatization stems from a belief that clearly-defined and enforced property rights are crucial for exchange. The view is that without identifiable ownership, ideally private and individual, we encounter the 'tragedy of the commons'.

However, the emphasis on property rights sits uneasily with the otherwise non-institutional conception of markets simply as the summation of isolated bilateral exchange. The very existence of property rights and the accompanying legal codes and contract laws provide market-wide institutions that support 'isolated' exchange. If agents were unboundedly rational, as they are in a Walrasian world, of course, there would be no need for institutional supports, and the unnecessary costs of setting up a legal code would be avoided. In the real world, where agents are only boundedly rational, however, the prior existence of a set of rules and codes defined by a 'third party' makes exchange viable as it obviates the need for the repeated determination of certain detailed aspects of the terms of trade in each case.

However, the intervention of a third party, in the form of the provision of legal institutions, while necessary on grounds of bounded rationality, is also *incomplete* for the same reason. It cannot cover the whole range of possible contractual eventualities. More precisely, the third-party institutional support – legal codes and contract law – is incomplete because of the fundamental juxtaposition of bounded rationality and uncertainty. In an economy of repetition where no new information is generated, legal institutions would be sufficient (though perhaps in the long run redundant). However, in a changing environment where new information is generated continually and where, moreover, this information is inherently of a local and dispersed character, the need to supplement the third-party support becomes paramount. *It is this fundamental fact that limits the efficacy of privatization in the process of systemic change*: private property rights can never be *fully* defined *ex ante*. They can only be *exercised ex post* and this depends on the ability of the owners, individually or collectively, to create appropriate institutions and patterns of behaviour.

Bottom-up Privatization

The problem of adequately defining property rights also confronts attempts to create a private-enterprise economy via bottom-up privatization. It is not existing organizations that are transferred into private ownership, but new private institutions and organizations that are formed. This is of particular relevance in terms of the encouragement of a fledgling small-enterprise sector in many socialist economies. Small enterprises are often thought of as being the most entrepreneurial types of firm. In this way the debate on bottom-up privatization ties together the discussion on entrepreneurship as a means of changing society, with small business as a mode of achieving such change. Entrepreneurship is regarded as an essential feature of reform in many socialist economies seeking to move towards market-type economies.[6]

Many academic commentators argue that encouraging entrepreneurship is vital for the development of socialist economies. In general, the lay meaning of entrepreneurship as innovative/risk-taking activity is left as an unstated premise in their arguments. In typical vein, H. Bannasch (1990) argues that three types of reform are necessary to facilitate entrepreneurship: 1. the creation of an economic environment conducive to entrepreneurial activity; 2. the removal of entry barriers facing new firms; and

3. the creation of institutions to promote and facilitate new businesses. In this way, they argue that entrepreneurship is probably best promoted through something like bottom-up privatization. From our perspective, their understanding of institutional change is somewhat narrow. By institutions they do not mean the pattern of routinized behaviour, but simply new legal organizations. Their emphasis is placed upon entrepreneurship by small-scale ventures as a means of overcoming systemic paralysis caused by monolithic monopoly enterprise. Small and medium-sized enterprises are seen as a crucial element in the successful demonopolization of economies largely devoid of competition (Hricovsky, 1990).

In many socialist economies in which highly concentrated industrial sectors have predominated, the basic problem with bottom-up privatization is seen to be the speed of transition towards an economy of private enterprise. Thus, even if the small-firms sector is actively encouraged, it will not have a significant impact on the structure of the enterprise sector in the short or medium term, given the dominant role of the state sector.

A more fundamental problem, however, lies in the relation which is posited between entrepreneurship and small business. Entrepreneurship, although often clearly aligned with smaller-enterprise activities, may be carried out inside larger-scale organizations – usually called intrapreneurship (Pinchot, 1985; Hisrich and Peters, 1992). As such, either top-down or bottom-up privatization may be appropriate, as long as it succeeds in promoting entrepreneurial behaviour. To discuss which type of privatization is best used as a means for encouraging entrepreneurship assumes, of course, that there is entrepreneurial spirit to be encouraged. As Kornai (1986) has noted, 'there is enterprising spirit in several layers of the population. The question is whether this spirit will be supported or cooled down by the administrative, legal and economic measures' (p. 102).

Although interest in encouraging entrepreneurship as a means of moving rapidly towards marketization is readily apparent in the literature, what many commentators proposing entrepreneurship in the socialist reform process fail to analyse in any systematic manner is how entrepreneurship is related to the idea of the market. An interesting and useful exception is provided by Y. Shiozawa (1990), who suggests that marketization may reveal hints for a new foundation for economic theory. He argues that 'entrepreneurship is a state of mind or rather a tendency to find and put into practice what is possible but is not yet included in the routines' (Shiozawa, 1990, p. 32). In this way entrepreneurship is innovative. He notes that the spirit of entrepreneurship is not restricted to the owners of business enterprises. It can be present throughout organizational structures. The extent to which such enterprise occurs depends on both the formal and informal institutions of the firm and on how these mould patterns of behaviour.

INFORMATION ASYMMETRY, BUYER'S RISK AND ENTREPRENEURSHIP

For economic development to occur, there must be an expansion of the level of existing trade, and particularly the development of new trading possibilities. Underpinning this process of development, it is usually argued, is entrepreneurship. The entrepreneur must be successful in removing various obstacles to trading. We have suggested that in a changing environment the obstacles to trade stem from exposure to the risks of opportunism and the very dispersal of information. The task of the entrepreneur is essentially to remedy or reduce these problems.

Dispersal of information can take two forms. One is the case where there is information which is complete but *asymmetric* – that is, one party to the exchange has information which the other party would value but does not possess. This type of information dispersal is the cause of the adverse selection problem that has received a lot of attention by economists (see also below). The other form of the dispersal phenomenon is the case whereby neither party to the exchange has the full information required for market exchange. This is the basis of the buyer's risk problem identified in this chapter.

Information Asymmetry

Where there is information asymmetry, as, for example, in relation to quality, there is G. Akerlof's famous 'lemon problem' (Akerlof, 1970), and market exchange breaks down. In the context of our discussion, the significance of information asymmetry is that it severely limits the scope of the application of property rights since, in practice though not in principal, no non-misleading description of the performance and characteristics of the object of exchange is possible.

In the context of the Akerlof-type model, the very asymmetry of information *may* also be the source of the solution to the adverse-selection problem. The party that is better informed may undertake to guarantee some level of performance for the commodity. The provision of a guarantee is, in a sense, a further clarification of the property rights exchanged but which is provided directly by one side in the bilateral exchange rather than by a third party external to it. The fact that the seller is better informed regarding the quality of the product does not automatically mean that he/she is *able*, or will find it profitable, to offer a guarantee. The ability to offer a guarantee depends, presumably, on control over the production process. It also depends, however, on some level of trust by the buyers. Akerlof (1970) implies that the solution of the 'lemon problem' lies in some sort of 'quality arbitrage'. Those who can assess quality at the purchasing stage can also guarantee products when selling. But why should buyers trust the guarantee? In practice, of course, the guarantee may be legally enforceable. But this only reduces, rather than eliminates, the necessity of trust. Ignoring enforcement costs (which can be substantial), the law can only enforce a bare-minimum standard of performance. Effective operation of guarantees involves some investment in the production of trust by the seller. There are various mechanisms for the production of trust (Zucker, 1986) but in the present context it is necessary for the supplier to undertake a commitment to the market in the long run. The existence of such a commitment means that co-ordination is not through price alone, nor is it purely *ex post*. Some bond or relationship, in addition to price alone, between buyers and sellers is implied. By contrast, behaviour implied in perfectly competitive or perfectly contestable models of the market (where there is freedom of entry and *exit*) will actually prove destructive in terms of the development of market-generating institutions. Were all agents to act as if markets were perfectly competitive or contestable, it is doubtful if effectively functioning markets would ever arise. In this context the paper by S. Rashid (1988) is particularly interesting. As Rashid argues, if the market is contestable, then who is to tell incumbent from transient suppliers in the industry? In fact, why is the entire industry not composed of transients? And if the industry is composed of a large number of transients, why should they care about how the customers regard the quality of the product? If no firm has a long-term commitment to the industry or is not prepared to forgo the opportunities for short-term gain (in the form of the adulteration of product quality, for example) as an act of investment in reputation, the prospects for the development of the market are not favourable. In a regime of perfect contestability, investment in quality is never an optimal strategy (see Baumol, 1990). A strategy of short-term profit maximization dominates a policy of long-term commitment.[7]

Buyer's Risk

So far we have been concerned with the institutional implications of the problem of information asymmetry. What if there is an expectation of performance failure, but neither party to the exchange (or, indeed, anyone else) has prior knowledge regarding the probability of failure? This is the basis of the general problem of buyer's risk already noted.[8] Although there is no information asymmetry – both parties to the exchange may be equally ignorant *ex ante* regarding the performance of the product *ex post* – the risk regarding the uncertainty is borne by the buyer as, in monetized exchange, the seller receives money which is by definition and function perfectly homogeneous and of invariant quality and performance.

The solution to the buyer's-risk problem also involves long-term commitment and the development of institutions that imply some shifting of risks to the suppliers. To get a more effective handle on this discussion, consider the following example of institutional practices that seem explicable only in terms of the concept of buyer's risk. In academic publishing we expect the regular provision of inspection copies; many retailers provide information for their customers, such as sell-by-dates; other firms allow their customers to have goods on approval. All these are institutional practices designed to reduce buyer's risk by shifting some of the risk to the seller. Although in all of these cases more information is generated for the buyer, in none of them is there a problem of information asymmetry as such.

However, the development of the types of institution that attenuate buyer's risk faces even more forbidding obstacles compared to the development of those relating to information asymmetry. Three related differences seem particularly important.

First, in the context of Akerlof-type models, the provision of a warranty is rather like an act of investment with a predictable, though uncertain, pay-off. At the very least, the calculation of the costs involved, reflecting the probability of performance failure, can be based on reliable data. On the demand side, too, the effect of the warranty in increasing the number of trades and repeat purchases can be predicted. By contrast, the kinds of institution that may remedy buyer's risk are not really acts of investment in the narrow sense of an activity with a predictable pay-off. The seller is not in a position to guarantee a level of performance, since by assumptions s/he does not have the requisite knowledge on the basis of which to define a 'normal' standard of performance. The *private* provision of a mechanism intended to attenuate the problem of buyer's risk in a particular market or segment of the economy is of a more speculative or 'entrepreneurial' character, the benefits (and clearly also the costs) of which are not known or even predictable *ex ante*.

Second, the 'quality arbitrage' implied by the provision of a guarantee and the accompanying investment in reputation and trust can take place within the given institutional framework of a basically market economy. The individual firm's investment in reputation creates local or 'second-tier', rather than systemic, institutions. This investment in fact creates 'good will', the benefits of which can be fully appropriable by the firm itself. This is very significant. If an individual firm fails to honour its guarantee, this does not undermine our faith in guarantees in general. No externalities are involved.

By contrast, the creation of institutions that attenuate buyer's risk are much more akin to the private provision of a public good. Any 'good will' generated is less likely to be appropriable privately and, unlike the institution of the warranty, the full benefits can only be appreciated if the practices achieve a critical mass in society. These practices perform institutional arbitrage by helping to spread the acceptance and legitimacy of the market system. The legitimacy grows in proportion to the growth in perception of entrepreneurs as people who devise new products, services and activities and in the process enrich not only themselves but also society (Nove, 1991).

Third, it follows from the above that so far as the problem of buyer's risk is concerned, the possibility of destructive as well as productive entrepreneurship must be taken into account. Of course, all entrepreneurship is necessarily destructive. In fact, the major problem with privatization of state assets is that its management is unlikely to be entrepreneurial in the sense of seeking to destroy the institutional practices and habits of a command economy. By contrast, the so-called 'bottom-up' privatization, which essentially promotes small businesses, is more likely to be entrepreneurial because small-scale business is likely to prove a powerful corrosive force so far as the institutions of a command economy are concerned.[9] But there is also a danger that entrepreneurship will be wholly destructive – not only undermining the institutions of command economy but also undermining the social acceptability of profit-orientated behaviour. We have argued that the institutions which remedy the consequences of information asymmetry, and particularly those that reduce buyer's risk, imply some departure from extreme individualism. They involve individual investment in the creation not only of purely private capital, but also of social capital. This social capital takes the form of an expanding network of trust in society. This is the essence of what may be called 'institutional entrepreneurship' – entrepreneurial behaviour that helps to create and spread the legitimacy of the market mechanism. However, as we noted in the introduction, the ideological and historical context within which the transition to the market is taking place makes this outcome increasingly less likely than it might have been. We may add, however, that this likelihood seems rather slim in any case. Only a few market economies have succeeded in developing the institutions that help to achieve the delicate balance between private rent-seeking and productive entrepreneurship.

Notes

1. Thus we are using the term 'institution' in the broad sense, to mean 'a social organisation which, through the operation of tradition, custom or legal constraint, tends to create *durable routinized patterns of behaviour*' (Hodgson, 1988, p. 10, our emphasis). In contrast to much of the Western literature on marketization, within the Soviet Union, at least, this point appears to be recognized. Mikhail Gorbachev, in discussing *perestroika*, states: 'We must ensure radical changes in productive forces and production relations, the revolutionary renewal of social and political structures and growth in the *spiritual and intellectual potential of society* ... In practice, one frequently runs into a negative reaction to initiative, a refusal to accept it ... We cannot put up with this state of affairs. If we do, restructuring will not succeed' (reported in *Current Digest of the Soviet Press*, 1988).

2. 'The East European industry, antiquated and inefficient as it is, has been built at the price of enormous sacrifice by the general population over the last 45 years...If this industry is now to be sold at prices which are seen as very low, the popular opinion might turn against the privatisation program as a whole...Great attention must therefore be paid to choosing a strategy of privatisation which will not exacerbate the anxieties of the population, but rather give it some tangible stakes in the success of the undertaking' (Frydman and Rapaczynksi, 1990, pp. 10–11).

3. Governance checks against not only the consumption of profits by managers but also against the possibility of sheer managerial incompetence.

4. 'Suppose there were apples in Krasmodor and no apples in Kharkov. An enterprising would-be trader could make a lot of money by buying them cheap in Krasmodor and selling them at a much higher price in Kharkov. Most of his fellow citizens, as well as the law-enforcing agencies, regard such activities as illegitimate speculation and the apple-merchant as "greedy" and a scoundrel' (Nove, 1991, p. 259).

5. Those who do make profit cannot really be considered as capitalists in the accepted sense of the term. Profits are likely to be regarded as a means of boosting consumption rather than accumulation: 'In historical accounts of capitalist economies, we are used to reading about the parsimony of the founders of family businesses who endeavour to bequeath their wealth to future generations ... By contrast, wasteful consumption in family business in reformed socialist countries often began on the very first day of their existence' (Kornai, 1986, p. 138).

6. In Hungary, for instance, the government recently stated that, 'It is the firm resolution of the government ... to create the most important elements of a contemporary market economy ... This market economy relies on entrepreneurial freedom, on individual initiatives and on a sense of mutual social responsibility' (reported in *East European Reporter*, 1991). Similarly, in the Soviet Union a new 'Law on Principles of Entrepreneurship' was introduced

(Gorbachev, 1991, p. 22) which aimed at 'creating conditions for the broad display of economic initiative and enterprise by citizens'.

7. Under these circumstances, even if markets come into being they are unlikely to be a vehicle for economic development. Not surprisingly, quality variation is much greater in the LDCs. Akerlof (1970) cites the example of Indian housewives 'who must carefully glean rice in the local bazaar to sort out stones of the same colour and shape which have been intentionally added to the rice' (p. 16). See also Rashid, 1988.

8. Note that with information asymmetry, the risks are not necessarily borne by the buyers. The classic examples of the adverse-selection problem, the insurance and credit markets, are cases where the risks are borne by the sellers.

9. The ideology and practice of classical socialism suppressing not only full-blown capitalism, but also small-scale production, has been very much influenced by V. I. Lenin's frequently quoted dictum that 'small production engenders capitalism and the bourgeoisie continuously, daily, hourly, spontaneously, and on a mass scale'. In the author's opinion, 'Lenin was absolutely right. If a society allows for a large number of small commodity producers ... a genuine group of capitalists will sooner or later emerge' (Kornai, 1986, p. 137).

Part IV

Part III

Eastern and Central Europe

5 Economic Transformation in East and Central Europe: An Overview
Peter Lawrence

This chapter presents an overview of the process of economic transformation in the former state socialist economies of Eastern and Central Europe.[1] It will be shown here that the central features of this process have been, first, the collapse of a large part of the traditional industrial base of these economies; second, substantial falls in GDP and living standards; third, the creation of, and significant increases in, unemployment; and finally, the failure of the economic reforms to generate, in the short run, the process of growth of alternative economic activities to replace those that have collapsed.

The chapter begins with a survey of economic performance in the former European state socialist economies, and goes on to examine some of the policy prescriptions and their implementation. Finally, it considers the prospects for further change in these economies. It will be argued that while the economic reforms have merit in improving the structure of incentives to all economic agents, too much faith has been put in the 'free market' model as a reaction to the former rigidly-administered system. This faith in the 'market' is not only misplaced, but needs to be replaced by a reassertion of a degree of economic planning and co-ordination so that the transformation process is consistent with political as well as economic stability.

ECONOMIC PERFORMANCE IN EASTERN AND CENTRAL EUROPE

A comparison of economic performance over time of Eastern and Central Europe shows evidence of a slow but steady decline in year-on-year growth since the 1970s, culminating in sharp negative growth-rate changes in most economic indicators after 1989 in most of these countries. Figure 5.1 shows annual percentage changes in net material product (NMP) for six of these countries since 1970. All these countries show a sharp fall in NMP after 1989, with only Poland showing some kind of recovery in 1991.

Figure 5.2 shows what has happened to industrial production over the same period. Poland and the former German Democratic Republic (GDR) showed the sharpest falls in industrial output in 1990, while Bulgaria, Czechoslovakia and Hungary registered sharp drops in 1991, showing the differences in timing over this period between the countries concerned. Figure 5.3 shows what happened to agricultural output over our six countries, with the sharpest fall being registered by the GDR in 1990.

Figure 5.4 shows the phenomenal drop in gross fixed investment in the period after 1989, with the usual lags for countries which introduced economic reforms later than others. Figures 5.5 and 6.6 show what happened to exports and imports over this period. A marked drop in export-volume growth appears in the late 1980s, with an upturn in 1988 preceding some dramatic drops in 1989–91. The introduction of import liberalization and exchange-rate depreciation has quite differential effects. Poland, which underwent a massive currency depreciation, showed high growth in export volumes and high negative growth in import volumes.

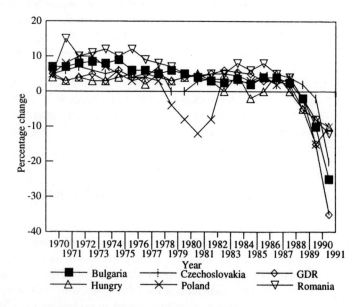

Figure 5.1   Net material product, annual percentage change
Sources: UNECE (1992); OECD (1992).

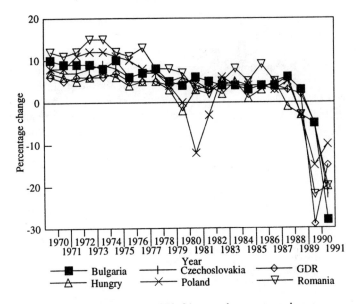

Figure 5.2   Industrial production, 1970–91, annual percentage change
Sources: UNECE (1992); OECD (1992).

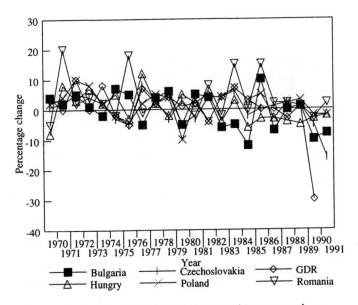

Figure 5.3   Agricultural production, 1970–91, annual percentage change
Sources: UNECE (1992); OECD (1992).

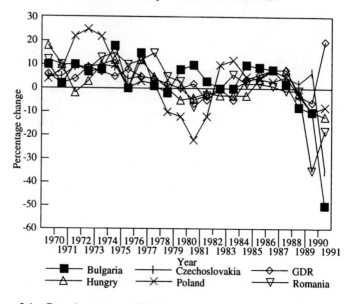

Figure 5.4   Gross investment, 1970–91, annual percentage change
Sources: UNECE (1992); OECD (1992).

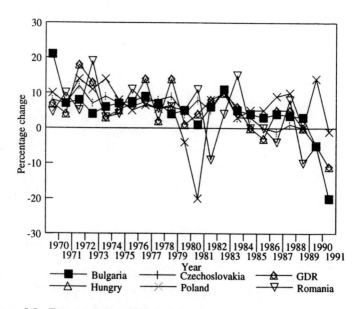

Figure 5.5   Export volumes, 1970–91, annual percentage change
Sources: UNECE (1992); OECD (1992).

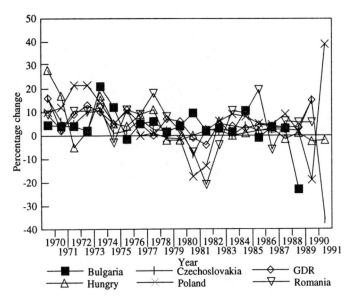

Figure 5.6   Import volumes, 1970–91, annual percentage change
Sources: UNECE (1992); OECD (1992).

The most important socioeconomic consequence of this process of output decline and structural change has been a massive increase in unemployment across Eastern Europe as enterprises close down or lay off surplus labour. Figure 5.7 shows the growth in unemployment over the transition period. Enterprises producing goods destined under the old system for other CMEA economies found demand for them cut off and were forced to lay off workers pending the introduction of rescue packages or bankruptcy laws. In any event, unemployment was likely to rise because of the substantial degree of hoarded labour, which was a characteristic of the old system. Enterprises always kept on more workers than they needed in case they were required to fulfil contracts additional to those planned or, in order to fulfil existing contracts, they needed to take on more labour (Gora and Rutkowski, 1990). The question of which workers would go in a 'dehoarding' process is answered partially by looking at the differences between male and female unemployment rates. Table 5.1 shows that female rates are much higher than male rates. This suggests that the process of labour dehoarding will be one in which more women are expected to leave the labour force, as both male and female labour is allocated more efficiently. Women in Eastern Europe have tradi-

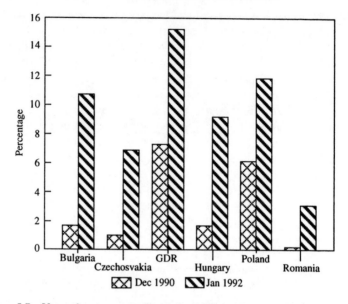

Figure 5.7   Unemployment rates, December 1990 and January 1992
Sources: UNECE (1992); OECD (1992).

Table 5.1   Eastern Europe: Male and Female Unemployment
Rates (September 1991)

Country	Total	Male	Female
Bulgaria*	10.7	9.5	11.5
Czechoslovakia	5.6	5.0	6.3
GDR	11.7	9.1	14.3
Hungary	6.1	6.6	5.5
Poland	10.4	9.2	11.8
Romania	2.4	1.8	3.2

Source: UN (1992); *December 1991.

tionally done two jobs: their paid work and their housework. The system
of crèches and nurseries has enabled a high female participation rate to be
maintained to support the system of labour hoarding.

However, cuts in public expenditure are already reportedly reducing
free or subsidized nursery places. Women may therefore be registering as
unemployed and looking for work, but may be unable to take up an
offered job because of the reduction in child-care facilities.

However, it has been observed that the process of increasing unemployment has been slowed by the cheapening of labour because of a decline in real wages. Figure 5.8 shows what has been happening to the inflation rate since 1989, while Figure 5.9 shows how this has affected the rate of real wage increase. It is clear that there has been a sharp decline in real wages since 1989, resulting from the rapid increases in prices that have taken place with the removal of subsidies and the depreciation of exchange rates. Most countries have brought the process of inflation under control, but at the cost of employment, as state subsidies to enterprises are withdrawn and enterprises themselves are scheduled for privatization or bankruptcy, once bankruptcy laws are introduced. The people of the Eastern *Länder* of Germany have been partly protected from this process because of the policy of gradual money wage equalization across Germany (OECD, 1992), although, as we have seen, they have not been protected from unemployment.

Paralleling the decline in real wages has been the erosion by price restructuring of the real value of social benefits, such as pensions (UNECE, 1992). Though these were always a relatively low proportion of the average wage, price subsidies on essential foods and other goods, as well as on energy prices and public transport, meant that pensioners could

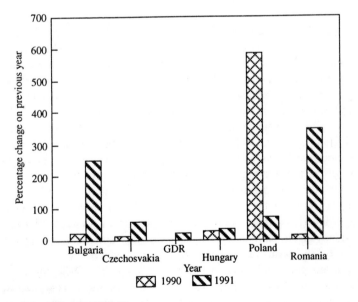

Figure 5.8 Inflation 1990–91
Sources: UNECE (1992); OECD (1992).

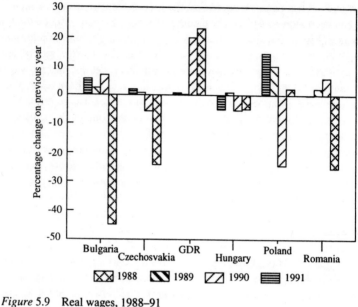

Figure 5.9   Real wages, 1988–91
Sources: UNECE (1992); OECD (1992).

maintain their living standards after retirement. With the removal of subsidies, pensioners have seen their living standards fall sharply. Taken together with the erosion of real wages, this leaves the lower-income groups and the unemployed open to increasing poverty and provides a backdrop for potential social unrest and dislocation, as discontent with the immediate effects of the reforms is more widely felt.

The growth of unemployment, together with social and ethnic tensions and the opening up of frontiers, has led to a massive increase in labour migration across the former state socialist countries. Apart from the migration of Eastern Germans to Western Germany after the opening of the border and subsequent unification, and the commuter traffic of cheap Eastern German labour to the Western *Länder*, there have been significant migration flows from Poland to Germany; from Russia to Poland and Germany; from Romania to Poland, Hungary and Germany; and, more recently, an exodus of migrants and refugees from the former Yugoslavia to various parts of Europe (UNECE, 1992; OECD, 1992). Much of this migration involves the search for jobs, but much also is generated by the development of informal commodity markets in goods and currencies, especially where internal convertibility of currencies is not fully fledged.

Thus traders come from non-convertible-currency countries to internally-convertible-currency countries, sell goods, convert into dollars and then re-exchange the dollars at parallel-market rates back home, or use the dollars to obtain goods and services not available for holders of the local currency.[2]

Reliable data on these migration flows are difficult to find. It is estimated that almost half a million people moved to Germany from Eastern Europe and the former Soviet Union in 1989, while less than 10 per cent of that number moved to other West European countries (UNECE, 1992:258). Within Germany, there has been a substantial increase in migration from East to West as unemployment rose in the Eastern *Länder*, although this migration mainly takes the form of commuting. By the end of 1991, there were up to half a million commuters travelling an average of 50 kilometres, with nearly half of these commuting weekly or at longer intervals (OECD, 1992:24).

All these developments have been concurrent with, and some have contributed to, a deterioration (with the notable exception of Poland) in the external balances of these countries, and an increase in their international indebtedness. Figures 5.10 to 5.13 show what has been happening to the external balances of four countries for which data are available from the

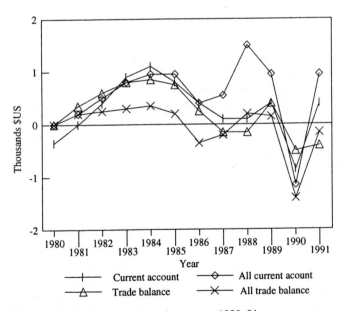

Figure 5.10   Czechoslovakia, trade and payments 1980–91
Sources: UNECE (1992); OECD (1992).

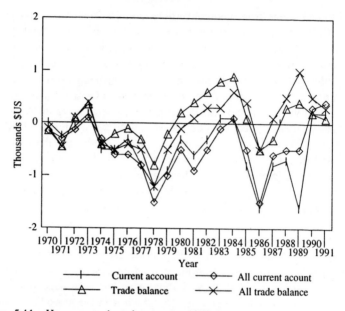

Figure 5.11   Hungary, trade and payments, 1970–91
Source: IMF (1992b).

International Monetary Fund (IMF). The external balances of these countries are complicated because, prior to the move towards trade exclusively
in convertible currencies, distinctions had to be drawn between trade in
convertible and non-convertible currencies. As the countries concerned
have moved to trade only in convertible currencies, the picture has become
somewhat clearer: the effects were already to be seen in 1991. For
Romania, Poland, and to some extent Hungary, there is convergence
between the convertible and all-currency account, indicating the shift
towards all-convertible currency trade, while Czechoslovakia's payments
accounts still reflect a larger surplus on non-dollar trade than on dollar
trade. It is also interesting to note that the trade and payments performance
seems to improve immediately after the implementation of devaluation,
but then slips back (Poland, and to a lesser extent, Hungary). It will be
instructive to see if Czechoslovakia and Romania follow that pattern, too.
If they do, this might suggest that regular currency devaluations (or freely
floating rates) are necessary to sustain improvements in payments balances. The reason for this could be that the short-run gains from currency
devaluation in the form of increasing (or more slowly decreasing) export
revenues and decreasing (or more slowly rising) import bills are dissipated

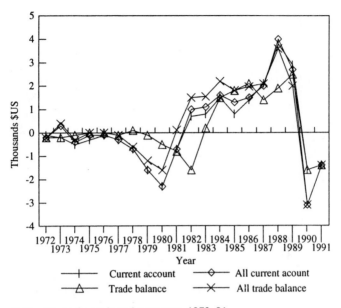

Figure 5.12   Romania, trade and payments, 1972–91
Source: IMF (1992b).

through the inflationary effects of increased import prices, bringing the effective exchange-rate back to its pre-devaluation nominal rate. The export-price advantage gained by devaluation has to be maintained to preserve a price advantage in buying goods from East and Central Europe in order to offset the quality gap between its manufactures and those of competitive Western products. The process of currency depreciation and inflation as a means of balancing the current external account can only be slowed by a closing of that technological gap. While it could be argued that a process of restructuring to raise productivity and quality will occur naturally by means of the operation of the market forces in the goods and currency markets, it is not clear whether an unstable exchange and price regime gives the private sector sufficient incentive to generate the investment necessary for restructuring. If enterprises can continue to export market advantage from further devaluations (and this partly depends on the effects of the current recession on demand for their exports), then they do not have much incentive to restructure either. There may well be more to restructuring than exchange-rate and other price reforms.

Figure 5.14 shows the extent of indebtedness of the four IMF members. With the exception of a small dip in the Polish debt in 1991, Eastern

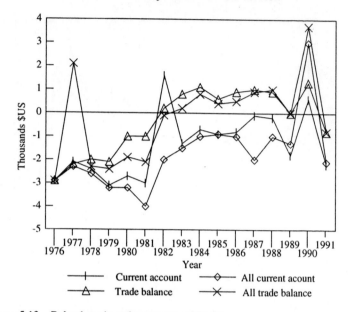

Figure 5.13   Poland, trade and payments, 1976–91
Source: IMF (1992b).

European convertible-currency debt has been increasing. Poland and
Hungary have, of course, been carrying a debt built up during the 1970s
and early 1980s, when it was thought that borrowing to finance industrial
projects could be repaid out of the profits of these projects. This debt over-
hang, which involved debt-service ratios of up to 20 per cent in 1991, is
likely to remain a burden throughout the 1990s for Poland despite some
rescheduling, and for Hungary which, with its small population carries the
higher per capita debt burden.

Such a debt burden, coupled with a probable deterioration in the
external-payments position, forces these countries to seek IMF assistance
in exchange for economic restructuring. All the countries surveyed here
now receive stand-by credits and other assistance from the IMF stabilization fund to enable them to continue with the trade-policy reforms without
the severe balance-of-payments constraints which these reforms induce.

THE ECONOMIC REFORMS

The explanation for these dramatic changes in output and trade growth
lies in the succession of political and economic changes following the

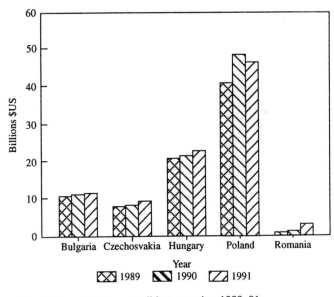

Figure 5.14   External debt, convertible currencies, 1989–91
Source: IMF (1992b).

break-up of the state socialist system dominated by the Soviet Union, and the subsequent implementation of economic-reform programmes linked to IMF stand-by credits and World Bank loans. Such reforms have been implemented gradually, as in the Hungarian case, or very rapidly, as under the 'shock therapy' of the Polish Balcerowicz plan (WERI, 1991).

The decision in 1990 to dissolve the Council for Mutual Economic Assistance (CMEA, or Comecon) trading system dominated by the Soviet Union generated a number of changes in trade and industry which have had profound effects on economic performance (WERI, 1991). Much of Eastern Europe's industrial output was directed to trade with the Soviet Union. In return for relatively sophisticated industrial goods from its partners, the USSR would supply raw materials, especially oil (Blanchard and Layard, 1990). For political reasons, the governments of Eastern Europe were concerned that contracts made with the USSR should be fulfilled. The existence of a secure market in the USSR meant that enterprises in Eastern Europe had no incentive to innovate, or in any other way improve efficiency. Furthermore it was easy for inefficient enterprises to get state credits in order to survive because of the political need to supply the USSR. The banking system also provided incentives for such enterprises since, in the Hungarian case at least, the value of contracts with the Soviet Union was credited to the enterprise account even before the goods had been supplied.

The major reforms that were introduced to this system after 1989 were the abolition of the transferable rouble as a unit of account for transactions between CMEA countries, and the introduction of a hard-currency trading system for all trade, from the beginning of 1991. Some exceptions were made to this by engaging in barter deals in bilateral trade (WERI, 1991), but the effect of this reform was to limit severely the USSR's ability to import. It also ensured that if the USSR had to pay for imports in hard currency, it made more sense to buy higher-quality goods from the West.

This reform was accompanied by exchange-rate restructuring that resulted in substantial currency devaluation and the introduction of internal currency convertibility across most of the countries concerned with single-exchange rates. Devaluations have ranged from 600 per cent in Poland (over the 1980s) and 900 per cent in Bulgaria (in 1991) to the small but regular devaluations by the Hungarian government (UNECE, 1992). Internal convertibility, that is the purchase with limited restriction of convertible currency by firms and households, was implemented in all countries, although some put very low limits on how much could be converted in one year.

The third plank of trade-policy reform was to implement import liberalization in a gradual manner, as in Hungary, or quite extensively, as in Czechoslovakia and Poland. In conjunction with devaluation and real-wage reduction, this has limited the deterioration in balance of payments positions feared by opponents of import liberalization. However, it has contributed to the decline in demand for domestically-produced, but inferior, goods which can now be imported, and therefore to the problems of falling domestic output and rising unemployment outlined above.

Together with the above policies to liberalize external trade, governments across Eastern Europe implemented price-liberalization reform, varying in 1990–91 from 70 per cent to 95 per cent, and in the case of Polish energy prices 400 per cent (UNECE, 1992). Accompanying these price increases have been highly restrictive wage policies, with in some cases taxes on 'excess' wage increases. Fiscal policy has included tax reform and the implementaion of income tax systems as well as cuts in public expenditure, while monetary policy has been dominated by the liberalization of interest rates, resulting in Poland, for example, operating a 36 per cent real interest rate (IMF, 1992b).

In the financial sector, the introduction of banking reform allowing the establishment of foreign banks and competition among state-owned banks has proceeded quickly in most countries. Meanwhile, stock exchange were established by Hungary in 1989 and Poland in 1991. The further introduction of capital markets will depend on the speed with which the state sector of these economies is dismantled and private companies seek share issues on local capital markets.

The privatization of state assets is therefore widely regarded by all the new governments as the favoured route to divesting the state of economic power and rescuing failing, inefficient enterprises (Hare and Grosfeld, 1991). However, the methods and extent of intended privatization vary between countries. Some countries, for example Poland and Czechoslovakia, have favoured the distribution of vouchers to the population, with which shares can be bought, while in Hungary, the favoured method is sale by auction or by stock exchange flotation (Hare and Grosfeld, 1991; Borensztein and Kumar, 1991). The variation in methods exposes the problems associated with privatization of state-owned assets. First of all, who has sufficient capital to buy these often very large enterprises? Private savings by individuals and private businesses cover a very small proportion of the asset value of state enterprises. Only foreign enterprises backed by financial institutions have the resources to buy. Given the strong streak of nationalism running through East and Central Europe, giving companies away through a system of vouchers is seen as being superior to selling to foreign enterprises. However, on what basis can voucher-owners make decisions about where to invest when information about companies is asymmetric, and when capital markets and associated financial institutions – investment trusts, for example – have yet to demonstrate their effectiveness?

Second, on what basis can the information about enterprises be regarded as being reliable? Accounting systems under the old regimes were based upon prices which were administered involving subsidies or hidden taxes and did not represent what could be obtained in a more market-orientated system. Costs were also distorted by the distortion of other administered prices which made up costs. So enterprises which appeared to be profitable under the old system could be loss-making when 'Western' accounting methods based on 'true' costs and prices were applied.

Third, who wants to buy large, inefficient enterprises producing goods which cannot be sold? Western companies were only likely to be interested in those enterprises, or more precisely those *parts* of enterprises, which would be profitable, thus leading to asset-stripping on a large scale. Even then, foreign partners would only be interested in acquiring a minority shareholding, leaving the state with the bulk of the shares. In Hungary, for example, despite its pioneering position in privatization (beginning before 1989), even after the privatization of 39 companies, the state still owned 70 per cent of the total shareholding (SPA, 1991).

It might therefore be concluded that privatization of these economies is unlikely to come from the sale of existing state assets, but rather from inward foreign investment, either directly or through joint ventures and through the expansion of small and medium-sized enterprises. Although foreign investment in Eastern Europe has been increasing since the end of the 1980s it is still a relatively small proportion of total inward capital flows, except in the case of Hungary, whose foreign investment and other private inflows in 1990 constituted 46 per cent of total foreign direct investment and other private inflows into Eastern Europe as a whole (UNECE, 1992).

Some of this direct investment is 'Third Worldist' in character, in the sense that the investment yields high returns for the investor but little benefit to the country concerned. Parts of existing state enterprises are 'colonised' by international companies, using cheap, often female, labour to assemble imported parts at inflated prices as a means of hidden repatri-ation of profits. Such an 'ideal type' example exists in at least one East European case observed by this author. Part of the plant of the Hungarian electronics firm Videoton was taken over by the Dutch multinational, Philips, as a video-recorder assembly line. Philips charged its Videoton plant three times the price it normally charges for its inputs and pays its largely female labour force one-eighth the wage it was paying in Austria (interview with Videoton manager, June 1991). It might be expected that, at some stage, Eastern Europe will become a base for serving the Commonwealth of Independent States' (CIS) market and might then attract not only investment from Western Europe and the United States, but also from Japan. The question will then be: how far can East European governments negotiate such investment deals so that more than simply employment at low wages is gained by the host country?

The clear hope for the future is the growth of small- and medium-scale enterprises and joint ventures between local private or state and foreign capital. There was a rapid spurt in growth of small and medium-sized enterprises and of joint ventures at the end of the 1980s as company law was changed to allow for limited liability and partnership enterprises. The privatization of small shops and restaurants has further contributed to the growth of small, privately-owned enterprises. In Poland, for example, there was a 2.5-fold increase in the number of private companies, and a fourfold increase in the number of joint ventures in 1990 (WERI, 1991). A similar story can be told for Hungary (CSO, 1991). One of the features of state socialism was the gap in industrial structure deriving from the domination of the large, state-owned trusts. Not only in the service sector but also in manufacturing, the absence of a strong small enterprise sector producing specialist parts and machines for small markets, increased the likelihood of shortages as large enterprises were ill-equipped to respond to orders for small production runs of a highly specialist product. So the expansion of the small-scale sector should provide the dynamism for the transition and the source of an increasing share of non-state activity in these economies.

Finally, there is the question of agriculture. The forced collectivization of much of East European agriculture, with the exception of Poland, has raised questions about whether to return the land to the former holders, if they can be found. Although opposed initially, a great deal of collectivized agriculture has been highly productive, even if the level of chemical input intensity has suggested that net returns to agriculture may not be very high (see, for example, Swain, 1987). The development of smallholder production alongside or within collectives has generated some degree of interdependence between highly mechanized large-scale production on collectively farmed land, and small-scale production on household plots. To what extent collective members want to overturn this system, which has generated some degree of security, and replace it with a fully-fledged smallholder system is debatable, and some governments have resolved this question by offering vouchers to former landholders rather than the land itself. To the extent that smallholdings become more prevalent, especially in such labour-intensive activities as horticulture, this will merely reflect the filling of gaps in the production structure, much in the same way as for the industrial and service sectors discussed above.

THE FUTURE

The early euphoria that accompanied democratization in 1989–90 has died down and been overshadowed by the harsh realities involved in transforming economic systems which had stagnated for nearly two decades and had failed to implement economic reform. It is becoming clear that in the midst of a world economic recession the task of transformation will be much more difficult than had been supposed.

The idea that the governments of Eastern and Central Europe could simply act as enablers to open the gates for foreign investors is giving way to the view that the state has an important role to play in easing the transformation process and itself taking initiatives where the private sector fails to do so. As dissatisfaction with the reforms increases, social discontent channelled into ethnic and nationalist movements itself reacts against the takeover of key industries by 'foreigners'. The problem associated with giving the state an interventionist role is that those who play this role are the very people who played it under the old regimes, thus giving rise to fears about the return of vested interests that once again might oppose reform.

However, it is evident that privatization will be a slow process, and that foreign investors are not queueing up to take over antiquated production facilities, especially in conditions of a major world recession and of uncertainty about the survival of the new democracies. It is also evident that restructuring has to take place, since the breakdown of the old Eastern Europe–USSR trading system means that factories are producing goods that nobody wants.

This situation calls for a new industrial strategy and for investment by the state to facilitate the implementation of such a strategy. Clearly, this has to be a different process from that which operated under the old regime. Accountability in its literal and general sense, competitiveness guaranteed by the gradual liberalization of imports, and an incentive structure which encourages high productivity and technological change, can all contribute to making such a state-led system work effectively.

In this context, some of the suggestions of reform economists under and outside the old regimes (Nove, 1983), in spite of the reservations (noted by Pat Devine in Chapter 2 of this volume) of Kornai (1986), might be more relevant than previously thought. For some time to come, the former state socialist economies are going to continue to have large state sectors that require restructuring and efficient management. Reforms based on enterprise autonomy from the state, already effected in many of the former state socialist economies, would need to be accompanied by the gradual imposition over a fixed period of 'hard budget constraints' – the slow withdrawal of state subsidies for these enterprises, thus giving breathing space to them to adjust to market price signals.

The promotion of subcontracting arrangements within enterprises, with semi-autonomous groups of workers competing for contracts to supply specific inputs and services might lead to the breaking up of the larger enterprises and the development of small and medium-sized firms in a more organic fashion. The liberalization of access to commercial credit at market rates of interest, of enterprise access to convertible currency and therefore to imported inputs, would provide state enterprises with the opportunities not open to them under the credit- and convertible-currency-rationed state socialist systems. Experimentation with different forms of ownership, control and economic planning (see Chapter 2 in this volume) as well as of contractual arrangements between public and private economic agents, is no longer constrained by the pace of change in the Soviet Union. Ironically, now the constraints on experimentation with reform may rather come from the side of the IMF and the World Bank, committed as they are to *de-ètatization* and rapid liberalization. However, even these organizations may begin to realize that the difficulties of making a rapid transition to Western-style capitalism may call for new solutions, which may indeed prove to be new versions of some of the old solutions made impossible under the old regimes.

Notes

1. Much of this article is based on interviews with economists and officials in Hungary and Poland, during research visits in November 1989 (Hungary, privatization) and June 1991 (Poland and Hungary, unemployment), funded by the British Academy and the Nuffield Foundation, respectively. The author is grateful to the many people, too numerous to name here, who gave freely of their time to explain the 'old' system and the effects of the reforms.
2. The very public 'Russian' markets, observed by the author in 1991, are a good example of this, as were the 'Polish' markets in Hungary, which sold Polish goods in Hungary. Hungary goods not available in Poland were then bought and resold in Poland for dollars.

6 The Impact of Economic Reform in East and Central Europe on Developing Countries

Mehdi Shafaeddin

INTRODUCTION

A number of significant institutional, political and economic changes have taken place in the USSR, Eastern Europe and China in recent years: *perestroika* in the USSR; abolition of the Council for Mutual Economic Assistance (CMEA) and termination of the barter system in trade among the countries of Eastern Europe; German unification; economic reform in China;and development of separatist fervour in the USSR and Yugoslavia.

Substantial work has been emerging on the nature of such changes and the future of East–West economic relations. In relation to their trade in general, and East–South trade in particular, many developing countries have voiced concern about the implication of economic changes in the socialist bloc, especially as they concern reforms in trade policies which will affect them. No analytical framework for studying such implications can be found in the literature.

The main purpose of this chapter is to outline a conceptual framework in which the impact of economic reform in the socialist economies in transition of Eastern Europe and the USSR (SET) can be assessed on developing countries. A framework for examining the short- and long-term consequences is provided in the next section. It is too early to provide a comprehensive statistical analysis of such an impact. Nevertheless, with the help of available data for 1990, some light may be shed on the pattern of development in the short run. This task will be undertaken in the third section. The final section draws conclusions.

A CONCEPTUAL FRAMEWORK

Economic reforms in the socialist economies in transition will influence East–South trade relations directly through changes in trade policies, trade institutions, exchange-rate policies and their overall international economic relations with developing countries. Economic reforms also have an indirect influence on the trade of developing countries through the impacts of domestic policies on foreign trade in general. The impact of such reforms would need to be examined separately, first for the interim (transition) period, then for the period near completion. This can be defined as a time when transition to a market economy has been achieved. The major preoccupation of SET countries during the transition period would appear to be on how to operate within a market economy, and how to put in place the necessary infrastructure for a market to function satisfactorily.

The main elements of economic reforms consist of privatization of ownership and appropriate decision-making; removal of rationing; reduction or cessation of state trading and preferential trading; liberalization of trade; currency convertibility; employment and wage policies; investment regulation and provision for technological changes. All these factors influence the magnitude, composition and geographical distribution of international trade, thus influencing trade of SET with developing countries both directly and indirectly. For example, the removal of rationing and the fixed-price system would tend to activate the portion of effective demand which used to be repressed before the reform. As a result, the excess demand will manifest itself, given the level of output, to a lower saving ratio and an increase in demand for imports. Other things being equal, developing countries may benefit from such an increase in demand for imports, provided imports can be increased. Other things, however, are *not* equal and developing countries may, in fact, lose as a result of diversion of trade away from these countries, as will be explained later in this section. It should also be mentioned that if imports cannot be increased due to the lack of foreign exchange, the removal of the rationing system would lead to inflation, unless domestic output can be increased sufficiently, which is a very unrealistic assumption in the short run.

Similarly, trade liberalization and currency convertibility has both direct and indirect influence on trade between SET and developing countries. As a result of trade liberalization, consumers would switch their demand towards imports. The increase in demand for imports would set in motion a similar mechanism to that mentioned above. In this case, the direct and indirect impact of all elements of economic reform in SET on the trade of developing countries could be measured.

The direct and indirect influences of economic reform in SET on the trade of developing countries explains the mechanism, or channel, through which changes in SET will affect trade of developing countries. For a more systematic analysis, however, such influences may also need to be classified according to their impact on trade flows and financial flows. The impact on trade flows can, in turn, be grouped into: trade creation effect, trade diversion effect, and competition effect.

While economic reform of SET countries might affect both the exports and imports of the South, the main emphasis in this chapter will be on the former: the exports from developing countries in the South to SET, as well as world markets in general. The impact these reforms might have will be analysed separately for the transitory period and for the longer term.

The *trade creation effects* of economic reform in general depend on two main factors: changes in the rate of growth of gross domestic product (GDP) or the corresponding indicator of gross material product (GMP); and changes in material intensity of domestic production and in the import intensity of domestic production and final demand. During the transition phase, the extent of trade creation would also depend on the speed with which 'demand repression' can be removed, and the speed of trade liberalization, both of which tend to increase the demand for imports.

It may be argued that during the transition period, the trade creation effect would be insignificant in most SET countries, except perhaps for the Eastern *Länder* of Germany. There would be little change in the material intensity of domestic production, significant increases in import intensity of production and final demand and hasty removal of 'demand repression'. Nevertheless, such positive tendencies for trade creation may suffer from an over-compensation effect, with significant declines in the rate of economic growth and a lack of means for financing imports. So far, there has been little sign of any sizeable increases in external sources of import financing. Moreover, the expansion of domestic demand would reduce exports, thus further affecting the domestic means of import financing.

In the long run, the extent of the trade creation effect would depend on the overall rate of economic growth – a matter of speculation – and changes in the technical coefficient of production. There will definitely be a reduction in material intensity of domestic production through the application of efficient technology, accompanied by an increase in import intensity of both domestic demand (caused by changes in taste and preferences) and domestic production (caused mainly by imports of embodied new technology). The prospect for high growth rates of output in China and Eastern *Länder* of Germany seems far better than other Eastern European countries and the old USSR.

The net *trade diversion* effects would depend on positive and negative elements. The positive elements will emerge from SET's diversion of intra-bloc trade to other areas as a result of the abolition of the CMEA. The negative elements will arise mainly through the reduction, or termination, of preferential trading practices. Decisions on trade with developing countries, which had been influenced to a large extent by political factors, would in future, if decisions on sources of supply are made mainly by the private sector, be influenced primarily by considerations of price and quality competitiveness. Further, negative elements may arise through internalization of international trade by the Eastern *Länder* of Germany, possible emergence of a new regional co-operation among Eastern European countries with the exclusion of the USSR, and the probable integration of some of those countries into the EC, EFTA, or other bilateral trade agreements among the Eastern European countries. Even more, the control of EC countries' quantitative restrictions by the Community, rather than by the individual member countries, is likely to work in favour of the exports of countries from Eastern Europe.

During the transition period, the positive effect may not be sufficient to offset the negative impact of the abolition of preferential trading. In the long run, other negative elements may dominate, particularly since the positive element of trade diversion (out of the CMEA in favour of developing countries) may be in the nature of a 'once and for all' type of occurrence. Further, such diversion may address itself mainly to developed countries because of their superior sources of embodied technology. Developing countries may, however, benefit from diversion away from the USSR of the supply of imported energy, and some other raw materials, to Eastern Europe.

The competition effect is related to the potential competition of SET goods with exports of developing countries in the third market – the North and China. During the transition period, the possibility of such competition having great consequence is slight. The inferior quality of consumer goods produced in SET and the existence of excess demand build-up, inherited from the old economic system's demand repression, are two important inhibiting factors. Excess domestic demand will offer little incentive to SET firms to develop their potential export markets. In the long run, however, the removal of repressed demand and trade liberalization will probably lead to lower export prices through pressure on the exchange rate and the need to expand export volume in order to finance imports. The resulting price competition and volume expansion would tend to affect the terms of trade of SET adversely, as well as affecting those of developing countries. Such competition could be exacerbated because of the Eastern European countries' (other than USSR) need for financing imports of oil and gas through the international market.

Previously, these products were imported from the USSR at subsidized prices through barter trade. The fact that, in the future, imports of oil and gas will be paid for at higher prices in hard currency would imply diversion of exports of manufactured goods away from the USSR to the rest of the world.

The competition effect could, however, be severe even in the transition period in the case of China, particularly for certain primary commodities: for example, cotton and traditional light manufactured goods.

While we have emphasized the impact of economic reform in SET countries on the exports of developing countries, it should be mentioned that these countries may also be affected by decreases in their imports from SET. Obviously, other sources of supply are available to developing countries to satisfy their demand. Nevertheless, imports of many developing countries from SET have been accompanied by favourable prices, credits and other forms of tied financial assistance which might not easily be available elsewhere.

This last point leads us to the impact of economic reform in SET on financial flows to developing countries and the resulting impact on trade flows. In addition to tied aid, some developing countries have received relatively small amounts of financial aid in cash or in kind. Lack of such facilities places an extra burden on the recipients, who have to risk means of financing imports from other sources. The flow of imports to developing countries may also suffer as a result of diversion of financial assistance, which they previously received from the North, in favour of SET.

So far, it has been assumed, implicitly, that the direction and volume of *international investment* would not change significantly. This may not, however, stand up to scrutiny. Eastern Europe could ultimately attract significant amounts of investment, particularly from Western Europe. The existence of markets and relatively cheap labour would probably induce gradual integration of Eastern Europe into the West, through direct and indirect foreign investment. Even if such capital flows do not take place at the expense of foreign investment in developing countries, they are likely to involve some diversion of trade, particularly to Western Europe. In fact, capital flows would create new trade opportunities, mainly as a result of higher GDP growth. Such trade will probably be, to a large extent, internalized within the foreign companies involved.

In the short run, however, large capital flows might not race to SET because of uncertainty that continues to surround the economic and political future of these countries. Moreover, the absence of market infrastructure stands as an inhibiting factor. In the long run, significant foreign investment could be attracted to these countries.

EMPIRICAL EVIDENCE

The economic reform in SET, which began in 1990 and was preceded by sociopolitical changes in the last quarter of 1989, have not progressed in a significant way. It is therefore too early to be able to undertake a sound empirical analysis of the impact of these reforms on trade in developing countries. Even for this short period, comprehensive data are not available. Nevertheless, certain inferences can be made by examining the relative importance of SET in the total trade of developing countries, and by assessing the impact of recent changes in SET's trade on developing countries.

THE RELATIVE IMPORTANCE OF SET IN DEVELOPING COUNTRIES' TRADE

It can be seen from Table 6.1 that developing countries' trade with the socialist countries before the political reforms was not significant either as a source of supply or as an important market for trade of developing countries. In fact, the socialist countries of Asia, represented almost entirely by China, have been just as important as SET for trade of developing countries. Hence, it may seem at first sight that any possible decrease in trade between developing countries and SET can be compensated easily by rapid expansion of their trade with China. This may not be the case, however, as will be explained shortly.

It should be mentioned that reliance of individual countries on SET varies from one country to another. For some countries, trade with socialist countries has been relatively significant: for example, the cases of Yugoslavia, India and Iraq, as shown in Table 6.2. Egypt, Cuba, Bermuda, Mali and Mauritius are among other developing countries with significant trade with SET. Moreover, the bulk of China's trade with developing countries consists of trade with Hong Kong. In 1988, Hong Kong accounted for 66 per cent of exports and 60 per cent of imports from China to developing countries. Singapore accounts for another 5 per cent of exports as well as imports from China to those countries. Hence China's trade with other developing countries is insignificant and does not seem to substitute for the decline in their trade with SET.

The Impact of Economic Reform

Table 6.1   Trade of developing countries (DCs) with socialist countries in transition (SETs) and socialist countries of Asia, 1980–9

	Eastern Europe	SETS USSR	Asia
Exports			
Value (US$ billions) (1987–9)	20.7	12.8	21.0
Percentage share in total exports (1987–9)	3.6	2.2	3.7
Annual average growth rate (1980–9)	3.6	4.6	21.7
Imports			
Value (US4 billions) (1987–9)	32.7	21.6	25.5
Percentage share in total imports (1987–9)	5.8	3.8	4.5
Annual average growth rate (1987–9)	1.7	1.3	13.8

Source: Based on UNCTAD, *Handbook of International Trade and Development Statistics*, 1990, tables 3.1 and A.1

Table 6.2   Trade of selected countries with socialist countries in transition (SETs), 1987 (values in US$ billions)

Country	Exports		Imports	
	value	percentage[1]	value	percentage[1]
Yugoslavia	3.3	26.3	2.8	21.0
India (1988)	2.9	21.8	2.4	12.6
Iraq	1.7	18.3	1.6	21.6

Note: 1.   Percentage share in total trade of the country.
Source: Based on IMF, *Direction of Trade Statistics Yearbook 1989.*

Developments in the International Trade of SET in 1990

The *trade creation effect* of sociopolitical and economic reform in SET has, so far, been negative, as has been the trade diversion effect against developing countries. According to Table 6.3, total trade, particularly exports, of Eastern Europe as a whole declined sharply in 1990 (see Note 3 of Table 6.3). None the less, as a result of significant *diversion of trade* against intra-trade among SET and other socialist countries and developing countries, developed market economies enjoyed a very high growth rate, particularly of exports to SET.

According to the same table, for the USSR, however, the picture is different as far as imports are concerned. Imports did, in fact, increase slightly

Table 6.3 Eastern Europe and the USSR: foreign trade by direction, 1988–90
(value in US$ billion; growth rates in percentages)[1]
Country or country group[2]

		Exports				Imports		
	Value	Growth rates			Value	Growth Rates		
	1989	1988	1989	1990[3]	1989	1988	1989	1990[3]
Eastern Europe,[4]								
to or from:								
World	81.1	7.5	–3.5	–13.4	75.8	3.0	–2.7	–6.2
Socialist countries								
(TR terms)[5]	45.3	5.0	–1.4	–9.2	41.5	–1.4	–2.3	–17.3
Eastern Europe								
(TR terms)[5]	14.2	5.8	–1.2	–12.8	14.2	0.3	–.5	–17.0
Developed market								
economies	28.6	10.7	6.5	7.8	27.9	10.9	4.8	24.2
Developing								
countries	7.2	1.8	–12.5	–19.8	6.5	0.5	5.5	–15.1
USSR, to or from:								
World	109.1	2.7	–1.3	–2.9	114.5	11.6	6.9	7.9
Socialist countries								
(TR terms)[5]	67.0	–3.0	–1.5	–13.8	70.9	3.0	3.0	0.9
Eastern Europe								
(TR terms)[5]	50.4	–4.6	–3.2	–17.3	56.8	2.6	1.7	–2.7
Developed market								
economies	26.0	7.8	7.8	12.2	32.5	22.6	21.1	10.1
Developing								
countries	16.1	2.2	2.0	–4.0	11.1	17.4	26.0	18.3

Notes: 1. Both export and import values are expressed fob, except for Hungarian imports
which are shown cif in the national returns. Growth rates are calculated on values
expressed in US$ for total trade with developed and developing market economies,
and on values expressed in transferable roubles (TR) for trade with 'socialist' countries, and therefore will differ from those shown in national statistics.
2. 'Eastern Europe' refers to the East European member countries of CMEA
(Bulgaria, Czechoslovakia, German Democratic Republic, Hungary, Poland and
Romania). The partner country grouping follows the practice until recently prevalent
in the national statistical sources, which differs from the breakdown usually employed
in UN publications. Thus, 'socialist countries', in addition to the East European countries, the Soviet Union, and the Asian centrally-planned economies, includes
Yugoslavia and Cuba. 'Developed market economies' exclude Turkey and
Yugoslavia and include Australia, New Zealand and South Africa.
3. January–September 1989 to January–September 1990. Data for Eastern Europe
include estimates for non-reporting countries.
4. Excluding Yugoslavia.
5. Transferable roubles, for growth rates only.
Source: Reproduced from the UNECE, *Economic Survey of Europe in 1990–91*, p. 63,
based on national statistical publications, plan fulfilment reports and (for 1990) in part
on trade partner data.

in the first nine months of 1990 and developing countries also benefited from the diversion effect of trade. More than developed countries, the growth of imports from developing countries stood, as in the previous year, above that of total imports, and it declined less than the rate of growth of imports from developed countries. Whether such a diversion is incidental in favour of developing countries, or is an indication of longer-term changes, remains to be seen. According to a more recent estimate by the UNCTAD Secretariat, the main beneficiary of Soviet Union trade diversion away from the CMEA countries has been China and developed market economies, particularly for imports (see Table 6.4).

Rapid import expansion in the case of the USSR was not a result of income and output growth. In fact, as is shown in Table 6.5, output did fall – though less than that in countries in Eastern Europe. The combination of output failure and increased consumption, mainly in personal consumption resulting from the easing of rationing, must have contributed to import expansion.

Such expansion has been made possible via financing by foreign exchange reserves, foreign aid and to some extent by borrowing abroad. In the near future, output is also very likely to continue falling because of the decline in investment (see Table 6.5) and the lack of a new industrial organization and management in the agricultural and industrial sectors. Nevertheless, import financing may become more difficult, particularly since it is very likely that exports will also continue to fall as a result of output failure.

The USSR is already facing debt-servicing problems and increasing net borrowing may not be easy. The USA and Germany have provided some

Table 6.4   Distribution of trade of USSR with major groups of partner countries, 1987–90 (percentages)

| | Exports | | | Imports | | |
	1988	*1989*	*1990[1]*	*1988*	*1989*	*1990[1]*
Developed market economies	22.0	24.0	31.5	21.4	24.4	26.6
Developing countries	27.5	27.6	26.3	27.8	26.8	27.6
China	1.5	1.9	2.3	1.1	1.7	1.9
Countries of Eastern Europe	48.9	46.2	39.9	49.6	47.1	43.9
Total	100	100	100	100	100	100

Note: 1.   Estimates.
Source: UNCTAD Secretariats based on national statistics of countries in Eastern Europe and CMEA statistical publications and ECE sources.

Table 6.5   Various economic indicators for USSR and other Eastern European countries

| | Growth rates | | Balance ($ billions) | | |
	Net material product	Consumption	Investment	Trade	Current account
USSR	−4.0	2.4	−4.3	−17.1	−4[1]
Others	−11.2	n.a.	−14.0	−0.8	−2

Note: 1.   Only with market economies.
Source: Secretariat of EEC, tables 2.2.1, 2.2.3 and 2.2.18.

financial aid, but not on a significant scale. Hence, the trade-creation effect of reform in the USSR is likely to be small – as with other Eastern European countries in the short run.

With the absence of data, it is not easy to analyse the competition effect on developing countries of reform in the USSR and Eastern Europe. All that can be said is that exports of these areas to developed market economies expanded rapidly, while their total exports declined. According to Table 6.3, in 1990, exports of the USSR and other Eastern European countries to the developed market economies accelerated to 12.2 per cent and 7.8 per cent respectively. Similarly, in the case of the USSR, for which data is available, in the same year exports to China increased by 65 per cent as against 24 per cent and 17 per cent in 1989 and 1988. Whether export expansion has been at the cost of developing countries or not has yet to be determined.

Some inference, however, could be made as far as the short run is concerned. First, the base of trade of both the USSR and Eastern Europe with developed market economies and China is small, so even a significant expansion of exports to these economies should not cause concern in the short run. Second, considering the structure of exports of the USSR, except for petroleum products, the competition effects of exports of the USSR cannot be significant. As is shown in Table 6.5, petroleum constitutes over half of the exports of the USSR to developed market economies. Otherwise, for main export items of developing countries, that is, light manufacturing goods (SITC 6+8–68), particularly textiles and clothing, agricultural raw materials, tropical foods and metals, the USSR does not pose a significant threat as an exporter for the time being.

The situation of Eastern European countries is, however, slightly different. The structure of exports of these countries, particularly for manufactured goods, is closer to that of developing countries. In such areas as light manufactured goods, particularly textiles and clothing, the competition effect of exports from Eastern European countries cannot be ignored even in the short run if they are able to accelerate their exports to developed market economies.

CONCLUSION

An attempt has been made in this chapter to develop a conceptual framework for the analysis of the impact of socioeconomic reform in socialist countries in transition in Eastern Europe and the USSR on international trade of developing countries. Empirical evidence was provided for 1990.

The various trade consequences were grouped into the trade-creation effect, the trade-diversion effect and the competition effect. It was also argued that the trade flows of developing countries would be affected by the changes in the financial flows into and out of SET. Distinction was made between periods of transition into market economies, and the longer-term completion of transition.

The chapter concludes that the trade-creation effects of economic reform in general would depend on changes in: the rate of growth of output; the material intensity of domestic production; and the import intensity of domestic demand. During the transition period, it would also depend on the speed of removal of demand repression, the pace of trade liberalization, and the availability of sources of import financing. The trade diversion effect would stem mainly from SET's diversion of inter-bloc trade to other areas, as a result of the abolition of the CMEA. Reduction of preferential trading in favour of developing countries, and decision-making on the basis of competitiveness of products offered, rather than on political considerations, are among other influential factors. The competition effect is related to the potential competition of SET goods with exports of developing countries in third markets – the North and China. Finally, diversion of international aid and investment flows in favour of SET, and against developing countries, and reduction in SET's financial assistance to developing countries, could have a negative impact on trade flows of developing countries. Yet the expansion of activities of transnational companies in SET could result in internalizing potential international trade opportunities.

The empirical evidence for 1990 indicates that the trade-creation effect of socioeconomic reform in SET has so far been negative . It also shows that some trade diversion has taken place against imports of SET from developing countries and in favour of developed ones, particularly in the case of Eastern Europe. The competition effect of reform in SET has not, however, been important in the third market, despite rapid expansion of exports of petroleum in the case of the USSR, and some light manufactured products in the case of Eastern Europe. Finally, it was shown that because of the closer similarities between the structure of exports of Eastern European countries and developing countries, possible expansion of exports by those countries could involve noticeable competition effects, even during the period of transition.

Part IV

Central, East and South-East Asia

7 The Democratic People's Republic of Korea: The Reluctant Reformer

Frederick Nixson and Paul Collins

INTRODUCTION

The Democratic People's Republic of Korea (hereafter DPRK) has long been one of the most isolated economies in the world. The Korean peninsular was occupied by Japan in 1905, formally declared a colony in 1910 and was integrated into Japan's 'highly militarised empire' (Halliday, 1983) until the end of the Second World War. The northern part of Korea was liberated by the Soviet Red Army in August 1945 and Soviet occupation continued until late 1948, when the DPRK was formally established, with the North and South (the latter called the Republic of Korea) divided at the 38th parallel. The regimes in both the DPRK and the Republic of Korea continue to claim jurisdiction over the entire nation.

The Korean War (1950–3) inflicted great damage on the North, with communist casualties estimated at between 1.5 and 2 million people, and with 1 million civilian casualties in the DPRK (Lowe, 1986). Aid from both the Soviet Union and China was crucial in the rebuilding of the economy, but Jon Halliday (1983, p. 131) argues that the real key to the DPRK's high growth rates in the post-war period lies in the 'combination of exceptional mass mobilisation and high domestic accumulation'.

This period also saw the consolidation of the principle of the *Juche* policy, meaning self-reliance, not autarky and not implying international isolation (Smith, 1992). The DPRK participated selectively in the CMEA (Halliday, 1983) and by the early 1970s, was relinking with the capitalist world economy through increasing trade and borrowing (and indeed getting into debt and defaulting on that debt in the early 1980s).

The late 1980s saw further changes in the DPRK's external relationships. The 1988 Olympic Games were held in Seoul and although the DPRK did not participate, the games were not disrupted in any way. Eight rounds of talks were held between the North and South Korean governments between 1990 and 1992. Both Koreas joined the United Nations in

109

August 1991 and attempts have been made by the DPRK to improve relations with the USA and normalize relations with Japan (Smith, 1992).

The government of the Republic of Korea has been following a policy of *Nordpolitik* with China and Russia, which both hope to benefit from greater trade and direct foreign investment by South Korean enterprises. The DPRK's position was weakened by the collapse of the USSR in December 1991, but it has so far survived these external shocks, even though there are reports that economic growth became negative in 1990 and 1991, that rationing of basic foodstuffs (rice and corn) has been tightened and that the regime and economy are on the point of collapse.

Clearly there will be major changes following the death of Kim Il Sung in 1994, and the succession of his son, Kim Il Jong, cannot be guaranteed. As outlined in this chapter, limited economic reforms and liberalization of the economy have already occurred, although it is still too early to determine the trajectory of the reform process. Whether the economy is on the point of collapse is a question that only time can answer. The view taken in this chapter is that collapse is not inevitable and that any analogy with the demise of the former German Democratic Republic (GDR) and the experience of German reunification would be misleading.

The major issue at present, however, relates to the DPRK's nuclear capabilities. The DPRK signed the Nuclear Non-Proliferation Treaty in 1985 and signed the Nuclear Safeguards Agreement in 1992 (after President Bush announced that the USA would withdraw short-range nuclear arms from its overseas bases). An inspection by the International Atomic Energy Authority took place in May 1992 (Smith, 1992).

Since then, the DPRK has withdrawn from the Nuclear Non-Proliferation Treaty (March 1993) and in mid-1994 faced possible international sanctions over its refusal to allow International Atomic Energy Agency inspectors access to secret reactor storage sites at Yongbyon, 60 miles north–west of Pyongyang. The outcome of this confrontation is clearly not predictable at present.

THE ECONOMY

The DPRK has a land mass of 122 762 square kilometres (approximately the size of Malawi) and a population of about 22 million, with a population growth rate estimated at 2.39 per cent per annum (for the period 1985–90). Its workforce is estimated at 8.95 million, of which 49 per cent are women. Estimates of per capita income vary widely, from US$ 1273 in 1990 (one-fifth of that of the Republic of Korea) to an implied per capita income for 1980 of US$ 2219 (Roy, 1990), the latter being above most previous estimates.

The DPRK has followed a development strategy that has given highest priority to the development of the heavy industry sector. The basis for this industrial development is the country's rich mineral resources (including coal, iron ore, magnesium and graphite, as well as lead, zinc, gold and silver) and its potential for hydroelectric power (a total installed capacity in 1986 of 8700 megawatts).

The development of the heavy industry sector is seen as being essential for the development of the whole economy. A statement by the late President (quoted in the 1988 edition of the *Korean Review*, p. 114) emphasizes this point:

> Our Party's line in the building of heavy industry was to create our own solid bases of heavy industry which would be able to produce at home most of the raw materials, fuel, power, machines and equipment needed for the development of the national economy by relying on the rich natural resources and sources of raw materials in our country.

The development of the heavy industry sector and its associated techno-logical base, is an essential aspect of the philosophy of *Juche* (self-reliance), associated with an almost total reliance on a highly centralized state planning system. A series of three-, five-and seven-year plans were implemented and the Third Seven-Year Plan (1987–93) had as its objec-tives continued modernization of the economy, 'placing the national economy on a scientific basis and making it more *Juche*-oriented' (*Korean Review*, 1988, p. 114).

Industrial production has experienced considerable growth in recent years, based in particular on engineering and machinery building, petro-chemicals and textiles. Iron and steel, cement and a variety of mineral-based products (asbestos, graphite) are also of significance. The investment goods industry is now capable of producing precision instru-ments and machinery, turning lathes, presses, macro-generators, trans-formers, etc. Shipbuilding, mining and transportation equipment are priority sectors, as, increasingly, is the electronics industry.

The light industry and consumer goods sectors produce a variety of goods, such as food products, glass, porcelain, textiles, shoes, refrigera-tors, radios and watches. This sector has been relatively neglected over the years, and this has led to shortages and low quality of consumer products. Light industry has recently been decentralized, with responsibility for the production of consumer goods delegated to each province. But unless central government assistance is provided to this sector, the problems that it faces are not likely to be overcome in the immediate future.

In his 1990 New Year Address, the late President emphasized that:

> Giving priority to the development of heavy industry and advancing light industry and agriculture simultaneously is the policy which our Party consistently maintains...We should make light industry factories more up-to-date and adopt positive measures to provide raw and other materials through a variety of ways so as to operate all light industry factories at full capacity. Light industry must...produce larger quantities of good-quality daily necessities and food-stuffs which cater to the tastes of the people.

With respect to light industry, attention in the Third Seven-Year Plan (1987–93) focused on textiles, footwear, food processing and domestic appliances. With respect to the agricultural sector, the objective was to achieve full self-sufficiency in food grains, via increases in yields (through the development and application of new technologies) and through increasing the area under cultivation via large-scale land reclamation programmes. In the case of the former objective, progress has been made increasing rice yields in particular, but although maize yields have risen, imports of this cereal are still required to meet domestic consumption requirements.

The DPRK development model is essentially inward-looking with trade policy emphasizing import-substituting activities within the overall framework of self-reliant development. Up to the time of writing, the bulk of the DPRK's trade (more than 60 per cent) has been in the form of barter agreements with other centrally-planned economies, with the (former) Soviet Union alone accounting for 43 per cent of its trade turnover in 1985. China and Japan are also important trade partners, and there are growing trade relations with Hong Kong, Singapore and Thailand.

The DPRK exports non-ferrous metals, steel, magnesium clinker, machine tools, coal, silk and cement. It imports petroleum, chemicals, grains and cereals, coking coal, machinery and capital equipment. By the late 1980s the value of exports was put at $10 billion by the government. The development of trade relationships has been inhibited by a number of factors, including failure to meet debt repayment obligations, the low quality and lack of diversity of exportable goods, failure to adhere to delivery dates and other contractual obligations, and limited transport and labour facilities.

It can be argued that the economy of the DPRK has reached a watershed. The economy's achievements in respect of the development of the heavy industry base and the engineering sector in particular, plus the development of physical infrastructural facilities and the meeting of the 'basic needs' (food and clothing, shelter, health and education) are considerable. It is likely, however, that the limits to inward-looking growth have been reached and it is argued in this chapter that the economic system must be made more flexible so as to raise quality, provide greater choice, modernize industry and make it more efficient and competitive. It should be noted in this context that the North Koreans have, since the mid-1980s, made limited attempts at enterprise reform (greater emphasis on financial accountability, material incentives for labour, greater relative autonomy for state enterprises) but these efforts have not overcome such problems as the soft budget constraint, ineffective worker incentive provisions and the hoarding of scarce inputs and raw materials (Kang and Lee, 1992).

Foreign trade has a vital role to play in this process. The earning of foreign exchange through the export of (largely) manufactured goods is essential if imports of advanced foreign technology and equipment, as well as fuels and other intermediate inputs, are to be funded. Joint ventures with foreign business partners also need to be given greater encouragement as, properly implemented, they can prove to be effective vehicles for technology transfer.

STATE MANAGEMENT

Management of the DPRK economy takes place within the overall framework of the central planning system and at the enterprise level through the 'Taean' work system.

Within the framework of long-term sectoral priorities and production targets, individual state enterprises are required to draw up their individual plans to meet these provisional targets. A process of consultation then ensues between the State Planning Commission and individual enterprises, resulting in a finally agreed production plan. Enterprises are then allocated resources on the basis of the latter. The system is a complex one, with many inherent challenges such as the need to marry effectively central directives and local enterprise initiative. A number of smaller enterprises report to provincial planning bodies, which have a degree of autonomy. Other larger, provincially based enterprises report directly to their Ministry or Commission. Among enterprises, an equally complex system of relations operates. Under ICAS (the Independent Cost Accounting System), enterprises are allowed to buy and sell goods among themselves (at centrally approved prices). Profits are retained and reinvested among the workers. Some major enterprises operate a worker production bonus system.

The 'Taean' management system was established by the late President when he visited the Taean heavy engineering works in 1961 and this has become the standard method for target setting (budget planning) for industrial and state planners. It is a three-stage process: (i) government targets for production as part of a seven-year plan; (ii) proposals by enterprise management based on available capacity; and (iii) agreement on target production figures after collective discussions with the workers, the secretary and factory manager. This is done through a series of committees in which plans are drawn up for achievement of targets.

Official policy, as expressed in economic plans and budget documents, has expressed dissatisfaction with existing managerial performance. In consequence of the need to return to earlier economic and industrial growth rates and especially to improve industrial performance for exports, stress is now being placed upon increased productivity, capacity utilization and the more efficient use of resources and assets. The key to this is felt to be the enhancement of management technology and 'placing production and management practices on an improved and scientific basis'. One consequence of the earlier inward-looking growth period has been the lack of inclusion of more modern management techniques into the productive sectors. A striking conclusion of the needs assessments conducted by two recent UNDP missions was that considerable improvement of resource use and output could be achieved by introducing a range of modern management techniques and systems into strategically placed DPRK enterprises. Critical among the former are decision-support systems to offer better management control over production activity and improved workflow. The introduction of such changes is likely to have important consequences for the existing economic management system of DPRK.

THE NATIONAL POLICY FRAMEWORK AND ECONOMIC REFORMS

The government of the DPRK has embarked upon a series of potentially far-reaching measures in a number of areas of economic management.

Management Development

While setting goals and objectives for public-sector management, the government has stressed the need for putting production and management on an improved and more scientific basis through automation and computerization. The government has emphasized the need for greater public sector productivity and optimal use of domestic resources. With regard to its strategic approach to management development, the driving force of the government's programme is the move to increase productivity by way of computerization. The overall benefits of modern management methods based on scientific and analytic management techniques involving computerization have been seen to offer better management control over production activity, an accelerated workflow, enhanced strategic planning and management capabilities on the part of management, and optimal use of installed production capacities, investments, men and material.

Trade Diversification and Liberalization

The objectives of trade liberalization are: the creation of a more 'open' economic environment within which the foreign trade sector is made more efficient and competitive; a more diversified export structure both in terms of export composition and markets served; and an accelerated rate of growth of foreign exchange earnings. Any anti-trade bias in the system of controls and incentives needs to be reduced or eliminated, any excessive over-valuation of the domestic currency in terms of the currencies of major trading partners needs to be corrected, and complementary measures need to be taken to increase profitability and reduce costs in both the import-competing and export-orientated sectors. The DPRK's moves to make direct contact with non-centrally-planned (that is, 'market') economies has underscored the need to increase the capacity of state officials in the Ministry of Foreign Trade and trading enterprises by way of their knowledge of the marketing, and perhaps also banking and insurance procedures, of non-socialist countries.

Direct Foreign Investment (DFI) and Joint Ventures (JVs)

The government of the DPRK wishes to encourage foreign investment and enacted (in 1992) three sets of laws: 'The Foreigners Investment Law of the DPRK', 'Contractual Joint Venture Law of the DPRK' and 'The Law of the DPRK on Foreign Enterprises'. The Government encourages investment on the principle of 'complete equality and mutual benefit' and is anxious that foreign investors become active in advanced technology sectors, those sectors that produce internationally competitive goods, and sectors of natural resource development.

Three forms of foreign-funded enterprises are defined:

(i)   *Contractual joint venture*: A business activity in which investors in the DPRK and a foreign country jointly invest, management is assumed by the partner from the DPRK and, depending on the precise provisions of the contract, the foreign investors' share of the investment is redeemed or profits shared proportionally to the investments made by the two partners.

(ii)   *Equity joint venture*: A business activity in which investors in the host country and foreign country invest jointly, operate the business jointly and share the profits according to proportion of investment contributed.

(iii)   *Wholly-owned foreign enterprise*: A business activity in which the foreign investor makes the investment and carries out management on his own account. Such enterprises will be located in the 'free economic and trade zone' in such subsectors as electronics, automation, machine building, food processing, garments and transport and service sectors.

In the remainder of this chapter, we look in more detail at issues of trade liberalization and DFI. Collins and Nixson (1993b) consider in greater detail management development issues.

INTERNATIONAL TRADE ISSUES

The DPRK has received technical assistance from a number of multilateral agencies in recent years, aimed at developing its international trade strategy. For example, an official mission from UNCTAD visited the DPRK in April 1989 and a subsequent programming mission visited in March 1990. It became clear during the latter mission that the government of the DPRK hoped that the mission would prepare the way for the development of very practical 'down-to-earth' technical assistance activities to develop exports by enhancing the capacities and capabilities of personnel in the trade field, and the international competitiveness of selected industries. The emphasis of the mission's report was thus on areas of technical assistance that would best contribute to export expansion, involving joint activities and co-operative arrangements between UNCTAD, ITC, UNIDO and possibly other agencies in the UN system.

The government of the DPRK indicated its priorities for technical assistance in the trade field and the manner in which they wished such technical assistance to be provided. UNDP finance could best be utilized by an emphasis on the training of personnel from the DPRK (manpower planning to include expertise in market surveys and back-up services) and/or on the provision of equipment to improve industrial performance. It was felt that the use of expensive foreign experts and consultancy services should be kept to a minimum.

The three main areas of concern to the UNCTAD mission were thus:

1. Enhancing the capacity/capability of Koreans on matters relating to foreign trade. This would involve:
   - updating theoretical knowledge and training;
   - intensive training in the procedures, practices and modalities of foreign trade as practised in actual or potential markets for Korean exports;
   - practical experience in banking and insurance services; and
   - training in marketing (considered to be perhaps the weakest link in the DPRK's approach to export-orientated industrialization).
2. The development of integrated programmes for the expansion of exports in specific sectors. This would involve:
   - an initial focus on labour-intensive or resource-based industrial exports (metallurgy — casting components; garments including silk garments; and electronics are all important in this context);
   - technical assistance to general policies of export promotion in chosen sectors, in, for example, product mix, links with foreign interests, etc.; and
   - targeted technical assistance to one enterprise in each sector to meet the specific needs of selected firms from the point of production to the point of sale of products (training of workers, technicians and management; assistance in design, use of appropriate technology and product adaptation; equipment for quality control; market surveys, marketing arrangements; identification of business partners and back-up services; assistance in trading, banking, insurance and transport needs; and study tours of collaborating partners.
3. The development of free economic and export processing zones (EPZs): the government of the DPRK requested technical assistance for the detailed examination of the issues relating to the establishment of EPZs. Two are currently under consideration: the Tumen River Area Development Programme, which it is planned to proceed with in co-operation with Mongolia, Russia, China and the UNDP (along with Japan and the Republic of Korea). Voices have, however, been

raised in Japan over the technical feasibility of this project. A second zone in an area of North Hamgyong Province has recently been proposed.

Overall, the above objectives could be achieved by placing Korean personnel abroad in target countries to gain practical experience ('learning-by-doing'); the running of highly selective training courses in the DPRK on specific aspects of foreign trade (for example, trade finance, banking and insurance); the availability of technical assistance to help in the development of an effective trade policy capacity (including the development of a computerized database on trade information, including trade barriers).

We have noted already the more uncertain external economic environment faced by the DPRK resulting from the collapse of its main trading partner and its attempts to respond to the Republic of Korea's *Nordpolitik* which partly accounts for its own efforts at trade diversification.

No country can anticipate all possible global developments and prepare itself fully to meet all new challenges effectively and efficiently. The DPRK, because of its past inward-looking trade policies, is perhaps less well equipped than other developing economies to respond to these new developments. Decision-makers in both government and state trading enterprises are not as informed as they could be and in any case do not have the experience of flexible response to rapidly changing situations. All kinds of constraints – marketing, credit, transport, insurance – inhibit rapid change at the level of the macroeconomy, and at the enterprise (micro) level, problems of pricing policy, quality control and marketing remain to be solved.

DIRECT FOREIGN INVESTMENT

Matters relating to DFI, joint ventures and what is called in the DPRK 'enterprise-to-enterprise co-operation' are the concern of the United Nations Centre on Transnational Corporations (UNCTC). The first UNCTC reconnaissance mission to Pyongyang took place in November 1989. In view of the limited experience of the government with Western business partners, the different economic sectors involved and the various types of foreign business relations envisaged, it was felt appropriate to start with some preparatory assistance. During this preparatory assistance period, UNCTC launched a number of missions to DPRK.

The first UNCTC consultancy mission, undertaken in June 1990, comprised legal, investment, trade promotion and tourism advisers, in addition to the UNCTC Project Co-ordinator. The mission held extensive consultations on three topics:

● legal aspects of joint ventures and related business arrangements;
● strategic issues for promoting trade and investment projects in DPRK; and
● perspectives for developing the tourism sector in DPRK with foreign partners.

Among the major findings from the discussions, three issues were singled out as being paramount, and the government expressed its wish that UNCTC and other UN agencies concerned with investment and trade in the DPRK focus their activities, at least in the immediate future, upon:

● concrete projects that would materialize in specific investment and training activities rather than on institutional, legal, policy or strategic aspects of foreign investment and trade (although it was recognized that this latter aspect should not be neglected in the long run);
● non-equity forms of foreign investment and non-traditional forms of investment and trade financing, such as the financing of equipment through buy-back arrangements; and
● a step-by-step approach resulting in a few successful projects.

This mission generated a number of follow-up activities dealing with legislation and promotion of contacts with foreign enterprises. Technical comments were submitted on the 1986 Foreign Investment Law and its implementing regulations, and together with the United Nations Industrial Development Organisation (UNIDO), a number of investment projects were identified.

As noted above, the DPRK now has in place legislation relating to the promotion and regulation of various forms of DFI. These laws together guarantee the legal rights and interests of foreign investors and foreign-funded enterprises: preferential treatment will be given to foreign-funded enterprises in priority sectors (including reduction and exemption of income tax and other taxes, favourable conditions of land use, and preferential supply of bank loans); foreign enterprises located in the free economic and trade zone will also enjoy specific benefits, including exemption from customs duties levied on export and import materials, a three year tax holiday and a further 50 per cent reduction in income tax for the following two years, at a concessionary rate of income tax; and guarantees covering the remittance overseas of profits and other income and guarantees of fair compensation in the event of nationalization of foreign assets are given. Overseas Koreans are to be encouraged to invest in the DPRK.

The legislation is comprehensive and follows that enacted in most countries anxious to attract DFI. The situation in the DPRK is, however, different from that in other countries and there are both general and specific factors that are likely to constrain inflows of DFI. The general factors relate to the DPRK's isolation from and suspicion of the outside (Western) world, the immediate problems relating to the nuclear issue (see page 110) and the continued pursuit of self-reliant development (*Juche*). The more specific problems relate to such factors as:

(i)   the DPRK's less-than-satisfactory international credit standing;
(ii)   the continued dominance of state enterprises, which will almost certainly restrict the possibilities for the development of JVs and will inhibit or prevent flexible decision-making by them;
(iii)   the absence of clear regulations and procedures with respect to foreign exchange transactions, labour–management relations, import–export operations, banking and financial arrangements and approval and monitoring of JVs;
(iv)   insufficient skill, information and management knowhow within the government and state enterprises to identify suitable projects, prepare and evaluate feasibility studies, and negotiate with foreign enterprises; and
(v)   lack of information about investment opportunities and economic conditions in the DPRK, and the absence of an overall promotional strategy.

There is some recognition in the DPRK as to the significance of these obstacles to the development of JVs, especially the incomplete legal, institutional and regulatory framework for the operation of JVs; the limited capability with respect to the preparation and negotiation of appropriate JV projects; and the general lack of experience in dealing with foreign enterprises, as well as problems relating to the credit-worthiness of state enterprises. Nevertheless, the DPRK feels (rightly or wrongly) that it offers a number of major attractions to foreign investors, including:

(i)   cheap, highly-educated and skilled labour which can produce high quality products; existing joint ventures, for example producing garments and pianos, are already an export success;

(ii)   good infrastructure and support facilities for joint ventures (customs clearance for imports and exports is being handled within one day); and

(iii)   ample natural resources.

CONCLUDING COMMENTS

Changes in the global economy, and in particular the collapse of the Soviet Union and the CMEA, have added urgency to the need to change trading practices and methods in the DPRK. Barter agreements with these economies have of necessity been replaced by more open and competitive exchanges, and the achievement of national economic objectives will depend to a greater extent on closer integration with the world economy and the development of a 'philosophy' of exporting. The economic conditions for a trade 'take off' in the DPRK exist – abundant high-grade raw materials, a broad industrial base, engineering capabilities, a highly skilled and disciplined labour force, and competitive labour costs – and a selective approach to export promotion will probably be the most effective way forward. This will permit concentration on a limited range of sectors and products including focused R & D and design efforts, more effective acquisition and application of production technology, greater efficiency in the organization and management of the selected export industries, and specialization in the establishment of marketing networks.

Unlike most other former centrally-planned economies, however, the DPRK is contemplating neither radical political and economic reform (following Mongolia and Poland, for example), nor radical economic reform with no political change (as in Vietnam and China). The DPRK does not intend to reform, restructure or liberalize its economy and, indeed, does not appear to accept that such changes are either necessary or desirable. The DPRK is a cautious reformer, with limited objectives in clearly defined sectors and activities.

Whether this approach, in contrast to the 'shock therapy' approach of Poland and Mongolia, will yield higher benefits and lower costs must remain, for the present, an open question. Given that the DPRK economy is at a watershed, and given that we cannot assume any significant improvement in global economic conditions in the immediate future, it may well be the case that the government of the DPRK may have to accept more radical changes if their development objectives are to be met. Indeed, the reform process may develop a dynamic of its own which, combined with possible future political changes, may well prove difficult to control.

This chapter has argued against the view that the economy of the DPRK is on the point of collapse. It is in no one's interests that the DPRK should collapse; and the government of the Republic of Korea has learnt from the German reunification and favours a policy of 'realistic incrementalism' towards the unification of the two Koreas.

Nevertheless, change is necessary and it will occur whether the government of the DPRK wishes it or not. It can also be argued that the extent of the changes necessary has not yet been fully appreciated in the DPRK. In a large number of important areas of economic life – exchange rate management and the balance of payments, export promotion and diversification with respect to both products and markets, the development of the financial sector, and the acquisition of the techniques of modern management – profound changes are needed. The DPRK has, in general, taken a positive attitude to the role that multilateral aid can play in promoting and facilitating such changes, but it wants aid to complement and not to undermine the *Juche* philosophy.

Self-reliance is highly commendable in a poor country. When self-reliance descends into paranoia (which many critics would argue is the case in the DPRK), necessary changes are prevented through fear and suspicion. The achievements of the DPRK, at least until the mid- to late-1980s should not be underestimated, and the country's extraordinary capacity for survival deserves recognition. Changes will come, however, and it is to be hoped that the transition in the DPRK will be a peaceful one. Economic, political and social collapse will benefit no one.

8 Lessons of Trade Policy and Economic Reform in China
Alasdair MacBean

The Open Door Policy was a key element in China's economic reforms. But its success can only be understood in the context of the other main areas of reform. Without the success of agricultural and rural enterprise liberalization, much of the impact of trade policy would have been lost. But equally, the trading opportunities, the foreign exchange earned, management know-how, technology transfers, and jobs created through the Open Door Policy have brought about dynamic change in China. Explaining China's success in exporting and attracting foreign investment requires at least a minimal grasp of reform in other sectors. This chapter looks first at China's economic performance before and after the pivotal year 1978, when reform began. Next, the main reforms in agriculture, industry, pricing and other changes in commodity and factor markets are set out. These are then related to the principal reforms in international economic policies in trade and finance. Finally, some implications are drawn for further reform in China and Eastern Europe.

CHINA'S ECONOMIC PERFORMANCE

Even though it was no slouch before 1978, China's growth rate increased dramatically during the 1980s decade of reform. National income growth rose from an average 5.7 per cent per year in 1953–78 to 9 per cent during 1978–87 (Nolan, 1990). Although the government reacted to rising inflation at the end of the 1980s with a credit crunch that squeezed growth down to 3.7 per cent in 1989, the economy bounced back to 9 per cent rate in 1990 (IMF, 1991b). Population growth was reduced from 2.2 per cent to 1.3 per cent per year in the 1980s. Absolute poverty was cut from 17 per cent of rural households in 1987 to 13 per cent in 1988 (World Bank, 1990a). Agriculture (the largest sector) was sluggish under Mao Zedong: its net material product grew at only 1.9 per cent per year in 1953–78, but surged to 6 per cent in 1978–87. Rural incomes doubled in the six years 1978–84, contributing demand as well as materials, investment and labour to the rest of the economy.

Industry, the favoured sector in pre-reform China, kept up its 10 per cent yearly growth, but with more emphasis on light industries, while construction, transport and commerce in the 1980s doubled or tripled their past rates of growth (Nolan, 1990; World Bank, 1990). Standards of consumption rose by 100 per cent for rural residents and 75 per cent for urban residents between 1978 and 1987 (Nolan, 1990). Total private consumption in 1980 constant yuan rose from 215 billion in 1978 to 488 billion in 1989 (World Bank, 1990, table 1.2). The improvements ran through every physical indicator, from grain to cloth, but are particularly marked for housing space and durable goods such as watches, bicycles, radios and television sets (Nolan, 1990).

The foreign trade ratio (weighted exports plus imports over national income) at 5 per cent was low even by the standards of large countries. In the 1980s it tripled. Merchandise exports rose from US$18.2 to US$52.5 billion, 1980–89, and China's share of world trade expanded from a mere 0.97 per cent to 1.7 per cent (World Bank, 1990a, table 1.1).

THE PRE-REFORM ECONOMIC SYSTEM (1949–78)

The birth of communist China in 1949 came after thirty years of political instability and war. There was hyperinflation. Outputs of steel, coal and electricity were about 80 per cent, 50 per cent and 30 per cent respectively below their previous peaks. The transport system was in ruins, grain output was 25 per cent down, and other major crops much worse (Hsu, 1989; IMF, 1991a). With substantial Soviet assistance, Chinese development policies in the 1950s achieved very respectable economic growth, with massive investment in physical and human capital.

This heavy investment (over 30 per cent of national income in most years), based almost entirely on domestic savings, is a characteristic of most of China's growth up to the 1980s. Efficiency in terms of output per unit of capital or labour was low (Hsu, 1989; Nolan, 1990; Naughton, 1989; IMF, 1991a). These were the benefits and the costs of the development policies of the Chinese government. The system lacked the information and incentives to become efficient. Moreover, the perceived external political threats led to heavy investments in defence-related industries, with the aim of self-sufficiency in all areas; and to regional dispersion of industry to ensure survival in the event of nuclear or conventional attack. Despite Chinese denials, it seems certain that China's defence industries had first claim on key inputs, including administrative and scientific talent (Naughton, 1989).

This, together with its isolationist policies after its break with the Soviet Union in the late 1950s, kept its industries starved of new technology and the spur of international competition. The policy of dispersal of industries and regional self-sufficiency meant that opportunities for gain from specialization, economies of scale and trade were forgone. Growth was also interrupted by the follies of the 'Great Leap Forward' in the late 1950s and the 'Cultural Revolution', which peaked in 1967–8. These did lasting damage to China's ability to manage development.

The early 1950s saw China's attempt to become a fully socialist, centrally-planned, command economy on the Russian model. The means of production, distribution and exchange were nationalized. Only small family plots and tiny businesses remained in private hands. By 1956 nearly all enterprises were in the public sector.

But the attempt to run a fully socialist economy in the First Five-Year Plan (1952–7) swiftly showed China the problems imposed on central control by the lack of information. At its height, only some 200 products were controlled by the central authorities. Key industries: coal, electricity, petroleum, machinery, chemicals and iron and steel were given targets, had centrally allocated supplies, and sold their outputs to the state for allocation to end users. Local planning authorities were given wide powers to control output targets and key inputs for non-key industries, to allocate investment to projects up to a certain value, and to control material balances and distribution of finished goods.

Large-scale industry in the 1950s was run on a Soviet pattern, with one-person management, piece rates, bonus systems and sizeable wage differentials. Agriculture was organized in collectives. But the Great Leap Forward radically changed both. In the industrial enterprises, management passed to committees of party members and workers. Managers lost power and were often humiliated, piece rates were abolished and earnings differentials reduced (Nolan, 1990). In the rural areas, Mao forced China's 700 500 collective farms into 24 000 rural communes with an average of 22 000 members. These conducted massive, labour-intensive rural public works, especially in irrigation. But they proved largely to be useless, as most projects that could be done by traditional methods had already been done (Perkins, 1969, quoted in Nolan, 1990). The private plots largely disappeared and all activities that could be communal were made so. Incomes were equalized. As a result of free-rider problems and lack of incentives, output dropped. The resulting economic chaos and terrible famine in 1959–61 led to a policy reversal.

The smaller collectives were restored, the production team became paramount, the private sector was partially restored, and economic incentives were reintroduced. Although the system in agriculture continued to swing between accentuating equity and incentives, no serious institutional changes took place there between 1965 and 1976. The Cultural Revolution largely bypassed the farmers. But at its height, Mao foisted similar policies on industry. There it had the same ill-effects on management and worker motivation. The resulting economic problems in the early 1970s led to a swing back to policies much like those of the First Five-Year Plan (Nolan, 1990; Hsu, 1989).

Under Mao, China sought to make itself as independent of foreign trade as possible. All trade took place through twelve State Trading Corporations organized mainly on product lines. Enterprises were cut off from contact with foreign customers or suppliers. The yuan prices facing exporters and importers had no connection with world prices. Trading was not seen as a way of using resources efficiently by exploiting comparative advantage, but purely as a way of obtaining investment goods and other essential imports. Until the 1970s, there was a high correlation between China's investment and imports (Hsu, 1989). China gained substantial inflows of capital and technology from the Soviet Union in the 1950s, but after the break, Mao placed his confidence in the development of technology within China. Despite a few dramatic successes, this proved illusory and after Mao's death China swung to the opposite extreme in the late 1970s in a desperate race to catch up on Western technology via wholesale importing of machines, complete factories and power plants.

Tax Revenues

Like many developing countries, China's massive investments in heavy industry were squeezed out of the agricultural and mineral sectors. At the beginning of the 1950s this was inevitable as 80 per cent of the population was rural. And it was made easier in that the long wars and inflation had turned the terms of trade against agriculture. By preventing the terms of trade swinging back to agriculture, the new leadership in 1949 was able to capture a good deal of the increase in production in the 1950s. This was done by keeping the prices of food and raw materials low relative to prices for producer goods, which in turn were kept low relative to the protected high prices for consumer goods. As all industrial profits were returned to the central authorities, the artificially high profits of state enterprises provided the bulk of the government's revenues. As industry grew, so too did this source of revenue. By 1957, it was 50 per cent and by 1964 more than 70 per cent of total revenue. The dangers of the system were that it held down incentives in agriculture, made for a very narrow fiscal base, feather-bedded manufacturing, and accustomed urban workers to low food prices. These features were stored-up problems for the 1980s.

China achieved much economic and social progress under the leadership of Mao Zedung: per capita growth of at least 3 per cent per year during 1953–78, and substantial improvements in nutrition, life expectancy and education. But by the 1970s several factors meant that the economic system was becoming increasingly wasteful. These factors included the long-term effects of the schism with Russia and the Cultural Revolution, both of which deprived China of educated, highly-trained administrators, managers and technologists. Lack of such people weakened both central and regional planning, so projects were wrongly selected, badly implemented and poorly managed. Many were never completed. Decentralization and regional dispersion were responses to external threats but led to enormous waste, duplication and loss-of-scale economies:

By the end of the 1970s, Chinese planners were struggling to get hundreds of unworkable, mid-designed, or incomplete projects into production ... in 1977, the stock of uncompleted construction projects amounted to 210 per cent of the value of that year's capital construction ... In other words, two full years' worth of investment was 'in the pipeline making no contribution to current production'. (Naughton, 1989, p. 28)

Barry Naughton claims that over a half of the extra output created by economic growth between 1953 and 1978 was wasted, in written-off construction and/or tied up in excessive stocks and military expenditure. Less than half of the increase in output went to increased consumption or new investment.

LEGACIES OF CHINA'S COMMAND ECONOMY

By 1978 China had passed the first phase of industrialization. Agriculture's share in national material product had fallen from 52 per cent in 1952 to 28 per cent in 1978 (Nolan, 1990). But this was achieved at the cost of neglect of agriculture and enormous waste and inefficiency in both sectors. Marginal output-to-capital ratios fell from about 32 per cent in the First Five-Year Plan to 16 per cent in the Fourth Plan (1971–75) (Nolan, 1990). A great deal of the capital stock was worthless. Grandiose plans for a massive leap forward with imported capital and technology, predicated on buoyant exports of petroleum, collapsed because of mismanagement and a failure of the petroleum industry to meet expectations. Huge investments based on expected piped gas from Sichuan were largely wasted when it was discovered in 1978 that there was insufficient gas (Naughton, 1989).

Chinese assessments in the 1980s blamed Soviet-style centralized planning:

> Such a structure put the national economy in a strait-jacket, discouraging initiative in all quarters, causing serious waste of manpower, materials and capital, and greatly hampering the growth of the productive forces. For many years, this was a major cause of the slow pace of the growth of the Chinese economy and the improvement of the living standards of the Chinese people. (Lin and Wang, 1984, quoted in Nolan, 1990)

But apart from the planning system, China's economy had been damaged by the loss of human capital caused by the Cultural Revolution and by the great costs of the regional autarky created in the name of defence and equity. It was not just central planning, it was bad planning that produced China's economic problems of the late 1970s.

Nevertheless, most of the problems were characteristic of those met by other centrally-planned economies. They are clearly summarized in a recent IMF study:

> irrational pricing stemming from controls, over-staffing and inefficiency in industry, an emphasis on product quantity and not quality, and isolation from foreign competition. These failings were exacerbated by biases against individual incentives, markets, and labour specialisation. In industry, there was effectively no link between individual productivity and remuneration. The labour market was virtually non-existent as a result of rigid restrictions on the geographical mobility of labour, the assignment of jobs to labour market entrants, and the system of lifetime employment under which enterprises provided housing, pensions, medical care, and other forms of welfare benefits. (IMF, 1991a, p. 3)

CHINA'S ECONOMIC REFORMS

By 1978, China's leaders had recognized that to use resources more efficiently was vital and that this required market-orientated reforms. But there was no master plan. Reforms were piecemeal, experimental, pragmatic, and gave local authorities much discretion in implementing them. China's reforms, it has been said, resembled a person crossing a river, moving from stone to stone with little idea where the next stone lies since it is hidden by the water ahead (Nolan, 1990). Various reforms were tried in all sectors, but agriculture, aptly, provided the most fertile ground.

Agricultural Reforms

From a system of collectivized farming with procurement through mandatory quotas at low fixed prices there was a rapid and progressive shift to contracts at higher prices and increased latitude to sell surpluses in free markets. In 1979/80 procurement prices for staples were increased by 41 per cent for grain, 62 per cent for oil and 47 per cent for cotton (Weiner, 1990). The Household Responsibility System was introduced. This gave family units contracts for their outputs and security of land tenure, initially for periods of three to five years, but extended in 1984 to fifteen years and even thirty years for tree crops. In 1985, farmers were freed from obligatory contracts and in principle allowed to sell to the market or to the state. In practice, pressure to deliver to official organs continued. In 1988, land-use rights were made legally transferable. Farmers were further benefited by administered price increases for raw materials (World Bank, 1990a; IMF, 1991a; Nolan, 1990).

The progressive moves towards a market-directed system were checked and even reversed somewhat in the 1988/89 atmosphere of panic buying, inflation, and Tiananmen Square. Despite this, in the early 1990s, only an eighth of farming output was still sold at government procurement prices (*Economist*, 1 June 1991).

The effects of reform in agriculture were dramatic. Growth between 1978 to 1984 was about 8 per cent per year compared to 1.6 per cent over 1971–7. The increases in labour productivity and profits released labour and savings to create or expand rural manufacturing and service industries, which under Mao had been discouraged as being 'bourgeois'. The expansion of demand and the release of resources from food production gave a boost to the development of small-to-medium private rural industries and town and village collectives.

Agricultural growth slowed to 3 per cent a year during 1985–8. This was partly inevitable: the easy options for expanding output were seized first. But also the initial short contracts gave incentives to over-exploit rather than to nurture the land, so some early growth was at the expense of conservation and the maintenance and expansion of common facilities, such as irrigation, flood protection, transport, processing and storage. Also, the attractive opportunities for investment in non-agricultural activities, such as rural industries and housing, diverted investment from land improvements. From 1987 the government increased state agricultural investment, particularly in irrigation, and on-farm investment was encouraged by the legalisation of transfer of land use rights in 1988 (IMF, 1991a). A bumper summer grain harvest was achieved in 1990 which helped to ease inflationary pressures (World Bank, 1990a).

Social Effects of Rural Reform

There have been a number of negative effects from the economic reforms. Inequalities have increased between families, villages and regions. The ending of the commune system has reduced medical and social services, and rural education has suffered as these activities were all financed by the communes. Women may also have lost status. They are once more working in the household as wives and daughters with no right to pay, whereas in the commune system they earned 'work-points' and had some independence (Bettleheim, 1988).

Enterprise Reforms

Before reform, state enterprises were centrally-controlled. Output, prices, sales and investment were all planned. All profits went to the state, and losses were covered by the state. Enterprise investments were funded by grants from the state budget. Working capital was supplied partly by grants from the state budget and partly by credits from the banking system. Wage rates were set on a centrally-approved scale with little scope for differentials and incentives. Workers and managers were often dependent on their work unit for housing, health services and other social benefits. Under the 'iron rice bowl' system, enterprises could not easily dismiss workers for inefficiency or through redundancy.

Since so little was under the control of enterprises, management could not be held responsible for financial results. Management's job was simply to meet physical output targets fixed by the plan. Neither managers nor workers had any incentive to improve efficiency.

The main aims of reforms have been to increase incentives to efficiency by giving enterprises more freedom to manage and more responsibility for their own profits and losses. The process of reform has involved trial and error and a gradualist approach.

Main Reforms of State-owned Enterprises (SOEs)

Between 1978 and 1983, enterprises were allowed to produce outside the plan, retain depreciation allowances, and a share of the profits, and there was a shift in financing from government to banks. Managers were given discretion over labour recruitment, and performance-linked wage bonuses were introduced.

These reforms were extended over 1984–6, allowing SOEs to sell surpluses over planned targets at negotiated prices. A major reform replaced profit remittances to the government with direct taxation. Banks were given greater freedom to act commercially.

Between 1987 and 1990 the job of enterprise directors was defined more formally and the Contract Management Responsibility System was introduced. Some 90 per cent of medium- and large-scale enterprises had signed management contracts by 1988. A national bankruptcy law was introduced in June 1988, but rarely used (IMF, 1991a; Hussain and Stern, 1991).

A pronounced pause in the reform process followed the events of June 1989, with some attempt to restore central control, but since then government policies seem to have become reformist once more (*Economist*, 1991).

Despite the reforms, the SOEs' inefficiency has proved to be relatively intractable. Some side-effects of the reforms have been counter-productive. Although SOEs have generally been favoured in the allocation of inputs and credit, their output in 1990 grew by only 3 per cent, compared with the industrial output of collectives, which were up by 20 per cent, and of foreign joint ventures, which were up by over 50 per cent (but from an admittedly small base). The share of SOEs in China's industrial output fell from 80 per cent in the late 1970s to 54 per cent in 1990 (*Economist*, 1991).

The shift from profit remittances to profit taxation without a properly designed fiscal system has increased China's budget deficits sharply. A uniform profits tax was not possible, because of the unfairness it would involve when there were substantial differences among firms with regard to location, capital equipment, and input and output prices. But this meant great scope for bargaining, which was exploited by SOEs to reduce their tax liabilities. Frequently, the results differed little from profit- or loss-sharing. SOEs have 'soft-budget constraints'; up to two-thirds of them have been described as 'chronically in the red' (*Far Eastern Economic Review*, 10 October 1991).

The existence of different prices (fixed prices, guideline prices and free market prices) for similar products, and large differences in profit retention rates between firms have led to substantial rent-seeking and corruption among enterprise managers (IMF, 1991).

Township and village enterprises, both collectively and individually owned, have prospered. Restrictions on their activities were relaxed after 1978. They generally operated in a more competitive environment for both inputs and outputs than did SOEs, and their budget constraints were harder. They have proved to be more flexible and more dynamic. Though often owned by municipal authorities, the latter's needs for revenue forced them to seek maximum profits so at the margin they operated much like private-sector firms (IMF, 1990; Thoburn *et al.*, 1990a). Their productivity has, however, often been low because of dated technology and the small scale of operation.

Prices and Wages

Before 1979, both commodity prices and wages were controlled by the state and rarely changed. After 1979 there were both administered changes and some price liberalization. Substantial increases in controlled agricultural prices were made in 1979 and subsequently. A two-tier price system was first introduced in rural areas. Farmers delivered quotas to the state at fixed prices and were then allowed to sell above-quota supplies to the state at negotiated prices, or in the free market. A few SOEs were given similar freedoms, but up to 1984 prices for important consumer goods, industrial raw materials and procurement prices for major agricultural commodities were still set by the state.

After 1984 the two-tier system was extended and more prices became market-determined or negotiable. As negotiations were generally left to local authorities, the 'guided' or negotiated prices have tended to follow market prices. The share of trade at state fixed prices fell from two-thirds of retail sales in 1978 to about one-third in 1988. The inflation which recurred in 1987–8 led to the reimposition of some price controls as the authorities sought to combat price increases. But in 1991 large increases in the subsidized prices of cooking oil and grain indicated a return to price reform (*Economist*, 1991).

Wage reforms have involved the linking of wages and bonuses to the value of sales, or to the profits of enterprises. By 1988 such wage systems covered a third of employees in SOEs. But most enterprises continue to distribute bonuses on an egalitarian basis. Despite taxes levied on excessive bonuses, enterprises have increased such payments significantly. Also, payments in kind have expanded to avoid tax penalties. Easy access to subsidies and credit in the late 1980s facilitated excessive payments to SOE workers and managers.

Labour was immobile in China. Up to the mid-1980s most jobs were assigned, employment was for a lifetime, welfare (including housing, health and pensions) was normally dependent on the work-unit, and there were severe restrictions on geographical mobility. Since 1986, SOEs have hired workers on three-to-five-year contracts, they have been given more freedom to select employees and, in principle, to dismiss them. In 1987, contract workers were about 8 per cent of the SOE workforce (IMF, 1991). Other measures to improve mobility have included experiments with pooling pension funds between several enterprises, creating unemployment insurance schemes, and housing reforms, including private ownership and some easing of restrictions on geographical mobility through a system of temporary residence permits. Despite these efforts, mobility remains restricted and underemployment is endemic in the state sector (IMF, 1991).

OPEN-DOOR POLICIES

China's pre-1978 trade policy has been likened to an airlock which sealed the domestic economy from the world. All trade was controlled exclusively by twelve state-owned foreign trade corporations (FTCs), each of which had a monopoly over particular products. The central plan set the levels of exports and imports for the year ahead and implementation of these targets was administered by the Ministry of Trade (MFT), later the Ministry of Foreign Economic Relations and Trade (MOFERT). The FTCs bought goods for export and sold imports at their domestic prices, which often bore little or no relation to world prices. The FTCs' profits were remitted to the state and losses were met by grants from the state budget. Imports were intended only to make up domestic shortages of goods and materials, and to provide those capital goods which could not be produced in China. These imports were financed by exports of commodities such as rice, petroleum, other minerals, and processed foods in which surpluses could be generated. The centrally-controlled trade plan aimed at balancing China's foreign trade and avoiding international indebtedness.

Trade Reform

The basic strategy of the reforms was decentralization. In 1979, part of decision-making power was distributed to local governments and enterprises. Since then MOFERT has been responsible for a foreign trade plan divided into a directive plan and a guidance plan. The first gives mandatory levels for exports of heavy industry such as petroleum, and for imports of raw materials and equipment for major state projects.

The guidance plan gives targets for the value of exports and imports to ministries and local administrations. They are allowed to form their own foreign trade corporations (FTCs) which have considerable discretion as how to meet their targets. Over the years the number of goods subject to the plans has fallen, and licensing, together with export and import duties, has become more important in influencing trade.

Since 1984, FTCs have become more responsible for their financial performance, paying taxes instead of remitting their profits to the state. In 1988, most local branches of national FTCs were made independent and responsible for their own finances. The number of FTCs expanded to over 6 000 and some domestic enterprises were authorized to engage directly in foreign trade. FTCs were encouraged to adopt the agency system where they received fees for handling trade instead of acting as buyers and sellers on their own behalf. These various reforms encouraged competition in foreign trade and some increase in the extent to which foreign prices were passed through to the domestic prices of imports and goods for export.

Enterprises were allowed to retain 25 per cent on average of foreign exchange earned for quota sales and 75 per cent above quota. In three sectors: garments, light industry, and arts and handicrafts, retentions were of between 60 and 100 per cent. At the same time, subsidies and official allocations of foreign exchange were ended in these industries, making them more-or-less financially independent. If enterprises or the local authorities with whom they shared exchange retentions did not wish to use their foreign exchange, they were allowed to sell it in the new foreign exchange adjustment centres (FEACs), where they could earn on average a 75 per cent premium over the official rate. These moves generated real incentives for enterprises and the provincial or town authorities to earn foreign currency. In the late 1980s and early 1990s there were several devaluations of the yuan which generally increased incentives to export and reduced the gap between the official and the parallel market rate to about 10 per cent (*Economist*, 1991).

The proliferation of FTCs and the incentives to export led to some excesses. It was alleged that competition between FTCs drove up the procurement prices of exportable goods – for example, silk products thus cutting the profits of some large state FTCs. More seriously, some export contracts were not met and some poor-quality products were exported. These damaged China's commercial reputation. The authorities responded by seeking to impose some quality control on the FTCs, withdrawing licences, and forcing some mergers.

Foreign Investment and the Special Economic Zones

The reformers saw attracting foreign investment as a way of gaining foreign technology and capital without adding to foreign debt. To experiment with this and more general economic reforms, five special economic zones (SEZs) were set up in 1980 as the main areas for foreign direct investment. Three of these are in Guangdong, the best-known being Shenzhen. They offered preferential tax and tariff rates, and tax holidays. In 1984 similar privileges were accorded to fourteen coastal cities and Hainan Island. Originally intended to attract joint ventures, especially from Western countries, foreign investors are present in a variety of relationships, from processing and assembly arrangements to wholly-owned ventures. In Guangdong, Hong Kong businesses have appeared far beyond the SEZs (Thoburn *et al.*, 1990b). The relationship with Hong Kong and overseas Chinese has proved to be enormously fruitful in attracting investment, and marketing and managerial expertise to assist China's exports. Hong Kong companies have created two million jobs in Guangdong. Output in Guangdong grew at 13 per cent per year in the 1980s, and in Shenzhen it reached 47 per cent a year. Guangdong has attracted over US$20 billion of foreign investment, most of it from Hong Kong, while Xiamen, in the neighbouring province of Fujian, has also been a major success, with over US$3.5 billion foreign investment, about a third of it from nearby Taiwan (*Economist*, 1991).

Conclusions on International Economic Relations

China's 'Open Door' policies have been a success. Since 1979, China's foreign trade ratio has tripled, reaching 29 per cent in 1989. The share of manufactures in total exports has risen to over 70 per cent. China's share of world exports doubled (1979–89) (World Bank, 1990a, tables 3–1 and 3–7). The average annual growth of China's exports in 1978–89 was 14 per cent. They slowed to 10 per cent in 1989 but surged to 20 per cent growth in 1990 (World Bank, table 3–3, and *Economist*, 1991).

There is a risk that China's foreign trade may nevertheless be inefficient, given the remaining distortions in the economy: multiple prices; soft budget constraints in SOEs; and incentives which vary across industries and regions. This is certainly the contention of John Hsu (1989). Without a detailed set of shadow prices and estimates of the domestic resource costs of China's industries, it is impossible to test this theory, but some casual observation of China's exports suggests otherwise. They are largely the natural-resource-intensive, or labour-intensive consumer goods and light-industries goods which conventional trade theory would predict. The rapid growth in manufactured exports has followed a similar path to the other successful Asian economies. The steps which China has taken to offset an import-substitution bias have been broadly correct; exports, on balance, are probably little, if at all, subsidized. Chinese labour seems to be highly thought of by overseas businessmen when comparing locations in Asia for overseas investment (*Economist*, 1991). Most of the increase in output and exports in recent years has come from the private or the quasi-private sector or collectives. They operate in a much more competitive, less subsidized environment than do the SOEs.

There may be greater risks of waste on the import side. Eagerness to use up foreign exchange allocations or currency retentions to avoid having to surrender them to the state did in the past lead to excessive imports of particular products and imported equipment being left idle, as Hsu argues. But the opening up of the FEACs must have reduced the incentive to use up foreign exchange surpluses when other enterprises, which really needed imports, were willing to offer attractive exchange rates for foreign currency.

SOME CONCLUSIONS AND IMPLICATIONS

Two basic lessons from China's economic successes since 1978 are the importance of early liberalization in agriculture and international economic relations. The combination of financial incentives and family or collective responsibility systems worked wonders in stimulating production and exports. The growth of farm production and incomes generated the demand and the resources necessary to stimulate rural, village and township enterprises. These in turn provided the main gains in manufacturing for both the domestic and foreign markets. The Open Door Policy encouraged the overseas Chinese to combine their talents in management, production know-how and marketing with low-cost Chinese labour, especially in Guangdong and Fujian provinces. The policy has been less successful in attracting the hoped-for Western technology. But recent changes to rules on foreign investment which allow wholly-owned subsidiaries may prove more attractive to Western multinationals. The relative abundance of food and consumer goods in post-reform China helped dampen inflation and is a major contrast with Russia and most Eastern European economies. No Eastern European economies have the great asset of a neighbouring Hong Kong or Taiwan to be tapped for capital and skills, but perhaps several could make more use of exiles who have successful businesses abroad.

The main weaknesses in China's economy are the slow pace of reforms in the state enterprises, the labour markets, and taxation. The SOEs remain overstaffed and heavily subsidized. Many continue to produce obsolete goods with out-of-date equipment. Reforms resulting in closures or mergers would convert widespread underemployment into open unemployment and naturally meet powerful resistance. Until proper employment benefit schemes are in place, such resistance is entirely understandable. But it would be wasteful to put increased finance into inefficient state enterprises when similar resources loaned to non-state enterprises could create real jobs and earn higher returns. New investment in the state sector should be confined to those activities which it is clear the private sector cannot handle in a more socially efficient manner.

The partial and incomplete nature of China's reforms stimulated particularly divisive forms of corruption. Decentralization put more power in the hands of provincial and local leaders. These, subject neither to the disciplines of central control nor of fully competitive markets, were able to exploit opportunities for buying at controlled prices and selling in free markets, and to extract bribes and favours for granting the various licences and permits needed to to business. Corruption, fraud and increased nepotism seem to have been widespread in the mid-1980s. These were widely reported in the press, and contributed to the discontent of students, teachers and workers on fixed incomes, which led to demonstrations and protests culminating in the Tiananmen Crisis (Meaney, 1991). The initial response of the authorities was to take back responsibility and control to the central authorities, but recent action to free more prices, raise controlled prices, devalue the yuan and widen access to foreign exchange have reduced some of the incentives to illicit arbitrage. More and better-trained auditors, together with incentives to 'whistle-blowing' are standard ways of dealing with fraud and other illegal business practices. But in China, with its long history of nepotism, special measures may be necessary to ensure that merit rather than connections gain advancement. Improvements in labour mobility could help.

Despite some reforms to ease geographical labour mobility, such as temporary residence permits, the present system gives individuals little choice of job or location. But requirements to advertise managerial posts widely, combined with transparent appointment procedures, and easier mobility for higher-grade personnel, would enhance efficient management. Special arrangements for mobility of key skilled workers, such as housing and attractive contracts, would also ease bottlenecks. For ordinary workers, mobility between work units can be improved by further social security reforms that transfer pension and health obligations from enterprises to the state. Similarly, existing and new housing should be removed from enterprises and transferred to municipal authorities with a view to developing a proper market for housing.

Fiscal reform is a key area. The reduction in revenues from SOEs has to be replaced. In China there may be a stronger case than in most developing economies for the introduction of an income tax, as 25 per cent of the labour force are in the state sector. Their incomes in cash and kind are more easily assessed (Hussain and Stern, 1991).

China's record under reform shows the dynamism which can be released when families in agriculture and small- to medium-sized enterprises in towns and villages are given responsibility and incentives. But it also shows the severe difficulties which face efforts to reform state enterprises. Similar problems have been met in Hungary and other reform-minded East European economies. It would be hard to deny that important lessons for the future of both China and other reforming centrally-planned economies can be learned from China's experiences since 1978.

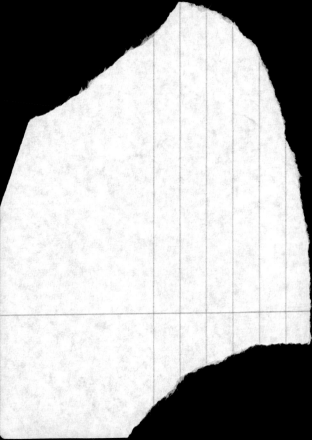

9 The Evolution of Chinese Foreign Investment Policy
Le-Yin Zhang and John Thoburn

This chapter traces the evolution of Chinese policy towards direct foreign investment (DFI) from the beginning of the economic reform period in 1978 to the time of writing, using mainly Chinese sources. The first section considers the role of DFI policy in the reform programme. The second looks at foreign investment strategies and their implementation, paying particular attention to the industrial and regional aspects of policy. The third discusses policy conflicts and inconsistencies; and the final section draws conclusions.

DIRECT FOREIGN INVESTMENT AND THE CHINESE ECONOMIC REFORM PROGRAMME

Attracting direct foreign investment, and 'opening' to the outside world more generally, have been central features of the Chinese economic reform programme that started in 1978 after the death of Mao Zedong. In the words of former Premier Zhao Ziyang:

> Invigorating the economy and opening up to the outside world are two basic guidelines for our modernization programme. They supplement each other and help each other forward ... China's modernization drive requires us to open up to the outside world and expand its economic and technical exchange with others. (BR, 18 June 1984).

Official thinking is that while economic reform would improve the efficiency of the economy by properly defining the economic relationships between the state and state-owned enterprises, and encouraging the latter to take initiatives in improving economic efficiency, the open-door policy would help in two principal ways: first, it would bring in much-needed foreign capital to help ease the shortage of domestic capital; second, it would bring in new technology and advanced Western management skills, and therefore help the growth of productivity.

The overall goal of encouraging DFI is to help attain the target of quadrupling China's gross industrial and agricultural output by the year 2000, under the Four Modernizations programme.[1] The Chinese government has not, however, defined with clarity the specific objectives of encouraging DFI. There has been no overall plan published elaborating the objectives of DFI policy and/or detailed measures for encouraging and utilizing DFI. Admittedly, it is difficult to define quantitatively the objectives of such a policy, since the inflow of DFI is largely beyond the control of policy-makers. This is particularly so in the case of China, because the country was for a long period insulated from the outside world and consequently the planners feel great uncertainty in dealing with DFI.[2]

Official speeches and articles in the press are useful sources of information none the less. A more authoritative source is the collection of some two hundred laws, regulations and provisions that have been promulgated in relation to DFI since 1979, when the first (the Law on Joint Ventures Using Chinese and Foreign Investment) was passed.

An examination of these sources suggests that the government's public economic aims in encouraging DFI are as follows: first, one of the most important objectives, and particularly so in the earlier years, has been to utilize foreign financial resources to expand China's capital formation. The late Secretary General of the Chinese Communist Party, Hu Yaobang stressed that 'it is because the top difficulty that we are facing in our modernization construction drive is the lack of capital that we have attached such an importance to attracting foreign capital'.[3]

Guo Mu, a state councillor, explained in greater detail:

> shortage of capital is a prominent difficulty in the economic development of our country. In every year's planning, there are always some projects that should be included but have to be dropped due to shortage of capital. How to solve the problem of capital shortage is a matter of significance to the pacing of the Four Modernizations Drive ... We ought to speed up utilizing foreign capital. (*SJD*, 5 November 1984)

However, the mere inflow of foreign capital is not enough, and a second objective is to introduce advanced technology and management skills through foreign capital. It is here that the advantages of DFI over other forms of foreign capital are recognized, as Hu Yaobang noted:

> As far as the near future is concerned, in my view, attracting foreign direct investment should be the most important form. It has two main advantages: firstly, the investment is directly linked with the interests of the investors, and the risk is shared; secondly, it puts us in a better position to learn advanced technology and management skills. (IIE, 1984)

Third, DFI has also been regarded as a powerful engine to expand China's exports, although the motives behind China's desire to increase its exports have undergone some change over the years. In the years immediately after the opening-up, the growth of exports was desired mainly to earn foreign exchange, to enable China to pay for the import of foreign goods. This perspective was changed somewhat around 1984 to a wider one, that is, China's participation in the international division of labour. Huan Xiang and Pai Lun-zhang, both prominent writers and high-ranking officials, wrote in 1984:

Implementing the open-door policy in our external economic work means not only openness to foreign capital and technology, but more importantly and more fundamentally, two other aspects, first, China's inevitably deepening involvement in the international division of labour; second, facing up to the increasingly fierce competition in the world market. (Yu and Xiang, 1985)

However, the aim of China's participation in the international division of labour is related to the improvement of economic efficiency:

the aim of external trading should not only be to realize the use value of commodities. It is inadequate to stress using our strong points to make up our weak points through exchanging alone. It should be viewed in the perspective of value adding and social labour saving. (Yu and Xiang, 1985)

The view that China should participate in the international division of labour was further developed in the following years and culminated in Zhao Ziyang's 'Coastal China's Development Strategy'. More specifically, the strategy proposed to take advantage of the opportunities provided by the international relocation of labour-intensive production from more-developed countries to less-developed countries using the advantages in China's coastal areas, such as rich labour resources and outside contacts, to develop an export-orientated economy there, particularly through the development of labour-intensive industries. The strategy was summed up as 'both ends abroad' (the two ends refer to material supply and product marketing), 'high volume of imports and exports' (*CEN*, 18 January 1988; 18 April 1988). In short, according to this strategy, China's coastal area was to become a huge processing and assembling site for the world market, and export growth was to become the order of the economy.

The fourth objective has been to enhance the growth of productivity and the improvement of economic efficiency through DFI. Indeed, the Chinese leadership went so far as for Zhao Ziyang to advocate that foreign investors should be allowed to manage or invest directly in existing Chinese state-owned enterprises so that the performance of these enterprises could be improved (*RR*, 26 December 1984).

More generally, it was hoped that the areas where DFI was concentrated could absorb selectively capitalist business management methods and skills introduced through DFI, and experiment in incorporating them with the socialist conditions in China to advance the reform process, both within and outside these areas.

There have also been important political goals such as promoting China's unification with Hong Kong, Macao and Taiwan. Perhaps, however, the ultimate aim of the DFI policy has been to maintain the CCP's political authority, as the party had come to realise by the late 1970s that a failure to promote economic growth would be fatal to its hold on power.

FOREIGN INVESTMENT STRATEGIES AND THEIR IMPLEMENTATION

In order to achieve the objectives discussed in the previous section, the Chinese government has adopted a strong regional policy to concentrate DFI in the geographically more accessible and economically more developed east coast areas, and has developed an industrial strategy to promote 'productive' (mainly manufacturing) DFI, particularly export-orientated and technically advanced DFI. It has also adopted various administrative measures, including increasing liberalization over investment forms; giving special encouragement to overseas Chinese investors; and administrative decentralization, to allow local governments to play an active role in encouraging and administering DFI.

To implement these strategies, the Chinese government has employed a wide range of measures, including improved application procedures, preferences, import and export controls, credit, foreign exchange controls and domestic market access.

Regional Strategy

By far the most coherent and consistent part of the Chinese government's strategy in encouraging DFI has been its regional policy. A limited number of areas, mainly on the east coast, have been opened for DFI earlier than the rest of the country, and these opened areas, with greater technical and policy capacities, were expected to absorb the foreign capital, technology and management skills first, and then transmit and spread the technology and experience to the less-developed inland areas (Wang, 1985).

The starting point of this strategy was the granting of 'special policy and flexible measures' to Guangdong and Fujian provinces by the central government in early 1979. This choice of locations was made for numerous reasons, as Vogel has suggested in relation to Guangdong (Vogel, 1989): first, to encourage national unification with Hong Kong and Macao. Since the majority of the residents in these two places are natives from Guangdong (and Taiwan, in the case of the natives of Fujian), 'What more could China do to win over the people of these three territories (Hong Kong, Macao and Taiwan) than to allow their native provinces special flexibility to gain their goodwill' (Vogel, 1989).

Second, to relieve the state's financial burden, Guangdong is the area of origin of the largest number of overseas Chinese and therefore more able to attract DFI from them. Third, it would reduce strains on national resources and the transportation system if Guangdong could develop into a more export-orientated economy, and earn more foreign exchange to support technology imports elsewhere. Fourth, Guangdong's great physical distance from Beijing reduces the political risks that changes in the province might cause in the central government. Fifth, Guangdong's 'modest' contribution to China's treasury reduces the risk that any failure on Guangdong's part would upset the national budget. Sixth and most importantly, Guangdong's cadres were thought of as being more receptive than others to trying new programmes, and there was access to world technology and management systems through Hong Kong.

Vogel has also provided a detailed list of those policies for Guangdong (Vogel, 1989). They included more independence in administering economic, social and cultural matters; more authority to determine the distribution and supply of materials and resources; and to determine wages and set prices. But the most important content of the policies are four elements, which Vogel describes as 'more freedom in managing foreign trade', 'fiscal independence', 'increased financial independence', and the establishment of the three Special Economic Zones (SEZs) on the province's coast.

Guangdong was allowed to take over many branches of the state-owned foreign trading corporations, to set up organizations in Hong Kong and Macao for trade promotion and information gathering, and to retain most of its increased foreign exchange earnings. The 'fiscal independence' allowed Guangdong, instead of sending to the central government a certain percentage of taxes collected (as was the case with other provinces), to pass on only a fixed, relatively low sum, which would stay the same for five years (this arrangement was renewed for a further five years (1985–9) in 1984) (*GGKY*, 1988). Moreover, banks in Guangdong were given more leeway to make their own investment decisions. As a result, the scale and direction of investment in Guangdong was no longer subject to state control. Vogel records:

> In order to begin Guangdong's banking independence with loans linked to deposits, the People's Bank agreed in 1980 to assign 400 million yuan per year to Guangdong for three years ... 700 million yuan were used ... From then on banks in Guangdong were allowed to link lending to deposits and expand loans as they acquired deposits. (Vogel, 1989)

A similar package was granted to Fujian province, which faces Taiwan. Due to the less-developed state of Fujian's economy, and the limited economic exchange between the province and Taiwan at the time (largely for political reasons, the Taiwan authorities banned direct contact with the mainland until May 1991), only one SEZ was to be set up in Fujian.

In the four SEZs (three – Shenzhen, Zhuhai and Shantou – in Guangdong; one – Xiamen – in Fujian), preferential conditions were offered to both domestic and foreign investors. A large amount of state funds was invested in the early stages in infrastructure. Within a few years, the areas where the SEZs, particularly Shenzhen and Xiamen, were located, were transformed dramatically.

Greatly encouraged by these changes, the conservative attitude within the party started to fade and the central government was soon calling for the SEZs to be 'windows' on the world and to play a 'demonstration' role on a wide range of matters.

The second step was then taken, with fourteen coastal cities and Hainan Island being opened in 1984 (of which Guangdong accounted for two open cities and Hainan Island, the latter then still belonging to the province). Fifteen Economic and Technological Development Zones (ETDZs) were set up in these fourteen open cities. Preferential policies were also offered. They were, however, less favourable than those in the SEZs. But significantly, the incentives offered in these areas distinguished between 'productive' DFI and 'other' DFI, and offered special incentives to the former.[4] Productive DFI is entitled to the same treatment as DFI in SEZs.

One year after the opening of these coastal cities, the Chinese government took a further step, in February 1985, by designating three Coastal

Economic Open Areas (CEOAs) – the Yangtze River Delta Economic Open Area (YRDEOA), the Southern Fujian Economic Open Area (SFEOA), and Guangdong's Pearl River Delta Economic Open Area (PRDEOA). Again, preferential policies on taxation, exports and imports were offered. In this case, energy, transportation and technology-intensive and other 'productive' projects were offered special incentives.[5]

The Open Policy gathered momentum in late 1987, when the Chinese government decided to expand the Coastal Open Areas into an area embracing virtually the whole east coastal area of China, extending from Liaoning Peninsula in the north-east to the Guangxi Autonomous District in the south-west.

Finally, in May 1988, Hainan Island obtained the status of a province and became the fifth (and largest) SEZ in China, although the financial commitment of the central government is believed not to be as substantial as to the other SEZs.

By the end of 1987, China's CEOAs included 288 cities and counties. They covered a total area of 320 000 square kilometres (3 per cent of the national territory) along a 18 000 kilometre coastline with a population of 160 million (14.5 per cent of the national population) (*CEN*, 25 April 1988).

The details of the treatment accorded to these different regions are numerous and sometimes confusing.[6] The overall feature, however, is that differences in treatment between the coastal regions have become smaller over the years. It remains the case, nevertheless, that the Open Policy is applicable only to a part of the country, mainly the coastal east. It is also evident, from the above account, that Guangdong has played a key role in the Chinese government's strategy of encouraging DFI.

During and after the political turmoil of June 1989, the commitment of the Chinese government towards the policy of encouraging DFI faced a major test. It was widely feared that the policy might be reversed. In the face of this, the Chinese government made its latest move in the regional strategy; that is, to establish the Pudong Development Zone in Shanghai in April 1990. The Zone is not only promised the same treatment as SEZs but also some new incentives. The latter include:

1. Foreign investors are allowed to engage in entrepôt trade and other service business;
2. Foreign-funded banks are allowed and offered special incentives.[7]

It seems that the government's intention is to develop this Zone into a financial and service centre for the surrounding Yangtze River Delta or even beyond, where a substantial amount of DFI is already in place and the potential for further inflows is still great. It is also evident that there is a shift in regional emphasis from the southern provinces of Guangdong and Fujian to the old industrial centres of the east and north-east.

Industrial Strategy

China did not have a general, publicly-declared industrial policy in the 1980s, until March 1989, when investments in agriculture, energy, transport and communications, and basic material industries, were given encouragement (*RR*, Overseas Edition, 20 March 1989). Inevitably, therefore, China's industrial policy towards DFI has appeared to be erratic, taking the form of a series of checklists issued by the state from time to time, about priority and demarcated areas for DFI.[8]

Indeed, before the promulgation of the Implementation Provisions of the Law on Joint Ventures in November 1986, industrial strategy was largely absent. The only trace of such a strategy then was that in the Joint Venture Law, it was stipulated that joint ventures using 'worldwide advanced technology' could apply for a tax reduction or exemption for the first 2–3 years (Xiang and Yu, 1988).[9]

In the Implementation Provisions of the Law, issued in 1983, however, the areas where Equity Joint Ventures (EJVs) would be allowed were specified as being energy, basic material industries, manufacturing, agriculture, animal husbandry, fishery, tourism and services. Any proposed EJV was required to meet at least one of the following four conditions:

1. Use advanced technology and scientific management methods, with the capacity to increase product varieties, improve product quality and output and reduce energy and material consumption;
2. Be conducive to technical renovation of existing enterprises and achieve economic efficiency;
3. Be able to expand exports and increase earning of foreign exchange; and
4. Be able to provide training for Chinese technical and managerial personnel.

This is an important clarification of the Law. But like the series of checklists, the Implementation Provisions do not attach any fiscal incentives to the identified priority investment areas. Their main significance is to provide guidelines for the government department in exercising its examination and approval power. Projects that do not meet the current criteria should be rejected.

In November 1984, however, the Provisional regulations were promulgated, on Reduction and Exemption of Enterprises Income Tax and Consolidated Industrial and Commercial Tax for Special Economic Zones and the Fourteen Coastal Port Cities. This offered distinctive tax incentives to productive DFI (Xiang and Yu, 1988).

The most important move in the implementation of the industrial strategy came in October 1986, when the Provisions on the Encouragement of Foreign Investment were promulgated.[10] The Provisions singled out two categories of Foreign Investment Enterprise (FIE); that is, export-orientated ones and technologically-advanced ones (referred to as 'two-type FIEs'), and offered incentive packages to them, including lower corporate taxation rates, prolonged tax holidays, exemption from paying part of the state subsidies that their employees receive, lower site fees, priority supplies of water, electricity, transport and communication facilities, and priority access to bank loans.

Rules for defining these two categories of FIE were announced shortly afterwards. An export-orientated FIE was one:

1. Whose products are mainly destined for export (usually 70 per cent of the output value); and
2. Which enjoys a foreign-exchange balance (or surplus) after deducting from its foreign exchange revenue foreign exchange expenditure and foreign currency remitted abroad.

A technologically-advanced FIE refers to one in which the foreign investor provides advanced technology for the development of new products, product upgrading and renewal, in order to increase exports or substitute for imports (*CBN*, January/February 1987).

In order to further encourage technologically-advanced FIE, the State Planning Commission promulgated additional Rules in October 1987. These stipulated that approved import-substitute products could be sold partly or entirely in the domestic market for foreign currency, and that, under similar conditions, domestic buyers must give priority to these import-substitute products over imports.[11]

In the general industrial policy published in March 1989, it was stated that an industrial policy for DFI would be drawn up soon afterwards. There is no sign of such a plan at the time of writing, however. One move was that a general FAI (Fixed Asset Adjustment) tax was introduced, which came into effect from 1 January 1991. This lays down five different tax rates, from zero to 30 per cent (*HKER*, 10 December 1990). It is not clear whether it applies to DFI.

Increasing Flexibility towards Investment Forms

One important aspect of the Chinese government's encouragement of DFI has been an increasingly liberal attitude towards the forms that DFI can take. China is rich in alternative forms of foreign investment contracts. There are five types:

1. Processing and assembly arrangements, under which a fee is paid in foreign exchange to the Chinese side for labour and other services, and materials and machinery are supplied by the foreign investor (PA);
2. Compensation trade, where the foreign side supplies machinery and is repaid with instalments of the product (CT);
3. Co-operative (or 'contractual') joint ventures, where the Chinese contribution is mainly in kind, such as buildings and a factory site (CJVs);
4. Equity joint ventures, where profits are split according to each side's equity contribution (EJVs); and
5. Wholly foreign-owned ventures (WFOEs).

Various features unique to the Chinese situation further complicate these arrangements and mean that contractual choice is still wider in practice.

The foundation of this flexible attitude was laid down in the first foreign investment law (the Law on Joint Ventures Using Chinese and Foreign Investment). No restriction was imposed on the maximum share of foreign investor's equity. On the contrary, there was a restriction on the minimum share of foreign equity, at 25 per cent. But in the early years, WFOEs were largely confined to the four SEZs. Moreover, applications for WFOEs could be handled only by MOFERT (the Ministry of Foreign Economic Relations and Trade). As a result, the number of WFOEs established before 1988 was small, totalling some 500 by the end of 1987.

The Law on Wholly Foreign-Owned Enterprises was promulgated in March 1986, which signified a significant improvement in the government's attitude towards WFOEs. Another positive move was made in 1988, when central government delegated to local government some of the power to examine and approve WFOEs.

Paradoxically, the austerity programme, started in late 1988,[12] seems to have provided a timely impetus for the Chinese government to encourage more WFOEs, since the economic contraction limited severely the ability of local partners to raise financial resources to join foreign investors in establishing joint ventures (*CEN*, 29 May 1989). The liberal attitude towards WFOEs appears to be fundamental rather than temporary, however. MOFERT in Beijing was reportedly acknowledging a wide range of benefits that WFOEs could bring to China. It is generally believed in China that WFOEs are associated with more advanced technology, although how such technology may be adopted in Chinese enterprises, without Chinese participation in the operation, is a matter of widespread concern.

The Chinese government's liberal attitude towards forms of DFI is also reflected in its adoption of the CJV. This investment form was initially a local creation from Guangdong province, later adopted by the central government.[13] The CJV is the most flexible of all the contracts. Different contracts require different levels of official approval. Until 1988, for instance, WFOEs required approval from Beijing, and some firms had set up *de facto* WFOEs in the form of long-term CJVs, which required only county-level approval. On the other hand, some CJVs were short-term (5–8 years), and were somewhat more like compensation trade, with the foreign (usually Hong Kong) partners being repaid their investment as a prior claim on profits, and the equipment belonging to China at the end of the contract.

Special Encouragement of DFI from Overseas Chinese

A major objective of the Open Policy in the beginning was to build prosperity in areas close to Hong Kong, Macao and Taiwan, and through this to promote the cause of national unification. However, although investment from these areas was regarded as being particularly desirable, no provisions were made at the outset to provide special incentives.

Special Incentives to Chinese investors from these three areas were first provided in April 1985, when the government issued the Provisional Regulations on the Encouragement of Overseas Chinese Investment (Xiang and Yu, 1988). But, interestingly, although Hong Kong rather than Taiwan was the main investment source, in July 1988, special provisions were passed to encourage investment from Taiwan (*RR*, overseas edition, 7 July 1988). In August 1990 the general Provisions on the Encouragement of Investment from Hong Kong, Macao and Other Overseas Chinese (*RR*, overseas edition, 28 August 1990), which extended in some aspects the previous provisions, were announced.

The most conspicuous special incentive offered to overseas Chinese is in terms of tax. FIEs of overseas Chinese investors, located outside the

SEZs and ETDZs in the fourteen Open Cities, are exempt from income tax for the first three profit-making years, and pay tax at half the normal rate in the following four years. Moreover, after the initial seven years, these FIEs pay tax at one-fifth the normal rate. In comparison, FIEs by other investors are exempt from corporate income tax for only one year, and can enjoy half tax reduction in the following two years only.[14] It is also stipulated that land use fees, charged on FIEs by overseas Chinese investors, should be 10–30 per cent less than normal.

Moreover, the Taiwan Provisions offer more special treatment to Taiwanese investors. First, they are allowed and encouraged to engage in exclusive land development in some separately designated coastal areas.[15] Second, they are allowed to purchase shares and stocks of existing Chinese enterprises, and freehold of real estate properties. The Hong Kong–Macao Provisions grant similar treatment to other overseas Chinese investors.

The Provisions even attempt to cater to the special needs of overseas Chinese investors whose business style is characterized by close family ties. For instance, it is stipulated that overseas Chinese investors can employ their mainland relatives as representatives. A special clause is also included to allow for transfer and inheritance.

The Chinese government seems not to want to stress the special treatment for overseas Chinese investors for fear that it might cause an unnecessary disincentive to other foreign investors. For instance, during an interview with reporters, the Head of the State Tax Bureau denied that overseas Chinese investors enjoyed more tax concessions than other investors by referring to the so-called 'basic principle of equal taxation obligation' (*RR*, overseas edition, 14 December 1990).

Decentralization

Finally, policy measures have been introduced in an attempt to create space for local governments to take initiatives. This dimension is, however, not peculiar to the DFI policy; rather, it is partly the consequence of the economic reforms. It can be argued, however, that the attempt of the central government to implement the Open Policy, mainly the DFI policy, by offering a special package to Guangdong and Fujian, initiated the process of decentralization, since many elements of this package were later extended to other provinces as they pressed for similar treatment.

Local governments can exert influences in the following fields with DFI.

Approval power

Since the early 1980s, central government has delegated increasingly great approval power to local governments.

Reduction or exemption of local income surtax

According to the Income Tax Law Concerning Equity Joint Ventures with Chinese and Foreign Investment, a local surtax of 10 per cent of the assessed income tax should be levied on EJVs (and other FIEs). Local governments, however, are given the authority to grant a reduction or exemption. It is apparent by now that most local governments offer the reduction or exemption of local surtax as an investment incentive. In some cases such as SEZs, local governments also have discretion over the reduction or exemption of the Consolidated Industrial and Commercial Tax on FIEs' sales in the local market.

Land-use fees and public utility costs

Land-use fees are decided by local governments, based on use, geographical position, environment and infrastructure conditions. Industrial joint ventures established in big cities such as Beijing and Shanghai pay annual land fees of about 15 yuan per square metre. The land-use fees vary greatly from place to place (*BR*, 21 January 1985). Charge rates on public utilities are also determined by local governments.

Wages

The total wage that FIEs have to pay to an employee can be divided into three categories: basic wage, bonus and subsidies. According to the relevant law of late 1986, wages in all FIEs must be at least 20 per cent above the 'average wages' of workers in Chinese state enterprises in the same localities and similar line of business. The term 'average wage' is, however, not defined. So localities have to formulate their own definitions as part of the legislation to encourage foreign investment in their areas (Horsley, 1988).

Comparatively speaking, FIEs retain greater autonomy over bonus payments. According to the 1980 joint ventures labour management regulations, the joint ventures' board of directors determines the bonus and establishes a bonus and welfare fund out of after-tax profits.

More recently, however, there has been pressure on FIEs to limit the upper level of wages paid by them, to avoid problems of competition for key personnel between FIEs and state enterprises (Greene, 1991).

Local legislation has significant power to influence other items such as subsidies, labour insurance and welfare, and pension payments. Subsidies fall into two groups: those paid directly to the worker, and those paid indirectly to the local government or kept by the trade union of the enterprise. The first includes money for such items as rent, transportation, sanitation, heating and food allowances, in total approximately 15 per cent of the average monthly wage. The indirect subsidy covers part of the cost of goods and services, including food and housing. Only export-orientated and technologically-advanced FIEs are by law exempted from payments other than labour insurance, welfare and housing subsidies.

Various other reforms

These include speeding up the handling of applications, curbing general 'red tape', providing supportive services such as special material supply channels, and improving infrastructure.

PROBLEMS OF POLICY AND IMPLEMENTATION

The problems of policy can be analyzed at two levels: one is operational, derived from faults in planning; the other is strategic, rooted in ideological and theoretical dilemmas.

From the point of view of planning, the greatest problem lies in the fact that the policy has too many goals. As shown earlier, the policy includes such diversified objectives as expanding China's capital formation, technology transfer, export promotion, national unification, and consolidation of the Party's authority in China. The problem is that not all the goals are consistent with each other. Furthermore, from the point of view of evaluation, the more goals there are, the less clear-cut are the criteria for judging the performance of the policy. In fact, various political or economic arguments are used to legitimize the failure of some aspects of policy implementation.

The major strategic problem concerns the relationship between industrial and regional strategies, and between these two and China's overall ownership strategy. It should be stressed that the Chinese government has not been very clear about how DFI relates to what, in principle at least, is still China's ultimate socialist aim, that is, complete public ownership in the economy. Indeed, there has been considerable confusion and uncertainty about this question among the officials and academic researchers.[16]

According to V. I. Lenin, to whose writings during the New Economic Policy period most Chinese writers have turned for ideological support, the role of DFI is transitory. It is allowed only to help develop the productive forces in the primary stage of socialism where these have not been sufficiently developed to allow full public ownership. Based on this point of view, Chinese writers have tended to agree with Lenin that DFI's presence in China is not permanent, although they have stressed carefully that this transitory period may be very extended.

What follows from the transitory nature of DFI is that its quantitative role is not without limits. Indeed, at a certain point, such a limit was defined. An important document produced in 1985 by the State Economic System Reform Commission, *Considerations of the Economic System Reform during the Seventh Five-Year Plan Period*, reads:

> While abiding by the domination of public ownership over the economy, we should continue to develop multiple economic forms and various management methods. By the end of the seventh five-year plan period [i.e. 1990], in gross industrial output value, the public sector is to account for about 60 per cent, the collective sector 30 per cent or so, individual and others about 5 per cent but not more than 10 per cent.[17]

It seems that the Chinese government intends to safeguard this principle,[18] although most of the collective sector has already surpassed the target. For instance, although many state-owned enterprises make heavy losses and although it has been suggested for a long time that DFI should be allowed to take them over and improve their operation, the Chinese government has not allowed this to happen.[19] On the other hand, DFI in some vital branches of the economy such as energy, transport and communications, is actually restricted due to the government's aversion to foreign control in those areas,[20] even though these are exactly the areas where the industrial strategy encourages DFI.

Contradictions between industrial and regional strategy are also evident. Although energy and raw material industries have since 1983 been earmarked among the priority investment areas, the regional strategy which favours the coastal areas, where there is little such activity, has resulted in limited flows of DFI into these parts. On the other hand, because of the massive inflow of DFI into light processing industries in the coastal areas, there is a growing imbalance between the underdevelopment of raw materials and energy, and the development of manufacturing industries. This relates directly to the very heart of the problems of the

Chinese economy, that is its irrational resource allocation and distorted pricing system.

The Chinese government seems scarcely to notice these contradictions. Instead, it has attempted to make Guangdong and Fujian, particularly the four SEZs, into an experimental ground for both economic reform and Open Policy, although these two provinces were neither technologically nor economically advanced. The question is: how far can a local economy with a considerable presence of DFI, such as Guangdong and Fujian, provide useful opportunities for China's economic reform?

One ultimate aim of the reform is to make Chinese enterprises independent (of the government) and, more importantly, efficient. How do FIEs help Chinese enterprises to become more independent and efficient? Given the nature of DFI and the existing liberal legislation towards FIEs, taking over existing Chinese enterprises with DFI will perhaps help. But, as shown earlier, this is thought to be ideologically undesirable (except for partnerships in the form of EJVs or CJVs with existing state enterprises).

Under the central government's regional policy, the areas where raw material industries are located (that is, the inland areas) receive less centrally-funded investment. In the meantime, because of lack of investment incentives and poor profitability, DFI is unlikely to invest in these areas either. Guided by profit maximization, DFI has been concentrated in the manufacture of consumer goods that fetch good prices in the market without the burden of price control. In doing so, they in fact add more shortages to domestic raw material supply, and cause more market distortions.

Thus, in this sense, the central government's expectation that the coastal open areas will play a pioneering role, not only in the Open Policy but also in economic reform more generally, is open to some doubt. Nevertheless, the expansion of labour-intensive manufacturing certainly has increased export earnings in Guangdong and Fujian, provided valuable experience of overseas standards of product marketing and quality control, and improved local management techniques. In addition, where foreign investors operate processing and assembly operations, these rely typically on imported materials and thereby avoid creating additional raw material supply bottlenecks.[21]

The regional strategy also raises some political problems. One of the most fundamental changes in the principles underlying China's development strategy since 1979 is its abandonment of egalitarianism, which had prevailed since the 1950s. It is official policy that some individuals should be encouraged in 'taking the lead to become rich'. The same policy also applies to regional units.

It can be inferred that, under this policy, there is likely to be a widening gap in the gains from economic growth between individuals and regions.

Furthermore, as administrative decentralization greatly increases the role of local governments in economic affairs, the implementation of such a policy and the resulting widening gaps may cause extensive competition between regional governments trying to expand their economic power. Ultimately, it could lead to regional rivalry and undermine the authority of the central government. The regional strategy, which is designed to implement the Open Policy, could thus in the long-term be divisive and, conceivably, politically unsustainable. However, regional divisions are much less a reflection of ethnic diversity than is the case among the republics of the former Soviet Union, for example, and this adds a certain stability to the Chinese scene.

CONCLUSION

This chapter shows that the goals of the Chinese government's DFI policy are not as simple as might at first be thought. While its overall economic goal is to promote economic growth in China through DFI's contribution to the expansion of capital formation, transfer of technology (including managerial skills), growth of exports, and the improvement of productivity and efficiency, its goal is also political. First, to enhance the Communist Party's political legitimacy and authority at home and abroad; and, second, to promote national unification with Hong Kong, Taiwan and Macao.

The policy also has certain less important goals such as creation of employment, or less-defined goals such as enhancing China's economic reform programme.

It is argued that, because of multiple goals, the policy on the one hand causes conflict and inconsistency in implementation, and on the other hand, makes evaluation difficult. The policy also suffers from various ideological, strategic and operational problems. From an ideological point of view, the policy-makers are not sure about the relationship between DFI and China's socialist aims, and tend to take a liberal or conservative attitude according to changes in the political climate. This leads to a situation where China's desire to attract more DFI in certain areas for economic purposes has to be compromised by its need to maintain the state's control over the economy through state ownership. In reality, this has made the absorption of foreign capital in the state-owned sector and in some vital industries, such as energy and raw material industries, difficult. In general, the regional policy has tended to overshadow the implementation of the industrial policy.[22]

Notes

1.   The 'Four Modernisations' refer to industry, agriculture, science and technology, and national defence. The programme was officially announced at the Eleventh Party Congress in 1975. In 1978, Deng Xiaoping, the paramount Chinese leader, indicated that the programme was designed to raise China's per capita income to US$ 1000 by the year 2000. In 1982, the Twelfth National Congress of the Chinese Communist Party stated that 'the overall target of economic construction in our country in the next twenty years between 1981 and 2000 is, while constantly improving economic efficiency, to quadruple the national gross industrial and agricultural output, ie. from yuan 710 billion in 1980 to yuan 2800 billion in 2000' (IIE, 1984, p. 223). In 1984, Deng Xiaoping mentioned a revised target of US$ 800 by the year 2000 (*RR*, 12 October 1984). To meet this target would require output growth of 7.1 per cent per annum between 1981 and 2000. Only a few countries, such as Japan and Korea, have sustained such growth rates for long periods. During the period 1953–78, China's gross agricultural and industrial output grew at 8.2 per cent pa, and domestic accumulation averaged 28.5 per cent (SSB, 1989). Nevertheless, total factor productivity growth during this period was either low or negative (depending on the weights attached to capital and labour inputs) (World Bank, 1985). In the World Bank's view, if productivity growth maintained its early 1980s growth, the achievement of the target would require domestic accumulation of 29 per cent of national income during the period to the year 2000, plus a stock of foreign debt of US$ 158 340 billion by 2000 (World Bank, 1985, annex 4). In 1988 China's external debt stood at US$ 42.015 billion, and long-term debt service absorbed 6.9 per cent of its export earnings, a low figure by international standards (World Bank, 1990a).

2.   Of course, China was not completely isolated economically between 1949 and the late 1970s. It continued to trade with the outside world and until the 1960 Sino-Soviet split it received aid and technical assistance from the Soviet Union. After the *rapprochement* with the United States in the early 1970s there was an expansion of trade. Nevertheless, the trade expansion of the reform period represents a distinct break with past experience. This is not only because the economy became far more open, with the ratio of exports to GNP rising from just 5 per cent in 1978 to 13 per cent in 1987 (see Nolan and Dong, 1990), but also because of the (partial) decentralization of trade decisions. In any case, there was no Western foreign direct investment between 1949 and the late 1970s.

3.   Hu Yaobang, 'On the External Economic Relationship', IIE, 1984.

4.   'Productive' DFI includes investment in industry, transport, agriculture, forestry, animal husbandry and the like.

5.   In fact, foreign investment, mainly from Hong Kong, was already going into the Pearl River Delta well before 1984; see Thoburn *et al.*, 1990.

6.   A survey of major differences in tax treatment can be found in Thoburn *et al.*, 1990a.

7.   According to a speech by Shanghai's mayor, Zhu Rongji, see *JD*, 18 June 1990.

8. See *CEN*, No. 30, August 1986; 4 January 1988; 14 March 1988; 17 October 1988; No. 41, October 1988; 3 July 1988.
9. See the third section (Problems of Policy and Implementation) for a discussion of the different kinds of foreign investment contracts available in China.
10. The 1986 Provisions were formulated in part to deal with serious problems, especially connected with foreign-exchange expenditure and the remission of profits by foreign investors, and a high perceived level of foreign investor dissatisfaction.
11. Xiang and Yu, 1988. Also see 'China's Import substitute Policy', *CFT*, No. 3, 1988.
12. The austerity measures introduced in late 1988 were designed to deal with powerful inflationary pressures building up in the Chinese economy, and bottlenecks in energy and infrastructure which had developed while the economy grew in the 1980s at approximately 10 per cent per year.
13. Interview by Le-Yin Zhang with an official from MOFERT in Beijing. For further discussion of contract types in China, see Leung *et al.*, 1991.
14. See 'The Law of the People's Republic of China on Corporate Income Tax of Sino-Foreign Equity Joint Ventures', in Xiang and Yu, 1988.
15. This right has only recently become available to other investors.
16. For a discussion of ownership issues in the Chinese economy, see Dong Fureng, ch. 3, in Nolan and Dong, 1990.
17. See Master Planning Group of the State Economic Reform Commission, in *SESRC*, 1988.
18. A conversation Le-Yin Zhang had with an official from the SESRC in early 1991 indicates that the above document was written at a time when policy towards ownership reform within the Commission was relatively more liberal than at present.
19. With the exception of joint ventures (usually EJVs) between state enterprises and foreign investors. However, these ventures have not been 'takeovers by DFI', and many problems have been encountered. (See Thoburn *et al.*, 1990, ch. 3.)
20. This information is derived from interviews by Le-Yin Zhang in Guangdong.
21. For further discussion of these issues (see Thoburn *et al.*, 1990c). Note, however, T. M. H. Chan (1988), has suggested that Guangdong's export expansion has been at high cost relative to production in more established industrial regions of China.
22. It is also worth noting that by the end of the 1980s, investment by mainland China in Hong Kong (the country that is China's largest foreign investor) was larger than the DFI that Hong Kong has made in China. See Hsueh and Woo, 1989.

10 Mongolia: The Painful Transition to a Market Economy

Frederick Nixson

INTRODUCTION

Mongolia (formerly the Mongolian People's Republic) is a landlocked country located in northern continental Asia, bordering on the Russian Federation to the north and on China to the south, east and west (Sanders, 1987, p. 1). It has a population of approximately 2.2 million people and a per capita income somewhere in the range of US$570–815 (an estimate made before the beginning of the reform process, and in large part depending on the rate of exchange used). This estimate puts Mongolia into the World Bank's lower-middle-income economies category.

Mongolia's large geographical size (at 1.6 million square kilometres, it is approximately the area of Western Europe), combined with its small population, gives a very low population density. Its landlocked geographical location and its poorly developed transport and communications systems exacerbate Mongolia's relative isolation from the world economy.

With the national revolution of 1921 and the establishment of the Mongolian People's Republic in 1924, Mongolia was the second country, after Soviet Russia, to establish a communist regime. For almost seventy years after 1924, Mongolia was an increasingly centrally-planned economy, closely associated with the Soviet Union. It joined the CMEA in 1962 and only gained international recognition as a sovereign state in the 1960s, with admission to the United Nations in 1961 (Sanders, 1987, p. xi).

The removal of Tsedenbal (Mongolia's leader for much of the post-Second World War period) from power in 1984 marked the beginning of the economic and political reform process (Gibbons, 1992a). The centrally-planned economy had become subject to increasing pressures and constraints, both internal and emanating within other CMEA countries, and in 1986, Mongolia launched its own programme of political reform and economic liberalization. The broad aims of these reforms were the acceleration of development, the application of science and technology to production, the reform of management and planning, greater independence for enterprises, and a more appropriate balance between individual, collective and social interests. There is general agreement, however, that these reforms were not successful and did not improve the economic and political situation (Gibbons, 1992a, p. 2).

Partly as a consequence of this lack of success, and partly influenced by changes that were occurring in the then Soviet Union, there were popular demonstrations in Ulaan Baatar in March 1990 which led rapidly to the first multiparty elections four months later. A new coalition government was formed, pledged to turn Mongolia into a 'market-orientated economy' and to create a pluralistic society with new political and administrative structures guaranteeing fundamental human rights, democracy and freedom of information (Collins and Nixson, 1991, p. 3).

Since 1990, Mongolia has undergone a profound and lasting transformation during a period that has seen the collapse of its major economic partner, the Soviet Union, the dissolution of the CMEA in April 1990, and the consequent cessation of most financial and technical assistance as well as the withdrawal of essential supplies (oil, spare parts, cement and fertilizers). It is estimated that real GDP fell by 2 per cent in 1990 and by approximately 10 per cent in 1991. A further fall was predicted for 1992. Inflation also accelerated over this period, with prices rising by approximately 120 per cent in 1991 and with an estimated inflation rate of between 100 and 300 per cent in 1992.

It is within this context that the political and economic reform process has been pursued. A new Constitution was adopted in January 1992 and a second general election was held in July 1992. Economic reforms have been implemented in all sectors and at all levels – price liberalization, privatization, fiscal policy, monetary and credit policy, foreign trade liberalization, devaluation, the encouragement of direct foreign investment (DFI) and legal and institutional reforms – as part of an ongoing process, the end of which is not yet in sight and the outcomes of which are still essentially problematic and uncertain. Mongolia's economy has undergone 'shock therapy' as dramatic and drastic as any applied elsewhere. The difficulties of the transition period and the economic crisis that has engulfed Mongolia are recognized by the Government, but policy goals largely remain unchanged:

> the main goals of the Mongolian Government are to overcome, in the shortest possible time, the crisis in economic and social life; stabilize the economy, and lay a sound basis for the future development. The Government regards the strengthening of the transition process to

market economy as one of the basic means to alleviate the production crisis and stabilise the economy. (statement by H.E. Prime Minister P. Jasray to IAMD/UNDP/MDP Seminar, 1992)

THE PRE-REFORM ECONOMY

At the time of the revolution of 1921, Mongolia's economy was in a state of chronic economic backwardness (Sanders, 1987, ch. 4). The main industry was extensive cattle breeding (with perhaps 50 per cent of cattle owned by feudal rulers, both religious and secular). Small Chinese-owned enterprises dominated coal and gold mining.

One of the first acts of the revolutionary government in 1921 was to nationalize foreign-owned coal mines, gold-fields, power stations, armouries and telegraph lines (Sanders, 1987, p. 84). In 1924, the decision was taken to take the 'non-capitalist road' of development and during the 1920s and early 1930s, the Soviet Union was active in promoting economic activities in Mongolia, in banking, transport, wool and wholesale trade. The period from 1921 to 1940 is referred to as the period of 'general democratic transformation' (Sanders, 1987, p. 86), with the gradual development of light industry and a food industry based on the processing of livestock produce, and the concentration of coal-extraction and electricity generation in the capital, Ulaan Baatar.

The period 1940–1960 was the era of the 'construction of the foundations of socialism' (Sanders, 1987, p. 87). This period saw the establishment of rural economy collectives, the collectivization of animal husbandry and the diversification of the economy into ore-mining, metal working, timber processing and consumer goods production. Full-scale industrialization accelerated in the 1960s (the period of the 'completion of the construction of the material and technical basis of socialism') with entry to the CMEA in 1962 (from which Mongolia greatly benefited, Faber, 1990) and the development of joint-stock ventures with the Soviet Union and a number of Eastern European countries. Mineral development encompassed oil, fluorspar, gold, copper, molybdenum and tin. Other industrial activities included meat packing, woodworking, cement making, wool-scouring, spinning, glue making, distilling and flour milling (further details can be obtained from Sanders, 1987, ch. 4).

Statistical data are not readily available (although 1991 saw the publication of an Anniversary Statistical Yearbook by the State Statistical Office (SSRMPO, 1991)) and are often ambiguous and incomplete. According to this Yearbook (table 5.2, p. 63), the annual average increase of 'Gross Industrial Products' was as follows

1976–80   8.4 per cent
1981–85   9.2 per cent
1986–90   2.4 per cent

In the 1986–90 period, there was negative or zero growth in a number of industrial branches, including engineering and metal working, wood processing, non-ferrous metals and the food industry. As of 1990, 'consumer goods output accounted for 43.7 per cent of Gross Industrial Product and output of the means of production accounted for 56.3 per cent (SSRMPO, 1991, table 5.4, p. 65).

UNIDO data present a slightly different but not totally inconsistent picture when compared to the above data. According to UNIDO, the rate of growth of Mongolia's GDP was 7.1 per cent in 1987, 6.4 per cent in 1988 and 6.3 per cent in 1989. Rates of growth of manufacturing value added (MVA) for the same years were 11.0 per cent, 10.1 per cent and 9.3 per cent respectively.

Clearly, there was a slowing down in the growth of the economy from the mid-1980s onwards and the Mongolian government was itself critical of both the industrial strategy pursued and the performance achieved. It was argued that the wrong priorities were selected (for example, too high a priority given to large-scale enterprises in the mining sector) that technologies utilized were out of date, and that the rate of growth of labour productivity was too low (all references taken from the *State of the Mongolian Economy in 1989*, mimeo, no date, as quoted in Nixson, 1991, p. 126). In addition, it was argued that the agricultural sector had been ignored, rural–urban inequalities had increased, and food shortages had emerged (especially of meat, the main food of Mongolians).

With respect to the composition of output of the manufacturing sector, it is clear that Mongolia was heavily dependent on relatively slow-growing industries (food products, leather and fur products, non-ferrous metals, glass and glass products, and timber processing) and in common with many other poor countries had not sufficiently diversified into more rapidly-growing sectors in capital and industrial intermediate goods (for example, paper and paper products, industrial chemicals, non-electrical and electrical machinery, and so on) (Nixson, 1991, p. 126). By the second half of the 1980s, therefore, Mongolia had, in a fundamental sense, reached the 'limits' of its chosen 'model' of development – limits imposed by geography, politics and history as well as those inherent in the 'inward-looking' heavy-industry model of industrialization. Dependence on the Soviet Union was almost total (75–80 per cent of Mongolia's trade was with the Soviet Union), an increasingly large debt with the Soviet Union was being built up (because of the imbalance in trade between the two countries) and the Mongolian economy was dominated by a (probably) inefficient public sector. Economic reforms were both necessary and inevitable.

OVERVIEW OF THE ECONOMIC REFORM PROCESS

The IMF (1991c) provides a useful overview of the reform process in Mongolia up to January 1991.

In 1986, there were increases in domestic wholesale prices, limited autonomy was granted to public sector enterprises for investment and long-term bank loans for investment were introduced. In 1987, there was a further expansion of the investment autonomy of public enterprises, a modification of the investment planning system for setting overall targets and a rationalization of a number of government ministries.

In 1988 there was a reduction in five-year-plan performance indices, limited liberalization of agricultural pricing and marketing in excess of state orders, the promotion of private sector co-operatives, the decentralization of budgetary operations to local levels and the introduction of a more depreciated non-commercial tugrik – US dollar exchange rate. In 1989 there was a liberalization of intra-public-sector enterprise pricing and expansion of enterprise autonomy; a modest easing of restrictions on private herd ownership; the elimination of monopoly of state trading corporations; increases in selected administered retail prices; the easing of foreign-exchange surrender requirements, and the introduction of preferential prices for exported goods.

Since 1990, the pace of economic reform has accelerated within a policy framework established by the coalition government formed in September 1990. Table 10.1 highlights the key reforms of 1990 and 1991. These reforms fall into three broad categories, namely (i) those designed to strengthen the government's ability to manage the economy through indirect means; (ii) those reforms required to enhance allocative efficiency and to increase the country's export potential; and (iii) those directed towards the creation of a 'social safety net' to protect the poor, the sick and the elderly.

Macroeconomic Management

The abolition of the system of economic planning means that the government must quickly put in place the new institutions required for the operation of a market-orientated economy through indirect means of macroeconomic management.

With respect to financial sector reforms, the new Banking Law became effective in May 1991, leading to the creation of a central bank (Bank of

Mongolia), a foreign trade bank (State Bank of Mongolia (International)) and seven new commercial banks. With respect to fiscal reform, tax reforms initiated in January 1991 have as their objective the expansion of the tax base and an improvement in the elasticity of the tax system. Reductions in government expenditure have largely focused on reducing the size of the bureaucracy and reducing subsidies.

Improving Incentives

These reforms are relevant with respect to enhanced allocative efficiency: the reform of prices and markets; the reform of the external sector; and the reform of enterprises.

Table 10.1   Mongolia, major economic and structural reforms, 1990 and 1991

1990
- Elimination of restrictions on private ownership of herds.
- Freeing of selected retail prices.
- Legislation of two-tiered banking system and establishment of two commercial banks.
- Rationalisation of government ministries; elimination of State Planning Committee.
- Establishment of Customs Affairs Department and Tax Service Department.
- Promulgation of new foreign investment law.
- Devaluation of tugrik *vis-à-vis* US dollar for commercial transactions.
- Introduction of foreign exchange auction system.
- Negotiation of most-favoured nation trade agreements with countries of the convertible currency area.

1991
- Increase in retail prices of most goods.
- Lengthened maturity structure of term deposits and increased interest rates.
- Substantial reduction of budgetary subsidy for imported goods and to loss-making enterprises.
- Devaluation of tugrik *vis-à-vis* US dollar.
- Adjustments to wages, pension benefits and private savings deposits to offset impact of price increases.
- Privatization law passed and programme for small privatization initiated.
- Banking law passed; Bank of Mongolia established as the central bank; separate commercial banks established.
- Direct export rights granted to selected manufacturers.
- Foreign trading rights issued on non-discriminatory basis.
- Stock market regulation established.

Source: IMF, 1991c; World Bank, 1991a.

As noted above, limited price liberalization measures were implemented from 1986 onwards, although major price adjustments were not made until January 1991. Controlled prices were limited to thirty-five categories of retail prices (down from a previous 220), ten categories of imported goods, and wholesale prices of certain basic goods. Rationing coupons covering ten items (meat, two grades of flour, rice, sugar, butter, vegetable oil, tea, soap and vodka) were also introduced at the same time.

In September 1991, the prices of half the remaining thirty-five commodities still under control were liberalized. The items that remained controlled included rationed goods, petroleum products, selected consumer goods such as tent covers, medicine, and rents and public utilities. It has been argued, however (Background Paper, IAMD/UNDP/MDP Seminar, 1992) that price liberalization proceeded rather slowly and that prices were only increased for rationed items in October 1992. Price liberalization and the elimination of state orders are a priority but it is not yet clear if this objective can be achieved.

As far as external sector reforms are concerned, Mongolia has of necessity been forced to reform its trade regime and diversify its sources of foreign exchange following the collapse of the Soviet Union and the demise of the CMEA. There have been a series of devaluations and Mongolia now maintains a multiple exchange-rate system. Export taxes have been abolished and most export restrictions removed (except for seventeen products of environmental importance or critical inputs for domestic producers (Batbold, 1992, p. 36)). A basic uniform tariff rate of 15 per cent has been established but it is estimated that approximately half of all imports are exempt from duties. State enterprises are allowed to retain on average 35 per cent of foreign-exchange earnings. Large, government-owned, foreign trade corporations continue to dominate foreign trade, but some liberalization and decentralization has occurred via the issuing of import licences to a number of public and private enterprises (Batbold, 1992).

Given Mongolia's geographical position, its previous dependence on the former Soviet Union, the collapse of the latter plus the major problems associated with the transition to a market economy, it is not surprising that the country is finding it difficult, to say the least, to restore external equilibrium. Foreign aid and loans were covering the current-account deficit but the government failed to meet IMF conditions and in September 1992 tranche withdrawals were suspended. The government is under pressure to unify the exchange rate system and permit the convertibility of the tugrik for current-account transactions. The shifts in relative prices brought about by a devaluation must also be allowed to have their full impact on the domestic economy and shift resources into the traded goods sector.

Enterprise Reform and Privatization

Privatization has been the centrepiece of the Mongolian economic reform process and has attracted a good deal of attention. A voucher system has been used, similar to that being implemented in the Czech and Slovak Federal Republics, Poland and Romania, and a stock exchange was established in February, 1992. The sequencing of privatization in the overall reform process attracted much discussion in the 1990 International Symposium (see Collins and Nixson, 1991) and has continued to be a controversial issue. There is general recognition that the driving force behind privatization is political rather than primarily economic (Batbold, 1992, p. 23) and the goal is to produce an irreversible change in the ownership structure of the economy.

The privatization programme is complex and full details are not given here. It has been implemented through the free distribution of vouchers (or coupons) that are used in the bidding for publicly-owned assets. There are two components: (a) small privatization, using green vouchers, later changed to red, each with three tickets to be used in the purchase of small assets; and (b) big privatization, using blue vouchers with one ticket for the purchase of large assets. Each citizen has been given two vouchers, with a face value of approximately 10 000 tugriks, and the total national voucher value is about 20 billion tugriks, which corresponds approximately to the book value of assets to be privatized (World Bank, 1991a, p. 44).

Small properties are sold at auctions, arranged by local authorities under the guidelines prepared by the Privatization Commission. The figures issued by the latter (Gerelchuluun, 1992) indicate that over 3 000 entities (including livestock), with an asset value of 3.7 billion tugriks had been privatized as of October 1992, and 65 per cent of the red vouchers that had been issued had been used.

Large enterprises (big privatizations) are also sold at auction, but with the use of brokers and the stock market. Enterprises to be privatized are first converted to joint stock companies and 10 per cent of their shares distributed to existing employees. The mechanics of the process are more complicated than with small privatizations but it is estimated that 430 enterprises (including agricultural co-operatives), representing assets worth 10.6 billion tugriks, have been privatized, and that 1.3 billion tugriks-worth of shares are in the hands of the population (Gerelchuluun, 1992).

Overall, the government's target was that by the end of 1993, approximately 45 per cent of fixed assets, in all sectors, should have passed into private hands. This compared to a figure of 3.5 per cent in 1990 and 30.7 per cent in September 1992. By 1994, it was hoped that agriculture would be completely privatized, construction almost completely privatized, housing and public services 60 per cent privatized and industry over 40 per cent privatized.

The mere fact that public-sector assets have been transferred to the private sector does not mean that privatization *per se* has been successful. A comprehensive legal framework has yet to be established, the development of commercial banking must complement and support the newly-emerging private sector, and enterprise managers must be equipped with the techniques of modern management. The use of the free voucher system has deprived the government of revenue from the sale of public-sector assets, and the initial dispersal of ownership may give managers too much freedom in the short run. Longer-run problems of the development of dominant shareholder groups, which would allow owners to exercise effective control, remain.

Above all else, the performance of enterprises is largely determined by the market structures within which they operate, and not by ownership as such. The Mongolian government must thus ensure the development of a competitive economic environment to encourage greater efficiency, higher productivity, enhanced quality and reliability of commodities and so on, and ensure that the regulation of natural monopolies, to prevent the abuse of monopoly power, is effective.

The privatization of state assets complements the development of the private-sector. Mongolia has no history of private-sector development (unlike other 'transitional economies', such as Vietnam, for example) and its long isolation from the outside world and its limited knowledge of the development of other economies (and the role that the state plays in the development process) all present obstacles to its development. The development of a dynamic private sector may well require the maintenal of a strong and dynamic state sector, and thus the reform and restructuring of enterprises that are to remain in the state sector, at least in the foreseeable future, should remain high on the reform agenda. The distributional consequences of privatization and private-sector development should also be given more explicit recognition and attention than they have so far received.

The Social Safety Net

Even if the Mongolian economy had not been subject to the shocks associated with rapid economic reform and restructuring, external shocks would still have destabilized the economy and led to severe problems. The rationalization of public sector employment, the break-up of state-owned enterprises and possible bankruptcies, the abolition of price controls, and rising prices coupled with falling output and increasing shortages, make the risks of social and political instability very real and require strong government action to establish a social safety net essential.

Batbold (1992, p. 40) presents figures which indicate that in 1992 there were 70 000 families (350 000 people) living below the official minimum income level, and social security payments absorbed over 20 per cent of state budget expenditure. Limited unemployment benefits are paid to those made redundant but new entrants to the labour force who cannot find jobs receive no financial assistance. Some retraining and job creation schemes have been put into operation but the problem of unemployment is largely structural in origin and its longer-term solution will only come through the emergence of a dynamic and growing private sector.

The maintenance of adequate health care and educational facilities is of importance in the transitional period, and some kind of cost recovery system may well be considered in the future.

THE REFORM OF PUBLIC ADMINISTRATION

While the reform of public administration is not of direct relevance to this chapter (for a fuller discussion of this issue and the role of international technical assistance, see Collins and Nixson, 1993a) it is necessary to make brief reference to it. The demise of the command economy and the highly centralized political system has triggered significant changes in public-sector organization. While the reform process in Mongolia placed initial emphasis on economic policy and management reforms, increasing attention has been paid to legal and structural changes within government administration itself.

Although the deteriorating macroeconomic situation described above occupies most of the government's attention, the three areas of public administration where reforms have been initiated are civil service management and structure; local government development; and the institutional framework for training. Gibbons (1992b) lists the main areas of reform which include, *inter alia*: the adoption of a new Constitution (January 1992), which created the basis for political and economic freedom; the Law on Central Government, adopted in 1990, establishing a new role and structure for central government and making a distinction between the powers of the Executive and Legislative bodies; the creation of a Ministry of Public Administration; and the adoption of the Law on Mongolian Public Administration, Territorial Division and their Governance which, among other things, defines the relationship between central and local government.

The reform and decentralization of administrative structures are ongoing processes, and need to be complemented by, most importantly, the creation of a legal framework appropriate to the market economy. The transition to the market economy also requires the retraining and reallocation of human resources within the public sector in order to enable it to adapt to changing administrative roles and functions. For redeployment and retraining to be effective, such activities must be accompanied by changes in government organizational structures, personnel management and so on, in order to ensure the more effective utilization of new skills. As the government adapts to its new role in a more market-orientated economy, it will lose some functions and acquire others, and the role of international technical assistance in these processes of reform will remain of prime importance.

CONCLUDING COMMENTS

The IMF, in its 1991 report on the Mongolian economy, was remarkably optimistic with respect to its development prospects, referring in particular to the rapid emergence of the private sector with the dismantling of controls, the growth in inflows of direct foreign investment, and the development potential of Mongolia's rich natural resource base (IMF, 1991c, p. 31). The World Bank (1991a) report was rather more cautious in its prognostications, emphasizing the severity of the external shocks that had affected the economy, and arguing that a substantial inflow of external resources, covering the initial phase of the transition period (up to mid-1992) and amounting to perhaps US$150 million, would be required to maintain production, consumption and investment at 'basic levels' (World Bank, 1991, p. 51). Both the IMF and the World Bank continued to emphasize the need for a rapid shift to a market economy.

Both the IMF and the World Bank could perhaps be forgiven for failing to predict the sudden and dramatic collapse of the Soviet Union in December 1991, although at least since the middle of 1991 Mongolia had been experiencing difficulties in securing supplies of essential commodities from the Soviet Union, including petroleum and explosives (for use in the coal-mines). Significant amounts of aid have been promised by both bilateral and multilateral donors and as of September 1992, approximately US$100 million (of a promised US$200 million total) had been utilized (Demberel and Ganzorig, 1992).

But to make these points is not to argue either that Mongolia's economic problems are largely the consequence of external economic shocks, or that salvation will come through increased inflows of foreign aid. The transition to a market economy would always be painful and difficult in the best of circumstances (given Mongolia's geographical isolation and dependence on the former Soviet Union), and external shocks obviously made matters worse. But the Mongolian government was clearly not persuaded by the arguments of the international participants at the 1990 colloquium (Collins and Nixson, 1991) that the reform process should be more cautious and more carefully sequenced. Rather, as noted in the first section of this chapter, the Mongolian reform process has been one of 'shock therapy', encompassing, *inter alia*, rapid and immediate steps towards price liberalization, foreign trade liberalization and devaluation, privatization, monetary and fiscal policy reforms, and institutional and legal change.

This is more than the merely 'technical' issue of the sequencing of the reform process (macroeconomic stabilization, liberalization and privatization – see Lipton and Sachs, 1990a and 1990b) although even the recommended reform sequence has not been followed by post-1990 Mongolian governments. A more fundamental problem is that most economic reformers seem to work with a textbook model of a market economy which is highly abstract, simplified and ideological, which ignores history, institutions and culture, and which admits to no alternative between the 'casino capitalism' of the UK and the USA and a return to the centrally-planned command economy (Nixson, 1995). Few economic reformers have a real appreciation of the role that the state has played in the most rapidly growing capitalist economies (Japan, the Republic of Korea and Taiwan) and the development of a new, dynamic commercial class is regarded by them as non-problematic.

These issues are best illustrated with respect to the question of privatization. We have noted above the high priority attached to the sale or disposal of state sector assets, and privatization has proceeded apace. It is important to note, however, that even though the transfer of state assets to the private sector might be successful, in the longer run what is of greater significance is the operational efficiency of the privatized enterprises, and this largely depends on market structure and the degree of competition, rather than ownership *per se*. This in turn relates to the development of the indigenous private sector and the role of foreign enterprise in the development of a dynamic and competitive business environment. It cannot simply be assumed that such an environment will develop of its own accord, that enterprise managers will acquire the necessary managerial, financial, organizational and marketing skills required, or that efficient and transparent equity markets will emerge. These are developments within which the state has an active role to play, and it is perhaps the case that this is not always fully appreciated by the Mongolian authorities.

Privatization is not the only reform measure that remains problematic and incomplete (the development of the financial sector, the design and implementation of appropriate monetary policies, fiscal reform and especially the control of government expenditure and the creation of new tax bases, all remain high on the reform agenda).

It is highlighted here to support the argument that at least some of the current problems of the Mongolian economy are self-inflicted and are the outcome of the complex interplay between political, economic and social forces within Mongolia. The move to the market economy has indeed proved to be painful in Mongolia. The transition is by no means complete and the external environment is even more uncertain at the time of writing than it was in 1991. Whether or not Mongolia will be successful in achieving the transition remains at present an open question.

Notes

This chapter has been written since the 1991 Workshop. At the latter, Mr Ts. Batbold, now Director, Research and Consultancy Centre, Institute of Administration and Management Development, Ulaan Baatar, presented a paper on the prospects for privatization in Mongolia. That discussion has largely been superseded by events. This chapter draws upon Batbold (1992).

11 Privatization and Private-Sector Development in a Transitional Economy: The Case of Myanmar

Paul Cook

INTRODUCTION

The economy of Myanmar has been controlled by military rule and organized through a centrally-planned system of economic management since the coup in 1962, when the Revolutionary Council government, led by General Ne Win, seized power and introduced the 'Burmese Way to Socialism'. This declaration rested on three ideals: the elimination of alien influence; the promotion of state ownership; and the promotion of Burmanization. This formed one of several policy statements outlining the new regime's ideology at the time, but which were never subsequently to be developed (Smith, 1991).

In 1963, the government introduced the Enterprise Nationalization Law, forbidding new private-sector activities. By the late 1960s almost all activities, including large-scale manufacturing, mining, communications, services and banking, were in the state sector. These were taken over and run by supervising committees. The state also controlled foreign trade and maintained extensive interventions in the private sector. Economic policies were formed in the framework of fixed plans which set targets for production, investment, trade, inputs, foreign exchange and domestic credit. Wages in the public sector were held constant from the 1970s until the late 1980s. The exchange rate has remained unchanged. Prices were controlled and, as a consequence, parallel markets existed for foreign exchange, credit and consumer goods (Cook and Minogue, 1993).

In 1987 the government began to remove restrictions on trade in agriculture, which allowed farmers to sell their output at market-determined prices and make decisions on the types of crop they should grow. More important reforms were announced when the military State Law and Order Restoration Council (SLORC) took over in September 1988 as a self-declared caretaker government following substantial civil unrest. These

171

reforms were introduced in response to the deteriorating economic conditions in the 1980s and to redress the imbalance of policies favouring public enterprises. In effect, they amounted to a survival strategy for the military rulers (Cook and Minogue, 1993).

The official view of private-sector development was declared when the government enacted the State Owned Enterprise Law of September 1989, which permitted private enterprises to engage in activities previously the exclusive province of the public sector; and the Private Industrial Enterprise Law of November 1990, which outlined the rules and regulations to be followed by the new private sector entrepreneurs. There has so far been no legislation permitting the sale of public assets to private buyers.

Although the government has in various press releases indicated its intention to privatize, the meaning attached to privatization at the present time embraces a wide range of measures. To many public officials, it indicates a desire to break with the past and to run publicly-owned enterprises according to principles usually adopted by private-sector businesses. It is also used to describe the various joint-venture arrangements, mainly with foreign partners, that the government permits under its recent spate of economic reforms. Since there have been no official pronouncements on privatization, the most commonly accepted interpretation, particularly in the Ministry of Industry, refers to the opening-up of existing industry to private-sector investment. Precisely what the implications of this are for the state sector can be inferred from one version of this view: this stresses that while the new policies may involve giving a larger role to the private sector, they certainly do not involve handing over state assets. Privatization, conventionally defined to mean 'changing ownership', is not yet on the agenda, and has so far been confined to returning some previously nationalized sawmills and rice mills to their original owners. A number of joint-venture arrangements have been entered into between state corporations and foreign and domestic entrepreneurs. A significant number are in trading, which in the present economic climate represents an activity where there are opportunities to make quick profits. There have also been a few cases of leasing arrangements and contracting out, in construction, for example. In some instances the private sector operates in parallel with the state sector. This trend is particularly noticeable in the field of medical care, with private wards and clinics being established in state-run hospitals. There has been deregulation of trade in agricultural rather than industrial products, although it has benefited manufacturing and processing industries indirectly. Finally, it is notable that present policy towards both the public and private sectors provides little effective legislation, institutions or mechanisms for competition.

In order to explore some of the issues raised by the recent changes in economic policy, and assess their implications for privatization and private-sector development, the chapter is divided into five main sections. The first uses a variety of indicators to examine the performance of the public enterprises, particularly those in the manufacturing sector. The second attempts to place the spate of current reforms, particularly those affecting state enterprises, in their historical context in order to develop an understanding of why they were introduced and to assess their direction and sustainability. The third extends the analysis by examining the impact of the recent reforms on the development of the private sector. The fourth focuses attention on the recent emphasis of government policy on foreign investment and looks at the relative advantages of this type of development. The final section highlights a number of key issues that are raised by the movement towards greater market-orientation and privatization, and draws some policy conclusions.

PUBLIC ENTERPRISE PERFORMANCE

At the macro level, public enterprises, or 'state economic enterprises' as they are referred to in Myanmar, constitute a significant proportion of government expenditure and revenue. Public enterprises account for two-thirds of public-sector investment and a half of total investment in the economy. In the manufacturing sector, publicly-owned enterprises produce around 40 per cent of total manufacturing output and, as shown in Table 11.1, are dominant in all sectors except for food and beverages, clothing and household goods. In turn, value added in manufacturing is dominated by the food and beverages industries, which account for nearly 40 per cent of total manufacturing value added (see Table 11.2). Adding clothing, construction materials and industrial raw materials, the percentage climbs to nearly 70 per cent. There is little evidence of structural change within the manufacturing sector since 1974.

Despite their importance in the overall economy, a longer view of the performance of state economic enterprises has revealed a bleak picture since the Revolutionary Council Government assumed power in 1962. This is reflected in the fact that although output of manufacturing under state control did grow initially at a modest rate of 2 per cent per annum, it resulted in a decline in per capita output. Furthermore, any growth in output required support of central-government to cover capital and operating costs. This poor performance could be explained by the heavy restrictions imposed on the operations of these enterprises, particularly over

Table 11.1 Relative shares of industrial subsectors in total gross value of industrial production, 1971/2 and 1983/4–1986/7 (percentages based on 1969/70 constant prices)

	1971/2				1983/4				1984/5			
	State	Co-op	Priv.	Total	State	Co-op	Priv.	Total	State	Co-op	Priv.	Total
Food and beverages	29.0	–	71.0	100	26.2	2.9	70.9	100	23.9	3.2	72.8	100
Clothing and wearing apparel	25.3	27.7	47.0	100	35.6	12.0	52.4	100	34.1	10.6	55.3	100
Construction materials	62.2	0.3	37.5	100	59.5	3.0	37.5	100	56.0	5.5	38.5	100
Personal goods	87.3	–	12.7	100	88.5	0.7	10.8	100	87.1	0.9	11.8	100
Household products	76.9	–	23.1	100	56.7	2.2	41.4	100	54.2	0.4	45.4	100
Printing and publishing	92.0	–	8.0	100	94.0	5.6	0.4	100	96.0	3.6	0.4	100
Industrial raw materials	89.5	–	10.5	100	80.4	0.2	19.4	100	76.3	0.2	23.5	100
Mineral and petroleum products	95.2	–	4.8	100	86.5	0.8	12.7	100	86.0	1.0	13.0	100
Agricultural equipment	100.0	–	–	100	100.0	–	–	100	100.0	–	–	100
Manufacturing machinery and equipment	100.0	–	–	100	97.9	–	2.1	100	92.4	1.8	5.9	100
Transport equipment	77.9	–	22.1	100	87.5	–	12.5	100	87.5	0.1	12.4	100
Electrical products	90.1	–	9.9	100	99.1	–	0.9	100	98.3	–	1.7	100
Miscellaneous	11.1	–	88.9	100	72.8	2.5	24.7	100	74.1	3.3	22.6	100
Total	42.6	3.6	54.8	100	42.5	3.3	54.2	100	40.5	3.5	56.0	100

Table 11.1 (continued)

	1985/6				1986/7			
	State	*Co-op*	*Priv.*	*Total*	*State*	*Co-op*	*Priv.*	*Total*
Food and beverages	21.5	3.7	74.8	100	21.7	7.1	71.2	100
Clothing and wearing apparel	30.0	13.1	56.9	100	23.2	11.5	65.3	100
Construction materials	60.7	3.1	36.2	100	59.3	7.4	33.3	100
Personal goods	86.5	1.5	12.0	100	85.3	1.4	13.3	100
Household products	53.0	0.4	46.5	100	39.3	0.4	60.3	100
Printing and publishing	89.0	7.1	3.9	100	92.8	3.0	4.2	100
Industrial raw materials	79.8	0.2	20.0	100	79.6	3.0	4.2	100
Mineral and petroleum products	85.8	1.1	13.1	100	85.8	1.3	12.9	100
Agricultural equipment	100.0	–	–	100	94.9	–	5.1	100
Manufacturing machinery and equipment	97.6	1.5	0.9	100	97.6	2.0	0.4	100
Transport equipment	91.1	0.2	8.7	100	88.2	0.2	11.6	100
Electrical products	99.2	–	0.8	100	98.8	–	1.2	100
Miscellaneous	73.8	4.4	21.8	100	11.3	2.4	20.3	100
Total	39.5	3.9	56.6	100	39.3	6.0	54.8	100

Source: *Report to the Pylthu Illuttaw*, various issues.

Table 11.2   Structure of manufacturing value added, 1974/5–1984/5 (percentages based on constant prices)

	1974/5	1980/1	1981/2	1982/3	1983/4	1984/5
Food and beverages	42.5	37.8	36.5	36.8	39.0	38.8
Clothing and wearing apparel	8.8	11.5	11.0	11.2	10.4	9.4
Construction materials	12.3	11.4	10.4	10.2	10.2	10.0
Personal goods	5.3	5.4	5.8	5.3	4.1	4.3
Household products	0.7	0.8	0.8	1.0	0.9	0.9
Printing and publishing	2.1	2.7	2.8	3.1	3.1	3.4
Industrial raw materials	6.4	9.6	10.2	10.1	11.2	11.4
Mineral and petroleum products	13.1	9.4	9.5	9.3	8.7	9.7
Agricultural equipment	0.9	1.8	1.4	1.3	1.2	1.1
Manufacturing machinery and equipment	0.4	0.3	0.1	0.3	0.3	0.3
Transport equipment	3.4	4.4	5.1	5.6	5.3	5.3
Electrical products	0.8	0.7	1.0	0.8	0.8	1.1
Miscellaneous	3.3	4.2	5.4	5.0	4.8	4.3
Total industrial sector	100.0	100.0	100.0	100.0	100.0	100.0

Source: Ministry of Planning and Finance, Planning Department.

pricing policy and access to foreign exchange. The government during these years also often failed to allow state economic enterprises to cover their cost increases (Hill, 1984).

In the mid-1970s, growth in manufacturing output revived to around 6.5 per cent annually. In part, the improved performance could be attributed to reforms introduced at that time. In addition, international lending agencies were applying some pressure for reform as the government had increased its external borrowing (Fenichel and Khan, 1981).

The overall financial position of the state economic enterprises improved after the reforms. This reflected rising current surpluses for enterprises and a reduced investment programme in manufacturing and mining, at least into the early 1980s (IMF, 1988). Inventories were also lowered during this period, which helped their cash flow considerably. As a result, the overall deficit for state economic enterprises was reduced.

The revival was short-lived, as overall deficits for state economic enterprises worsened during the 1980s. This time, current surpluses fell as capital expenditure revived. Since the accounts of state enterprises are consolidated with those of central government and local authorities, the overall budget deficit largely reflects conditions facing public enterprises.

The budget deficit expressed as a percentage of GDP hovered around 7–8 per cent between 1983 and 1986, improved marginally in 1987 but rose to over 8 per cent in 1988. In 1989 it climbed further and in the following year reached nearly 14 per cent. The official estimate for 1991 was between 6 and 7 per cent. Financing these deficits, given the relatively weak taxation base, ultimately places a heavy strain on the domestic banking system and was a contributory factor to the increase in external debt arrears in the latter part of the 1980s.

The efficiency of public enterprises is monitored on the basis of operating ratios. This is the ratio of operation and expenditure (excluding financial costs, but including depreciation allowances) to operating revenue. Ratios of this kind can only provide an imperfect guide to financial performance. Most operating ratios, as Table 11.3 indicates, are less than 100, except for those enterprises required to provide goods and services at less than cost. Most ratios, however, appear to have risen in the latter part of the 1980s, indicating a deterioration in financial performance. This is mainly attributed to the rising costs of imports used as inputs for the enterprises (IMF, 1988). This is particularly the case for those in the manufacturing sector.

The case of the pharmaceutical industry under Ministry of Industry No. 1 illustrates the range of performance that exists within a state economic enterprise and the conflicting objectives it is obliged to meet. This enterprise currently has a number of units which are loss-making in a wide range of products. Almost 70 per cent of its raw-material inputs are imported. It has a workforce of over 2000 and its technology and capital stock is of an old vintage, dating from the pre-1962 era. Most of the recent equipment acquisitions have been donated by various aid and charitable organizations. Nevertheless, the government requires the enterprise to fulfil social objectives, with the provision of low-cost medicines, but at the same time not to operate at a loss.

Caution must be exercised in interpreting operating ratios and current surpluses, since they exclude financial costs (IMF, 1988). Data on the profitability of individual establishments under the umbrella of state economic enterprises are not available. It is probable that a higher proportion of enterprises will be seen to have deficits if financial costs are taken into account. It has been estimated that interest costs on loans were equal to around 90 per cent of their current surplus between 1980 and 1988 and if interest costs on foreign debt were added, total interest costs would have exceeded the current surpluses throughout the 1980–88 period. In fact, some state economic enterprises had resorted to domestic bank borrowing to service their foreign debt.

Table 11.3 Operating ratios of state economic enterprises, 1982–9 (per cent)

	1982/3	1983/4	1984/5	1985/6	1986/7	1987/8 Revised	1988/9 Revised
Non-financial enterprises							
Printing and Publishing Corp.	82	83	85	83	72	87	85
News and Periodicals Corp.	81	71	65	75	82	87	87
Film Corp.	80	82	81	82	81	88	88
Agricultural Corp.	224	194	250	243	232	248	191
Fisheries and Pearl Corp.	91	110	99	93	100	86	87
Timber Corp.	61	55	57	58	65	58	57
Salt Corp.	97	153	113	17	102	87	83
Livestock Development Corp.	105	128	123	108	106	98	98
Mining Corp. No. 1	110	105	145	155	171	158	137
Mining Corp. No. 2	102	117	113	148	97	110	102
Mining Corp. No. 3	100	105	101	112	94	75	70
Myanmar Gems Corp.	71	61	72	59	75	70	72
Foodstuffs Industry Corp.	90	90	83	92	96	97	98
Textile Industry Corp.	94	93	91	94	95	106	93
Jute Industry Corp.	–	–	87	87	85	92	92
Metal Industry Corp.	88	88	86	87	93	113	108
Ceramic Industry Corp.	98	100	99	103	99	106	111
Pharmaceutical Industry Corp.	84	90	93	92	89	102	104
General Industry Corp.	95	93	95	94	91	104	93
Technical Services Corp.	52	39	39	75	89	94	166
Electric Power Corp.	67	65	66	63	72	63	71
Paper and Chemical Industries Corp.	81	89	83	91	101	94	94
Heavy Industries Corp.	83	84	87	86	88	85	83
Petrochemical Industry Corp.	108	116	117	117	131	126	101

Table 11.3 (continued)

	1982/3	1983/4	1984/5	1985/6	1986/7	1987/8 Revised	1988/9 Revised
Petroleum Products Supply Corp.	99	100	100	106	106	104	102
Myanmar Oil Corp.	135	131	125	114	125	130	125
Construction and Electrical States Corp.	54	94	94	93	93	93	93
Five Star Shipping Corp.	82	74	73	86	89	110	105
Inland Water Transport Corp.	95	73	85	77	77	83	81
Road Transport Corp.	92	90	91	101	98	95	95
Burma Railway Corp.	77	75	80	75	70	77	77
Burma Airways Corp.	104	113	115	116	126	133	119
Ports Corp.	45	54	55	55	55	61	60
Dockyard Corp.	90	89	86	87	87	92	93
Post and Telecommunications Corp.	50	44	49	48	52	55	55
Agriculture and Farm Produce Trade Corp.	93	94	94	105	109	107	100
Foodstuff and General Merchandice Trade Corp.	90	90	91	91	82	88	89
Restaurant and Beverage Trade Corp.	79	79	76	76	79	83	85
Textile Trade Corp.	82	81	81	82	87	88	84
Paper, Stationery, Printed Matter and Photographic Stores Trade Corp.	93	95	93	89	86	93	93
Medicine and Medical Stores Trade Corp.	86	88	87	90	94	93	94
Vehicle and Machinery Stores Corp.	86	84	84	84	83	83	85
Construction and Electrical Stores Trade Corp.	81	84	87	87	86	85	88
Hotel and Tourist Corp.	77	73	72	72	72	73	73

180

Table 11.3   (continued)

	1982/3	1983/4	1984/5	1985/6	1986/7	1987/8 Revised	1988/9 Revised
Inspection and Agency Corp.	34	40	39	40	59	45	47
Myanmar Export and Import Corp.	26	27	29	39	66	85	75
Financial enterprises							
Union of Burma Bank	20	22	21	19	19	21	26
Myanmar Economic Bank	58	59	60	61	63	67	68
Myanmar Foreign Trade Bank	39	38	38	37	36	40	40
Myanmar Agricultural Bank	56	57	57	57	56	64	65
Myanmar Insurance Corp.	35	38	31	43	38	64	49
Wasi Project	79	78	77	72	71	72	73

Source: Union of Myanmar and IMF (1988).

Other indicators of performance are capacity utilization and output. Data provided by the Ministry of Planning and Finance show a fall in both indexes for output and capacity utilization over the period 1985–9, with a modest revival in 1990 (see Table 11.4). It is also notable that the table shows output revived towards the end of the 1980s even though the overall financial position of state enterprises continued to deteriorate. The absence of political disturbances after 1988 is the most plausible explanation for the rise in output. Capacity utilization is also affected by a wide range of factors, including uncertainty over the supply of raw materials.

In addition to the current surpluses, the aggregate level of contributions paid to the government from the state economic enterprises has been used as a loose indicator of profitability. Again, indications are that these declined from the mid-1980s but, with the extensive controls over pricing and the preferential treatment given to state enterprises, the association between these contributions required by the Budget Department of the Ministry of Planning and Finance and profitability is highly suspect.

Several reasons can be given for the relatively poor performance of state enterprises in Myanmar. Clearly, government restrictions over their operations have been a significant ingredient and, as indicated earlier, this is especially important in relation to price policy. Contrary to recent claims, there is virtually no autonomy exercised by enterprise managers regarding pricing. A scheme was introduced in 1980 for trading enterprises and extended in 1982 to manufacturing to allow enterprises to pass on automatically to users price increases of imported raw materials. In practice, there have been few price adjustments of this nature and, given the present concern for inflation, the infrequency of automatic adjustments is likely to continue.

Indeed the number of adjustments, both automatic and otherwise, fell from 2924 in 1982 to 169 in 1988. This reflected not only the reluctance of the government to change prices, particularly as nominal wages had not been changed between 1972 and 1987, but also the declining importance of

Table 11.4 Output and capacity utilization of state enterprises, 1985/6–1989/90

	1985/6	1986/7	1987/8	1988/9	1989/90
Output	100	79	63	46	56
Capacity Utilization	57	48	35	25	32

Source: Union of Myanmar and World Bank (1990c).

imports in total domestic costs as imports were deliberately curtailed. This point is reinforced by the fact that, in 1988, 70 per cent of the price adjustments were made in the highly import-sensitive pharmaceuticals industry.

The system is even more rigid with regard to changes in purely domestic input costs. Any price modification, originating from an increase in domestic input costs, requires formal approval. Even the so-called automatic price-adjustment process can be considered illusory, since changes still require the agreement of an inter-departmental price committee. Admittedly, this is lower than Cabinet level, but it is still part of a formal procedure. In any event, the number of permissible applications for price increases for a given item in any year is severely limited. Indeed, if there has been any liberalization in this area, it has been modest and confined to a change in procedure rather than in real autonomy, since price changes now require only Ministry rather than Cabinet level (and beyond) approval.

It is difficult to interpret the information available on performance measures because of the distortions caused by market structure and the questions that have been raised conerning the appropriateness of the measures themselves. It is clear that factory performance within a particular sector can vary widely. Financial statistics and calculated operating ratios relating current expenditures and revenues of individual enterprises provide only an incomplete picture since they exclude capital-investment costs which are funded as interest-free grants through the government's central budget. While many enterprises make surpluses, mainly as a result of their market position and preferential pricing policies which keep input prices artificially low, a significant number in jute, pharmaceuticals and foodstuffs continually maintain losses.

Similarly, it is difficult to infer profitability from operating ratios and even more difficult to infer economic efficiency, which must be low with large labour forces, outdated technologies, declining investments and supply difficulties, because of the lack of foreign exchange and lack of managerial autonomy over investment and pricing issues.

PUBLIC ENTERPRISE REFORM

Some indication of the government's commitment to the current economic reforms and to their likely effect on public enterprise performance can be gained by reviewing the earlier attempts to modify enterprise behaviour. The first significant reforms for state-owned enterprises following the 1962 take over occurred in 1975. The motive for reform resembled that which induced the current measures. The previous government introduced a number of liberalizing measures in the mid-1970s, primarily in response to the slow industrial growth. The most notable was the 'Guidelines for Operating on Commercial Lines' for the state-owned enterprises, introduced in 1975. This was designed to link financial rewards more closely to the state enterprises' financial and production performance, and to give management a greater degree of autonomy. A bonus system tied to the targets set for operating ratios was also established.

A further response to the indifferent industrial performance of the state sector was the encouragement of state-sponsored industrial co-operatives. These were concentrated in the food and textile sectors. In effect the co-operatives were made to compete more fully with the state and private sectors. The co-operative enterprises did not fare very well, suffering from sub-standard products, produced by the low-quality workforce. In part this was because the better quality labour was absorbed by the state and private sectors.

The overall effect of the earlier reforms appears to be confined to financial improvement within the public enterprise sector. According to Hill (1984), the reforms constituted only a very limited degree of increased autonomy, because all major decisions continued to be made at the corporation level or higher, and because bonuses were paid at the corporation level, rather than at the enterprise level. Granting greater autonomy to enterprises while still preserving the concept of state ownership would be contingent on removing other exogenous constraints facing enterprises, to allow managers to operate in a manner that relates commercial to financial ideals. These constraints, as now, would have included foreign-exchange shortages that affect capacity utilization, restrictions on price changes, and indirect and direct subsidies. Market structure would also have been a factor, since managers have little incentive to operate efficiently when heavily subsidized or earning monopoly profits. It was not until 1976 that the state economic enterprises were given a limited degree of decentralized discretion by being allowed to engage in external trade. Prior to that, all trade was in the hands of the Myanmar Export and Import Corporation.

With hindsight, it is likely that the modest growth in manufacturing achieved after the mid-1970s was attributable to growth elsewhere in the economy, and to the favourable world market prices for teak and rice. It is difficult to ascertain the contribution to economic growth made by the institutional reforms introduced in the public sector, but it is clear that many of the complaints concerning the lack of autonomy granted to enterprises in the mid-1970s were to repeat themselves in the era of reforms in the late 1980s.

Similarly, it can be claimed that the spate of reforms following the 1988 crisis continues to leave unanswered many of the questions posed during the earlier period. There has been little change in the legal basis of state-owned corporations except when joint ventures have been formed, and none of the enterprises under the control of the two Ministries of Industry have been converted to state-owned company status, with complete ownership by the government. In other countries, this has often been used as a prelude to privatization.

The government continues to control the prices charged for goods produced by the state economic enterprises, and in many respects the situation has worsened since the 1970s. The parallel market has grown in importance and official prices for state enterprise transactions now differ significantly from the higher prices in parallel markets. In this situation, managers of state enterprises are encouraged to perpetuate the system of low official prices. Managers want to keep their own costs down to help them fulfil their targets for operating ratios and for the contribution to be transferred to central government. They have been able to accomplish this by restricting the supply of raw-material exports by private sector traders and producers to ensure adequate low-cost supplies for the state sector. Sometimes indirect coercion is used to acquire low-priced goods from the private sector, although in some instances the private sector is compensated by gaining access to low-priced products produced by state enterprises.

Two further areas where it is difficult to appreciate the logic of the policy changes concerns the writing-off of debt and the reduced financial autonomy granted to the state enterprises. State enterprises were relieved of their domestic bank debt when the government converted it into state-owned equity. The liabilities of the public enterprises at the Myanmar Economic Bank, itself a state-owned enterprise, amounting to 49 billion kyats, were converted into equity. In fact, liability was transferred from the enterprises to the banks. The Central Bank has relieved the Myanmar Economic Bank of loans totalling 28 billion kyats but still retains liability for a further 21 billion kyats in the future. As a result, public enterprises are virtually debt-free, although potentially these could build up again in one form or another, since the underlying causes of escalating debt have not been tackled.

Instead of devolving financial responsibility to the enterprises, the government has placed all financial matters for the state enterprises in the hands of central government. This is the case for current and capital expenditure. All expenditures and receipts, whether in domestic or foreign currency, go to the government's State Fund Account. In effect, this policy removes autonomy from the state enterprises in current expenditures, which now need government approval. But more importantly, central government retains strict control of investment expenditure and the allocation of foreign exchange. The Budget Department in the Ministry of Planning and Finance operates a version of zero-based budgeting, overseeing the allocation across industries. The enterprises make cases for capital expenditure, and the government supplies funds according to centrally determined priorities. Unlike the private sector, state enterprises cannot automatically retain their foreign-exchange earnings to purchase imported inputs.

Clearly, this represents one way of controlling increases in expenditure that may be inflationary, but by making funds available, the state enterprises are in effect obtaining 'interest-free' loans, which means in turn that the association between the decision to invest and the real rate of return facing enterprise managers is weakened. Decisions over capital expenditure have therefore become more arbitrary, which represents a precarious situation in the present political climate, when general investment is competing with military claims. The situation facing managers of state enterprises is further distorted because they are required not to make losses on their current operations which exclude capital costs.

Similarly, the system of incentives offered to enterprise personnel, based on the fulfilment of production and operating-ratio targets, is distorted. Instead of creating incentives, the system works in the opposite direction, since enterprises cannot retain their surpluses for investment but have to surrender them to the central government. Even increasing the size of the surplus does not appear to provide enterprises with preferential access to investment funds in the future, and therefore acts as a disincentive to raise profits. Within this framework there is no guarantee that incentives will enhance efficiency, since a large number of the state enterprises benefit from their monopoly position.

PRIVATE-SECTOR DEVELOPMENT

Since the 1970s the private sector could be described as being durable rather than dynamic. It has accounted for a high proportion of the output and employment in the manufacturing sector and exists alongside the public sector but with few linkages to it. The state enterprises predominantly engage in inter-firm trade within the public sector. Final goods are handled through state distribution networks and, in the main, consumers are public-sector workers and public-sector enterprises. Similarly, the private sector predominantly trades with itself. Enterprises in the private manufacturing sector, while being vast in number, are all extremely small. Some aspects of liberalization since 1988 have increased access to raw materials, enabling private-sector enterprises to compete more effectively with state-run organizations. This is particularly the case in the food-processing sector.

Following the 1975 reforms for the state-enterprise sector, the government, in an attempt to provide greater security to the private sector, introduced the 'Rights of Private Enterprise Law' in 1977. This law defined the activities that private enterprises could undertake and established a registration system for private businesses. In theory, this meant that enterprises could acquire officially-controlled inputs from state enterprises, and finance from the Myanmar Economic Bank. The law also guaranteed freedom from nationalization until 1994.

Despite these measures, confidence among private-sector investors was low, and correspondingly domestic investment also remained low. Indeed, Hill (1984) claimed that the law may have undermined confidence as it gave the impression that the government's tolerance of the private sector might well be short-lived. The preamble to the law stated that it was designed to encourage private-sector activity in the areas which could not as yet be operated by state economic and co-operative organizations.

As with the present programme of reform, the law did not specify how the objectives of encouraging private-sector activity were to be subsumed into the targets of the twenty-year plan. The private sector appears to be left with the same degree of uncertainty in the wake of current economic reforms and it is difficult to say whether the uncertain climate created by ill-defined policy is deliberate or is a result of the lack of knowledge about what to do next. Interpreting the present climate from historical experience might indicate the former, since there was little further encouragement to the private sector following the changes introduced in 1977.

In the period prior to the most recent reforms, private enterprises were not subject to direct controls over production, pricing and employment, although many of their day-to-day operations were strictly illegal. This was particularly the case with purchasing inputs. State enterprises were officially responsible for the supply of all inputs subject to government control. These included all imported and some locally produced goods. In practice, supplies from official sources were insufficient to meet the demand from the private sector. As a consequence, the private sector obtained inputs from the so-called parallel market. This introduced a considerable amount of uncertainty for the private sector, which was reflected in the prices paid for inputs and the availability of their supply. The fact that this had become significant for private-sector development was attested to by the periodic official crackdowns on these alleged illegal market activities.

The Private Enterprise Law of 1977 was eventually repealed in 1988, when the Ministry of Trade abrogated a number of orders, directives and announcements which had limited the activities of the private sector. Some of these dated back to 1963. As mentioned earlier, two Laws were passed in 1989 and 1990 respectively, the State Owned Economic Enterprise Law and the Private Investment Law. Both of these provide the present framework for private-sector development. Despite the opening-up to the private sector of activities previously confined to publicly-owned businesses, private enterprise continues to operate under a system of strict registration and licensing, including the possibility of registration under the Companies Act, the Partnership Act, the Special Companies Act and an annual export and import licence for each traded item. In some cases, enterprises need the approval of the newly-formed Capital Structure Committee.

Besides the extensive array of bureaucratic controls, licenses and approvals, many of them requiring annual renewals and the payment of fees, private enterprises suffer from restricted access to credit from the state-owned banking system (World Bank, 1990c). Access to imports and local supplies also continues to be limited. This was in part due to the practices of state enterprises and despite the liberalization in trade and the foreign-exchange retention policy for private businesses. The lack of credit availability particularly affects the working capital requirements of private firms.

The constraint on credit may eventually be lessened as the government modernizes the banking system and carries out its plan to introduce a greater degree of competition. This is to be achieved by establishing privately-owned banks alongside state-run financial institutions. The supply situation could, however, go in the opposite direction if the rule which permits private-sector businesses to retain all their foreign exchange earnings is reversed. This may happen if the government's demand for foreign exchange outstrips its current availability (Faber, 1991). This type of situation could arise if the present policy of acquiring foreign exchange through joint-venture arrangements falters. A policy reversal would have the added effect of further damaging the restoration of confidence within the private sector.

Finally, the private sector could be affected adversely by the changes recently introduced in the system of taxation. The previous Commodities and Service Tax was replaced by the Commercial Tax in 1989. The former used to apply only to state enterprises and co-operatives, but its replacement has a wider coverage, applying to all enterprises. It is, however, a multi-stage tax that tends to favour importers and vertically-integrated producers, namely the enterprises in the public sector. The government has provided some tax relief for private sector-operators, although many of the tax concessions are not utilized, either because private entrepreneurs do not know what they are entitled to receive, or the procedures to acquire relief are too cumbersome. In addition to the Commercial Tax, there are income and profit taxes which also, following amendments in 1989, give tax exemptions to smaller enterprises.

One of the main contentious issues, as far as the private sector is concerned, is the wide degree of discretion the government exercises in the application of the tax rules. This is compounded by the distortions created by the differences in tax rates between the Income and Profits Tax laws which apply to different types of businesses (World Bank, 1990c).

Overall, there are weaknesses in the policy and legal framework for private-sector development that hinder its growth. The private sector is not represented in policy-making circles, and earlier attempts to strengthen the Chambers of Commerce as a major lobby representing the interests of the private sector have been thwarted by government intervention in the selection of key members of these organizations. There is a feeling in the private sector that any representations that could be made which reflect the grievances of the private sector would be 'watered down' when presented to government. This concern is heightened with the recent vigorous campaign by the government, accusing domestic private-sector joint ventures of forgetting their social responsibilities and fuelling inflation through excessive profiteering.

The balance between the public sector and the private sector is slowly changing although, as indicated earlier, this appears to be due to declining capital expenditure by public corporations rather than to substantial growth in the private sector. This is to be expected when the overall investment climate remains uncertain, and infrastructure underdeveloped.

FOREIGN INVESTMENT AND JOINT VENTURES

It was indicated earlier that there has been little conventional divestiture. Instead, the government has introduced measures that encourage more indirect privatization through joint-venture arrangements. The government, following the 1988 crisis, has encouraged foreign investment with the enactment of the Foreign Investment Law in November of that year. This permitted foreign investors to operate enterprises in Myanmar as either wholly or partially foreign-owned enterprises.

Under the rules of this law, a joint venture can be established with domestic investors as long as a minimum of 35 per cent of the capital is held by the foreign party. The investors on the domestic side may come from either the public or the private sector. There are no restrictions on the form of capital coming into the economy, which could be foreign currency, equipment or intellectual property rights.

Foreign investment, has however, played an insignificant role in the development of Myanmar since the 1960s. The level of foreign investment had been reduced to a very low level during the late 1950s and early 1960s. After 1962, the government sought to eliminate alien influence and promote state ownership and indigenization. Consequently, there was only one joint venture with a foreign party operating prior to 1988. Immediately after assuming power, the SLORC declared an 'open door' and 'market-orientated policy', and socialism was officially relinquished. Precisely what the government meant by 'open door' was always in doubt, and in 1990 it ceased to use the term to describe the direction of its economic policy. Despite the passing of the Foreign Investment Law, the government has never stated clearly its objectives for foreign investment. Obviously, the foreign-exchange shortage caused by the low level of export earnings, which fell by 44 per cent between 1984 and 1989, and the need for access to capital and technology after prolonged isolation, have been major factors, although the foreign-exchange constraint has been partially alleviated by the substantial sales of natural-resource concessions.

To date, almost all of DFI has taken the joint-venture form with a domestic partner. The record reveals that most foreign companies have established themselves where natural-resource rents, such as fishing, timber, mining and oil and gas can be exploited, or where they can benefit from the under-utilized export quotas, particularly for textiles and footwear. The latter largely operate on a commissioning basis, bringing materials into Myanmar for processing, to take advantage of the relatively low cost of labour, and then exporting processed goods. The enterprises in the natural-resource field operate mainly on a production-sharing basis, by establishing domestic subsidiaries with a 100 per cent ownership in Myanmar. Prior to 1988, foreign investment was negligible, but as Table 11.5 shows, it reached over US$ 650 million by 1991, which represents a substantial increase from a low base. It is noteworthy that the share of foreign investment in manufacturing is low, and investors in this sector find it profitable to engage in a mixture of activities, including trade.

Foreign investors require the approval of the Foreign Investment Commission, established in 1989, to receive the incentives offered under the Foreign Investment Law. The Commission itself consists of all the

Table 11.5   Foreign investments in the Union of Myanmar by sectors,
1989/90–1990/1

	US$ *million*
Energy	317.10
Hotel and tourism	101.40
Mining	105.97
Fisheries	77.15
Foodstuffs and beverages	36.50
Industry	16.93
Livestock breeding	0.25
Total	655.30

Source: Data supplied by the Union of Myanmar Foreign Investment
Commission and UNDP, Yangon.

Ministers in the Cabinet and is chaired by the Minister for Planning and
finance and for Trade. The secretary to the Commission is the Director
General of the Planning Department in the Ministry of Planning and
finance, and Planning Department staff are responsible for scrutinizing
foreign-investment proposals. The Foreign Investment Commission has
established a set of criteria for foreign investment based on net profitability, employment, impact on national income and technology, and foreign-
exchange requirements. The Commission uses these criteria to approve
investments and determine the basis for the share of ownership in joint-
venture proposals. Foreign investors do not need the approval of the
Commission if they forgo the investment incentives, but they do need a
licence to operate, which is granted by the Capital Structure Committee,
and they are required to register under the Companies Act. In some cases,
proposals by foreign investors have fallen in areas officially reserved for
the private sector and, under the provisions of another law, the State
Economic Enterprise Law, have had their case referred directly to
SLORC.

   The scrutiny of proposals for foreign investment in practice is done on a
case-by-case basis, and in some instances Ministries have established
special committees (as in the case of oil and gas) and sought specialist
outside advice (for example, from Indonesia) to promote foreign investment. Joint ventures between state economic enterprises and a foreign
partner fall under the jurisdiction of the Special Companies Act and not
the Companies Act. The latter applies to domestic firms who enter into
private-sector joint-venture arrangements.

There are a number of advantages for foreign investors entering joint-venture arrangements. They receive a package of incentives which includes tax holidays, accelerated depreciation allowances, exemption from import tariffs, and tax relief. The Foreign Investment Commission has a considerable degree of discretion in granting benefits in particular cases. Foreign investors under joint-venture arrangements also have access to local finance through the Myanmar Investment and Commercial Bank but, as shown in Table 11.6 they have not so far been significant borrowers on the local market. Indeed, although private-sector borrowing as a whole has grown since the introduction of reform, total private-sector lending as a percentage of total domestic credit remains low. and a high proportion is for working capital rather than fixed investment.

Foreign investors entering joint-venture arrangements with state enterprises, as opposed to private-sector partners, also benefit from access to relatively cheap inputs that can be acquired through the links that the joint venture maintains with state economic enterprises. The latter benefit because, by entering a joint-venture arrangement, another entity different from a state enterprise is formed. Under this new form, at least in theory, joint ventures have autonomy over wage setting and labour practices. Further, joint ventures can take advantage of property-leasing arrangements with the government since, at the present time, foreign investors and the private sector cannot own land.

Alternatively, foreign investment as a form of privatization has a number of apparent disadvantages. A joint-venture arrangement, once entered into, does not necessarily involve restructuring on the part of the

Table 11.6   Private commercial loans and advances outstanding, 1989/90–1990/91 (Kyat in millions)

| | 1989/90 | | 1990/1 (prov.) | |
	MICB	MEB	MICB	MEB
Foreign and local JVC	0.1	–	5.7	–
Local JVC	2.0	–	0.5	–
Private industry	–	57.3	0.5	83.6
Private trade	17.1	50.3	29.8	49.6
Total	19.2	107.6	36.0	133.2

MICB = Myanmar Investment and Commercial Bank.
MEB = Myanmar Economic Bank.
JVC = Joint-Venture Corporation.
Source: Compiled by Central Bank (1991).

state economic enterprise since, in practice, only parts of a state corporation are involved in joint-venture arrangements. In most cases, state-sector
assets, revalued after 1988, have been used as the public sector's share of
equity and therefore the question of inefficiency is not confronted. Without
significant growth in the private sector, the greater autonomy over shed-
ding labour provided to joint ventures may place an even larger onus on
the state sector to absorb displaced workers. This would place those state
enterprises not entering joint-venture arrangements in a difficult position,
since they are already suffering from a decline in investment rates, and the
result may be that general government administration has to absorb labour.

Despite the relatively generous incentives for foreign investment,
however, foreign entrepreneurs have not established themselves other than
in joint-venture arrangements. The investment that has taken place has
been confined to a limited number of activities and in general, foreign
investors continue to operate in an uncertain environment. This is not
helped by the fact that many government bodies are highly politicized and
decision-making is secretive. This is compounded by the vagueness of
much of the economic legislation, making it difficult to interpret the
meaning of some regulations. In particular, private-sector confidence is
adversely affected by public-sector decision-making, which has the pre-
tension of being economic but instead is highly politically motivated. For
example, there have been instances of joint ventures between private,
foreign and local partners being refused, only to be replaced later by the
state as a partner to the foreign investor. The absence of guarantees for
foreign investors in comparison to other countries may represent a further
reason why foreign investment has not grown more rapidly in Myanmar.

An interesting development taking place within the present emphasis on
joint ventures is the formation of a sizeable domestic joint venture, the
Union of Myanmar Economic Holdings Ltd. In this company, formed in
February 1990 under the Special Companies Act, ownership is shared
between the Ministry of Defence, military personnel, and military veter-
ans. It uses subsidiaries to establish joint ventures with foreign companies
and in some cases has established a monopoly position, particularly in
areas associated with the oil and gas industries. In many respects, this
could represent the seeds for what Killick and Commander (1988) referred
to in the Philippines as 'crony capitalism'.

Given the administrative and political obstacles which have to be overcome to gain approval for joint ventures, and the uncertain environment as
perceived by domestic entrepreneurs, it is not uncommon to find small
domestic enterprises being formed with more informal ties and associations with overseas entrepreneurs. This is particularly the case where

advanced technology and techniques are an important element in the overall business. It is also probable that there is a growing imbalance between the kind of incentives that favour foreign investors with their domestic partners, and those that apply to the domestic private sector. It is further likely that the same imbalances exist between incentives for public enterprises, and those that discriminate against the domestic private sector. This can partly be seen in the recent open hostility to the private domestic joint ventures by SLORC.

CONCLUSION

It is evident from this review that a constructive re-drawing of the boundaries between public and private ownership, and between bureaucratic action and market processes will require careful policy design. In considering what is appropriate policy design for Myanmar, it needs to be emphasized that this is a system which reflects the typical problems experienced by those countries which in different ways are attempting a transition from socialist planning to a less interventionist form of economic policy-making and practice. In such economies, the economic and institutional constraints, the lack of a formal capital market, the low level of per capita income, and the poorly developed financial infrastructure will undoubtedly make conventional market-orientated reform and privatization difficult.

Indeed, despite the declaration by the Myanmar authorities that they are moving towards a market-orientated economy, reforms have had a limited effect and uncertainty continues to exist over their sustained commitment to the reform process. State-owned enterprises currently operate in a confused policy environment in which some reforms are making managers question the way they conduct their business, but since so little has happened, interventionist methods of the old kind to control their activities continue to predominate. This is understandable in the context of socialist economies in transition, as shown by the recent experience in Russia, where government officials, although wanting to open up the economy, have often continued to respond with an interventionist approach (Nellis, 1991).

There is a danger, however, to infer too much from the limited degree of economic liberalization and deregulation that has taken place. Privatization, as it is understood, has been very limited, but in this respect, Myanmar is not untypical of many other developing countries in which the debate on privatization is proceeding without much actually happening. How is this implementation gap, then, to be explained in the context of Myanmar, and what recommendations could be made? It is partly explained by differences of opinion as to what constitutes privatization. But a full and more convincing explanation requires the incorporation of administrative and political factors.

The administration in Myanmar reflects the organizational weaknesses found in many developing countries. The arrangements for controlling and sponsoring public enterprises are piecemeal and unsystematic. In some cases, there is a failure to recognize that problems exist and therefore require solutions. In part, an explanation for this relates to the lack of incentives provided to those charged with responsibilities for public enterprises, but it also relates more generally to problems about the structure of government involving too many agencies with ill-defined responsibilities.

Government departments in Myanmar collect information on public enterprises without either knowing what to do with it or having much authority to use it decisively. Obviously, these limitations could be overcome through a process of structural rationalization which ties both organizational and management reforms in public enterprises to more widespread changes in government administration as a whole. But implementation would challenge the sources of both bureaucratic and political power.

These issues have profound implications for privatization and public enterprise reform, since it is the defective bureaucracy that is the principal instrument for implementing reform policies. It is therefore likely in these circumstances, as in South Korea for example, that the bureaucratic machinery will only deliver reforms effectively when driven hard by a political leadership that is strongly committed to specific reforms. However, it has been shown by Shackleton (1987) that, in general, military governments similar to Myanmar's are not great supporters of the free market. They use orders and regulations in their own field and too often view similar controls over economic activity as being appropriate. In this respect, they are themselves the major beneficiaries of statism. In Myanmar, there are convincing reasons to believe that similar styles of political leadership exist and that, as a consequence, a gradualist survival strategy is being pursued. This type of strategy is likely to imply that features of a state-led planning system will continue alongside a limited re-orientation to a market economy.

In these circumstances, privatization and public-enterprise reform cannot be expected to be wholeheartedly embraced. In this context, reforms are more likely to proceed if political leaders have sufficient technical and organizational capacity to formulate and successfully implement innovations and if they have sufficient political authority to sustain the political costs.

When the political and administrative constraints are overcome, Myanmar, unlike many of the countries of Eastern and Central Europe, can use the stock of entrepreneurial skills and talents that exist within its private sector to run the state enterprises more commercially, whatever their ultimate form of ownership. Appropriate rewards would have to be provided to capitalize on the ingenuity that undoubtedly exists within the private sector, having survived nearly thirty years of state-led development. Confidence is low among the highly fragmented private sector and will need restoring before that sector can be expected to play a significant role. It will be necessary, given the small size of enterprises in the private sector, to develop schemes that bring together like-minded investors in developing new businesses. With the fragmentation that exists in the private sector, however, it is unlikely that privatization of large-scale state organizations will be widespread. Consideration could be given to dismantling state enterprises into forms that will make either divestment or internal reform easier to implement. Given the paucity of information concerning the precise nature of the skill base in the private sector and the lack of knowledge about entrepreneurial behaviour in Myanmar, the government, in conjunction with the international aid agencies, could undertake studies in the private sector to facilitate the development of policy initiatives in this area.

The absence of an official view on privatization, and the limited evidence of it happening in the form of joint ventures, begs the question of what is the underlying motive. If it is to improve the performance of the public-sector enterprises, then it is unlikely to be successful given the highly selective approach to joint-venture partnerships concentrated in a narrow range of activities. Similarly, if a partial approach to privatization is being combined with foreign investment policy, its present form is likely to undermine confidence within the domestic private sector. The unclear nature of scrutinies and decisions made by the Foreign Investment Commission, and the dominance of state owned enterprises in joint-venture arrangements, will encourage those domestic entrepreneurs who fail to gain investment approval to continue to seek quasi-legal associations with foreign partners. These arrangements limit the transfer of skills and inflows of capital investment. It is practices such as these that suggest the process of joint-venture formation needs to be made fair and open to competition.

Note

This chapter is based on a report written by the author for UNCTAD, Geneva 1991.

12 Perestroika in South-East Asia: Industry and Trade in the Lao People's Democratic Republic

Ian Livingstone

INTRODUCTION

Since the establishment of the Lao People's Democratic Republic in 1975, the Marxist government has operated a tightly-controlled socialist economy under Soviet influence, dominated by a state enterprise sector. Since 1985, however, the *politburo* has been introducing a series of fundamental reforms which are now being accelerated as Soviet financial assistance, on which the economy's finances have largely depended, reduces rapidly to what will be virtually zero in the near future. The Third Five-Year Plan is likely to carry this process much further. This chapter focuses particularly on the industrial sector at this time of reappraisal, and considers what the options might be.

HISTORICAL BACKGROUND

Laos suffers from two kinds of handicap: historical, and geographical or physical. The current Republic was formed in 1975, but formal independence from the French had been secured in 1949. During the colonial period, commerce was controlled largely by Chinese and Vietnamese, with the minimal administration required supplied by the French, using largely Vietnamese civil servants. Communications, education and health services remained undeveloped: the difference between Laos and other developing countries, however, is that the position in respect of these areas in Laos is essentially unchanged.

This has been the result, first, of the twenty-five years of conflict between Pathet Lao and Royal Lao forces, a cause of instability which precluded any serious economic development. As much as a quarter of the rural population is said to have suffered displacement from homes and

196

land during this time, requiring a subsequent major programme of resettlement for nearly 800 000 people.

Second, around 100 000, largely middle-class, people abandoned Laos with the advent of the communist regime, with a further 250 000 leaving over the next seven or eight years. The substantial Lao population resident outside the country is of some importance now, being reponsible for a substantial inflow of remittances and foreign exchange, and representing a potentially valuable source of new money capital. While the period from 1975 has been one of complete political continuity, it has also been one of isolation, apart from Soviet aid and influence. The government was established on Soviet lines, under the control of a *politburo*, party/government objectives being to transform production relations into state-run enterprises or co-operative and collective modes of production.

The new regime in 1975 had begun economic life in difficult circumstances. Previously, the main source of budgetary and balance-of-payments support was provided by the Foreign Exchange Operations Fund, which had been set up by the IMF and relied on subventions from the USA, UK, France, Australia and Japan. This fund, and most existing foreign aid, ceased in 1975, producing immediate hardship. While little development effort had been made nationally, the large expatriate population in Vientiane had given the capital a service-based economy of some local prosperity, but this localized prosperity collapsed with the overnight departure of the expatriate population in 1975, creating a problem of urban unemployment, together with inflation that had risen to 400 per cent by mid-1976. Thailand closed its border with Laos in November 1975, and the economy of Laos was further affected by severe droughts in 1976 and 1977, and by large-scale floods in 1978.

GEOGRAPHICAL OBSTACLES TO ECONOMIC DEVELOPMENT

Irrespective of whether a socialist or capitalist development path was being followed in Laos, this development would face major and basic physical and economic obstacles which reduce the options available. It suffers first from 'smallness', with a population of only 4 million which, combined with a low income per head (estimated at US$180 in 1988, placing it within the category of least-developed countries), creates a very small domestic market. This smallness is accentuated by the fact that many parts of the country are mountainous and that the internal road system is substantially undeveloped, resulting in fragmentation of the already small market. It also suffers, from 'landlockedness', producing major export disadvantages and increased costs of imported inputs. Lastly, Laos suffers from 'remoteness': from being away from the main international transport routes, which can have its own influence on transport costs. The latter two related disadvantages involve in this case dependence on communications through a coastal country or countries.

As in the case of other landlocked countries, this has placed Laos in an extremely vulnerable position, which Thailand has exploited. Thus all goods through Thailand have been made to use the Thai State Transport Company, resulting in delays, additional loading and reloading costs, and non-competitive charges, which together constitute significant non-tariff barriers for exports to Thailand, and increased costs for exports as a whole. Second, while Laos needs to make the most of opportunities for resource-based exports, particularly agricultural products, Thailand imposes a 40 per cent *ad valorem* duty on the latter. Third, although the number of products completely banned from transit has been reduced from some 250 items during the period of isolation, this still applies to about sixty commodities. Fortunately, the impact of these barriers has been limited – though not equally for different types of item – by the very large unofficial trade that exists.

The transport handicap affecting exports has contributed to a chronically adverse balance of trade. Thus over the four years 1984–7, official exports amounted to only 27–30 per cent of imports (see Table 12.1). As can be seen, this deficit was accommodated by transfers on current account (remittances from abroad) and transfers on capital account, these largely from non-convertible areas, namely the USSR, in the form of foreign loans and bilateral clearing arrangements. The real situation may be much less serious because of the substantial volume of unoffical trade, in both directions, referred to above. Nevertheless, in the light of the prospective rapid elimination of Soviet financial support, the situation is undoubtedly critical and highly dependent on the extent of new assistance which might or might not be forthcoming.

PAST NATIONAL DEVELOPMENT PLANS

Following an interim three-year development plan for the period 1978–80, the First Five-Year Plan was initiated, covering the years 1981–5. Although major structural changes were carried out during this time, particularly in industrial structure, problems of internal management multiplied, while factors beyond the control of government, as indicated earlier, made effective planning difficult. The economy was in so much difficulty

Table 12.1   Lao PDR: balance of payments, 1984–7 (millions US$)

	1984	1985	1986	1987
Exports	43.8	53.6	55.0	64.2
Imports	−161.9	−193.2	−185.7	−216.2
Trade balance	−118.1	−139.6	−130.7	−152.0
Services (net)	−9.8	−7.2	6.6	7.2
Transfers	45.0	53.1	34.2	30.5
Current account	−82.9	−93.7	−89.9	−114.3
Capital account	86.0	101.9	106.7	115.0
Convertible area	7.6	4.3	15.9	9.6
Non-convertible area	78.4	97.6	90.8	105.4
Loans (net)	(28.3)	(46.8)	(33.1)	(50.3)
Bilateral clearing arrangements	(50.1)	(50.8)	(57.7)	(55.1)
Errors and omissions	−9.1	10.5	−7.7	−11.8
Change in reserves (− = increase)	6.0	−18.7	−9.1	−11.1

Source: World Bank (1988b).

that a new approach was initiated in 1985 with the introduction of the New Economic Mechanism (NEM), formalized at the Fourth Party Congress in November 1986, and put into effect progressively since then.

Nevertheless, the targets for the Second Five-Year Plan, (1986–90), were not reached: recent calculations, using preliminary estimates for 1990, show a major shortfall in the overall growth rate during this Plan period, in agriculture especially, and in industry. This is shown in Table 12.2, along with tentative Third Five-Year Plan Targets. Large year-to-year variations in sectoral values make GDP projections extremely difficult: drought, for example, not only affecting agriculture but also producing large changes in the value of the main export, hydro-electricity. However, actual central government allocations to industry, for instance, also diverged enormously from the planned proportion of the available budget during the Third Five-Year Plan.

While national accounts and sectoral growth rate measurements underlying previous plans were based on the Material Product System (MPS), the Third Plan is based on the UN System of National Accounts (SNA). More fundamentally, it is an indicative plan, specifying general objectives, the policies to be adopted in respect of the various sectors, and the choice of incentive mechanisms, which will be set 'within a market-orientated framework'. Considerable emphasis is being placed on generating consistent GDP estimates and projections, despite serious problems of data. Components will thus be a macroeconomic framework; an outline of strategies, policies and programmes, with sectoral and regional dimensions as well as national; and a medium-term government budget programme for the five-year period, with a list of major investment projects. Its nature will be very different, therefore, from the previous ones, which followed the Soviet model, with detailed production and consumption targets for implementation by particular ministries, other government agencies and state enterprises. A progressive but thoroughgoing transition from a controlled economy to a market economy is envisaged.

THE STRUCTURE OF INDUSTRY

Before making any suggestions regarding a possible industrial development strategy for Laos, it is important to inspect closely the existing structure. Industry in the Lao PDR has been developed largely under the auspices of the state, such that practically all enterprises, even quite small ones above the level of microenterprises, are state-owned, whether coming under the authority of one or other of the central ministries, or a provincial government. A large number come under Vientiane Municipality.

Surprisingly, although most industry is state-owned, it is not possible to obtain from the state a complete list of manufacturing or other enterprises – statistical services are seriously underdeveloped – let alone figures for gross output, value added, employment and so on. Statistical recording of

Table 12.2   Sectoral growth rates, planned and actual, in Lao PDR's Second Five-Year Plan, 1986–90

Sector	Second 5-Year Plan Planned (%)	Actual (%)	Third 5-Year Plan Planned (tentative) (%)
Agriculture	9.85	3.4	5.7
Industry	13.65	7.7	9.6
Transport	11.30	15.2	11.1
Construction	12.55	8.6	11.1
Commerce	7.70	6.5	6.1
Services	–	7.1	7.8
Total	10.35	5.0	6.9

Source: Uses preliminary estimates for 1990. Third 5-Year Plan targets represent minimum possibilities. World Bank (1990b).

industrial output tends to be in physical units appropriate to each industry, rather than in value terms. The list of public-sector industrial enterprises of 1987, given in Table 12.3 (which does not include trading establishments) gives some idea of the pattern of ownership, and the unusual way in which

Table 12.3 Public-sector industrial enterprises 1987

	Manufacturing	Mining	Construction	Electricity	Total
Administered by Provinces					
Prefacture Vientiane	27	1	5	–	32
Province					
Phong Saly	8	–	1	1	10
Oudomsay	5	–	1	1	7
Bo Keo	4	–	1	1	6
Luang Namtha	6	1	1	1	9
Luang Prabang	8	–	2	1	11
Hua Phan	6	–	2	1	9
Sayaboury	9	–	1	1	11
Xien Khouang	4	–	2	1	7
Vientiane	4	1	2	1	8
Bolikhamsay	2	1	1	–	4
Khammouane	8	–	1	1	10
Savannakhet	10	1	3	1	15
Saravane	13	1	3	1	17
Sekong	2	–	1	1	4
Champassak	14	–	1	1	16
Attapeu	7	–	–	–	7
Subtotal	137	5	28	13	183
Centrally administered					
Ministry of					
Industry	13	4	–	1	17
Agriculture	14	–	–	–	14
Construction	5	1	2	–	8
Transport & Ports	2	–	6	–	8
Commerce	–	–	–	–	–
Defence	12	1	–	–	13
Interior	5	–	–	–	5
Education	3	–	–	–	3
Health	2	–	–	–	2
Other organisations	3	–	–	–	3
Subtotal	59	6	8	1	74
Total	196	11	36	14	257

Source: State Planning Committee, Ministry of Industry, Vientiane Prefecture, reprinted in Girard and Correa (1989).

responsibility for different industrial establishments is allocated among central sectoral ministries. A pharmaceutical industrial establishment, for instance, comes under the Ministry of Health rather than the Ministry of Industry.

These state-owned enterprises have absorbed the bulk of domestic credit in the past (see Tables 12.4 and 12.5), with consequently very little credit reaching agriculture or private, small-scale enterprises.

The historically developed pattern of ownership of industry disguises what appears in fact to be a not very surprising or unconventional structure – not surprising, at least, in terms of the constraints on the economy already described. As Table 12.6 shows, though only for enterprises under the Ministry of Industry excluding electric power and other items, major consumer items account for perhaps two-thirds of the value of manufacturing output. A substantial proportion of this is accounted for by cigarettes, beer and soft drinks; while wood products, metal products, construction materials and miscellaneous products account for much of the remainder.

Fuller coverage of the (formal) industrial sector is given in Table 12.7 which, unfortunately, is given only in physical units. The list comprises electric power; standard consumer goods (cigarettes, beer and soft drinks, food processing, clothing/fabrics, plastic goods); and tin plate and metal products. These are mainly for the small domestic market: electric power, and timber and wood products are also exported. Table 12.7 also allows examination of the recent growth or otherwise of different industrial sectors, by comparing levels of physical output in 1980 and 1990. Plans

Table 12.4   Distribution of domestic credit, 1982–7, as at end December

		1982	1983	1984	1985	1986	1987
Government (net)	Kip mn	10	–13	–109	–273	–484	–706
	Per cent	0.7	–0.8	–5.3	–10.0	–11.2	–9.6
Public enterprises of which:	Kip mn	1312	1585	2031	2740	4044	6935
	Per cent	94.5	94.9	98.8	100.9	93.4	94.2
Commerce	Kip mn	(–)	(–)	(530)	(725)	(1999)	(–)
	Per cent	(–)	(–)	(25.8)	(26.7)	(46.2)	(–)
Private sector	Kip mn	66	98	134	250	769	1135
	Per cent	4.8	5.9	6.5	9.2	17.8	15.4
Total domestic credit	Kip mn	1388	1670	2056	2717	4329	7364
	Per cent	100	100	100	100	100	100

Source: Government of Lao PDR.

Table 12.5 Composition of credit extended by State Bank of Laos, 1983–7

	1983		1984		1985		1986		1987	
	Kp mn	%	Kp mn	%	Kp mn	%	Kp mn	%	Kp mn	%
Investment capital	135	100	207	100	322	100	663	100	984	100
Agriculture	40	29.6	50	24.2	71	22.0	119	17.9	141	143
Public enterprises	88	65.2	145	70.0	229	71.1	496	74.8	780	79.3
Government	–	–	–	–	–	–	–	–	–	–
Other sectors	7	5.2	12	5.8	22	6.8	48	7.2	63	6.4
Working capital	995	100	1 062	100	1 580	100	2 963	100	4 297	100
Agriculture	42	4.2	55	5.2	122	7.7	546	18.4	701	16.3
Public enterprises	744	74.8	870	81.9	1 423	90.1	2 361	79.73	3 517	81.8
of which commerce	(472)	(47.4)	(538)	(50.7)	(725)	(45.9)	(1 999)	(67.5)	(3 015)	(70.2)
Government	200	20.1	120	11.3	–	–	–	–	–	–
Other sectors	9	0.9	17	1.3	35	2.2	56	1.9	79	1.8
Total	1 130	–	1 269	–	1 902	–	3 626	–	5 281	–

Note: Data refers to December, except for 1987 where it refers to June.

Table 12.6   Main product composition of output values of industrial enterprises supervised in 1982 by the Ministry of Industry (only) 1982–7 (percentages)

	1982	1983	1984	1985	1986	1987 (est.)
Major consumer items	69.3	44.2	86.3	62.7	66.7	57.1
Wood-related products	6.0	21.1	4.5	10.0	6.7	7.6
Metal products	20.5	18.7	1.2	17.2	13.2	10.0
Miscellaneous industrial products	4.3	10.0	4.5	2.5	5.1	16.8
Total	100	100	100	100	100	100

Source: Government of Lao PDR.

exist for substantial expansion of electric-power supply and exports, but it may be noted that the figure for 1990 was slightly down on the earlier one. Looking at the indices, one observes a large increase in timber and wood production as Laos's major natural forest resource is exploited; big increases in output of standard consumer goods for the domestic market (indices are 205 for cigarettes, 566 for beer, 287 for soft drinks, and 332 for clothing); and big increases in construction-related items, especially bricks, reflecting a building boom. In the absence of tourist-industry development, there has been no expansion in handicraft production, while experience with miscellaneous industrial products has been mixed. There has not, however, been significant diversification of industrial production.

The pattern of electricity consumption over time (Table 12.8) is not indicative of any major progress in the area of industry: indeed, the amount of electricity consumed by industry in 1989 was about the same as consumed in 1980, and was substantially down over the whole period 1984-88 on the figure attained in 1980. As a proportion of total energy supplied, industry accounted for only 1.6 per cent at the end of the period.

INDUSTRIAL DEVELOPMENT STRATEGIES

Industrial Development Strategy (1): Resource-Based Industry for Export

What kind of industrial development strategy should be adopted in Laos? If we refer back to the identified constraints, a priori considerations seem to point to two categories of industry, suggesting a two-pronged strategy focused on (i) resource-based industry, directed towards the export market; and (ii) the encouragement of small-scale enterprise, exploiting supply-and-

Table 12.7   Laos: principal manufactured products, 1980 and 1990

Item	Unit	1980	Alternative Year	1990	Alternative Year	Index 1980–90	Alternative Index
Electric power	mn kwh	901.0	–	844.0	–	94	–
Cigarettes	mn packs	14.6	–	30.0	–	205	–
Beer	000s HL	7.6	–	43.0	–	566	–
Soft drinks	000 HL	13.4	–	38.5	–	287	–
Liquors	000s HL	0.9	–	1.7	–	189	–
Bread, confectionery	tons	316.0	–	155.0	–	49	–
Noodles	tons	154.0	–	–	1987:64.8	–	1980–7: 42
Coffee	tons	23.0		8.0	–	35	–
Fermented fish	tons	131.0		121.0	–	92	–
Fish sauce	000s HL	1.5	–	1.2	–	80	–
Salt	000s tons	4.5	–	11.6	–	258	–
Ice	000s tons	7.0	–	13.7	–	196	1987–90: 84
Fabrics	000s m	1 044.0	–	368.8	–	35	–
Clothing	000s pieces	260.0	–	863.5	–	332	–
Leather	tons	179.0	–	–	1989: 70.0	–	1980–9:39
Plastic goods	tons	47.0	1986:584.0	281.7	–	599	1986–90: 48
Soap	tons	1.7	1986:2 223.0	1 000	–	–	1986–90:45
Detergent powder	tons	602.0	1986:2 631.0	2 000	–	332	1986–90:76
Notebooks	mn	1.5	–	1.2	–	80	–
Chalk	000s boxes	18.0	–	75.0	–	417	–
Tin plate	000s sheets	981.0	–	498.0	–	51	–

Table 12.7 (continued)

Item	Unit	1980	Alternative Year	1990	Alternative Year	Index 1980–90	Alternative Index
Nails	tons	60.6	–	114.0	–	188	–
Electric wire	000s m	7.8	1985:474.0	254.0	–	–	1985–90:54
Barbed wire	000s coils	3.7	–	6.0	–	162	–
Buckets, watering cans	000s units	81.5	–	11.1	–	14	–
Agricultural tools	000s pieces	62.8	–	10.0	–	16	–
Iron goods	tons	11.8	–	–	–	–	–
Timber	000s m	54.5	1986:335.8	310.4	–	570	1986–90:92
Lumber	000s m	11.2	–	78.4	–	700	–
Plywood	000s sheets	76.0	–	1 000.0	–	1 316	–
Thin wood	00s m	–	1985:143	1 600.0	–	–	1985–90:1 119
Wood flooring	000s m	15.5	1986:57	47.1	–	304	1986–90:83
Furniture	mn kip	13.7	–	678	–	4949	–
Rattan furniture	mn kip	0.4	–	93.7	–	–	–
Oxygen	tubes	3.1	–	7.9	–	255	–
Insecticide	cans	29.5	1985:44.4	–	1988:22.6	–	1985–8:51
Drugs	mn kip	11.8	–	659.2	–	5 586	–
Vaccines	mn am	3.0	–	2.0	–	67	–
Alcohol 90	HL	261.0	–	277.1	–	106	–
Battery acid	HL	61.0	1986:200.7	39.6	–	65	1986–90:20
Handicrafts	mn kip	1.2	1985:50.8	50.0	–	–	1985–90:98
Animal feed	000s tons	1.8	1987:6.8	2.5	–	139	1987–90:37

Table 12.7 (continued)

Item	Unit	1980	Alternative Year	1990	Alternative Year	Index 1980–90	Alternative Index
Bricks	mn	3.3	–	21.0	–	636	–
Blocks	000s	–	1985:346.0	120.6	–	–	1985–90:35
Concrete	000s m	–	1985:5.9	12.9	–	–	1985–90:219
Stones	000s m	4.6	–	160.0	–	–	–
Porcelain	000 units	46.5	1985:53.0	41.3	–	89	1985–90:78
Lead	tons	417.0	–	480.0	–	115	–
Coal	tons	67.0	–	3000.0	–	4478	–
Gypsum	000s tons	20.0	1985:100.0	80.0	–	–	1985–90:80

Source: *Basic Statistics About the Socio-Economic Development in the Lao PDR for 15 years (1975–1990)*, Ministry of Economy, Planning and Finance, State Statistical Centre, Vientiane, 1990.

Table 12.8   Distribution of total net energy supplied, by end-use, 1980–1

Year	Gross energy generated (GWh)	Total net energy supplied (GWh)	Local energy consumption by sector						Energy exported	
			Domestic/ commercial		Industry		Agriculture			
	(GWh)	(GWh)	(GWh)	(%)	(GWh)	(%)	(GWh)	(%)	(GWh)	(%)
1980	886.2	851.6	72.5	8.5	10.0	1.2	2.7	0.3	766.4	90.0
1981	846.5	813.7	92.8	11.4	10.6	1.3	1.6	0.2	708.7	87.1
1982	910.4	857.0	92.4	10.8	10.4	1.2	4.5	0.5	749.7	87.5
1983	863.4	818.3	110.0	13.4	10.1	1.2	3.8	0.5	694.4	84.9
1984	891.0	836.9	114.1	13.6	8.1	1.0	5.0	0.6	709.7	84.8
1985	906.6	846.5	118.7	14.0	6.4	0.8	5.1	0.6	716.3	84.6
1986	867.3	805.9	109.6	13.6	7.2	0.9	5.6	0.7	683.5	84.8
1987	567.0	513.4	113.1	22.0	8.6	1.7	3.7	0.7	388.0	75.6
1988	552.8	502.6	124.2	24.7	9.3	3.8	5.5	2.3	363.6	72.3
1989	698.0	639.5	133.2	20.8	10.3	1.6	5.5	0.9	490.5	76.7

Source: Government of Lao PDR.

demand linkages with agriculture, with both interacting to increase progressively rural incomes and purchasing power.

The case for resource-based industry follows from the fact that transport costs arising out of landlockedness have been shown to swamp what would otherwise have been a cheap labour advantage (Livingstone, 1986), disallowing the standard labour-intensive exports strategy. Emphasis on resource-based export industry is then indicated if any specific comparative advantage is to be secured. This is especially so as Thailand itself has advantages of cheap labour without Laos's transport cost disadvantage. This is a common situation between coastal and landlocked developing countries. A further comparative disadvantage for Laos is that Thailand has developed a relatively efficient manufacturing sector capable of providing manufactured goods to the Lao PDR at competitive prices.

Even resource-based industrial exports are not straightforward: given Laos's forest resources, this would point first to the export of processed wood, raising manufacturing value added by processing wood to the highest degree possible, rather than exporting logs. An Asian Development Bank analysis of financial returns from processing, however (ADB, 1988, vol. 2), shows much higher returns from the export of logs than from sawn timber and only the slimmest margin over processing costs in the case of plywood (returns from veneer, on the other hand, are good). It should be said that this calculation reflects operating costs and levels of efficiency which, according to an assessment in the late 1980s (World

Bank, 1988b), are unfavourable right across the country, because of obsolete equipment, excess capacity and poor management.

Laos's present principal export, electric power, is, of course, a resource-based industry with, moreover, low international transport costs, once connected with the importing country's grid. Export demand can only expand, given the momentum of industrialization in adjacent Thailand.

Tourism is another resource-based industry in that it 'exports' local scenery and culture, as well as labour services, paid for in foreign exchange. This particular export industry does not suffer from the transport disadvantage of landlockedness, though it may suffer from 'remoteness'. Two arithmetical ratios are also favourable to it. First, the diversion of only a small percentage of tourists from Thailand (5 million visitors in 1990 generating tourism earnings of US$ 5.3 billion) would produce substantial absolute earnings for Laos. Second, this volume would not need to be high, set against Laos's small population. Tourism can, moreover, be expected to have linkages with small-scale manufacturing, agriculture and construction.

Industrial Development Strategy (2): Encouraging Small-Scale Enterprise Within an Expanding Domestic Market

There are a number of arguments in favour of small-scale industry promotion in the Laos context:

1. The fragmented domestic market and constraints on internal transportation indicate a need to give attention to local production employing appropriate technologies.
2. It might be considered that the subsistence nature of the domestic economy, caused particularly by the transport factor, would limit possibilities for such development. In fact, the domestic economy appears to be more commercialized than frequent descriptions suggest: the obvious capacity to buy cheap imported goods throughout the rural areas indicates the existence of considerable cash purchasing power and foreign exchange, and probably reflects the existence of substantial unrecorded exports and remittances, both of which make foreign exchange available. Various indicators suggest population and purchasing power are relatively well-distributed across provinces.
3. Basic-needs considerations favour the promotion of local small industries (as well as, critically in Laos, health and education provision). Casual observation of the rural scene in Laos is sufficient to call into question its image as a 'least-developed country' represented by GDP per capita figures: while not all areas are as active as the Vientiane

Plain, one observes an evident building boom; often quite substantial rural houses, increasingly of brick; intensive agriculture supplemented by small livestock; bicycles and motorcycles enjoyed in rural as well as urban areas; substantial ox-carts widely used for rural transport; frequent ownership of sewing machines; and cheap imported Thai consumer goods in the rural shops and markets. A possible objective would thus be to supplement this by encouraging additional rural enterprise which can supply important needs, not at present covered, for the rural population as a whole, as identified in each province.

4.   Another reason for focusing on widely distributed small-scale industries is to take advantage of the rural electrification system extensions which are in the pipeline. These will soon reach Luang Prabang while, following the construction of the Xeset Dam, new systems will cover the provinces of Saravane and Xekong in the south. The marginal cost of providing power for rural industry can be considered to be low, once initial capital outlays (dams) are justified by exports, and transmission lines by perceived social benefits enjoyed by rural communities.

5.   It is easy to underestimate the importance of small-scale enterprises (SSEs). While any quantitative statement here is difficult to make in the absence of accurate statistics, it is useful to compare tentative figures for numbers employed in industrial, trading and service enterprises of all sizes (but, as can be seen, mostly very small) in Vientiane Municipality only (see Table 12.9), with figures for large establishments under the authority of the Ministry of Industry (together with four establishments under the Ministries of Culture and of Public Health) (see Table 12.10). Total employment in the enterprises of the Municipality amounted to some 26 000 in 1990, about 5400 of this in industrial and artisanal industries. The relative importance of all types of SSE as creators of employment can be gauged from the fact that these account for 22 000 out of the 26 000 employed in private (small-scale) and public (large-scale) establishments. Among SSEs, industrial and artisanal activities accounted for only 21 per cent, compared with 42 per cent in commerce and 24 per cent in services and hotels. An heroic extrapolation, based on an official provincial survey in Bolikhamxay province in 1990 at the national level (Livingstone, 1991), suggests that the national total for people engaged in small-scale industrial and artisanal activities would be 50 000 at the very least, and eight or nine times that in the main industrial establishments.

6.   There appears to be considerable scope for the development of SSEs linked to the domestic market (some also for export, such as made-up furniture), and linked to agriculture. Some indication of this is given

Table 12.9   Estimated employment in state and private establishments, Vientiane Municipality, 1990

Activity	State-owned establishments		Private establishments			Total employed	
	No. of estabs	Nos emp'd	No. of estabs	Est. mean no. emp'd	Nos emp'd	No.	%
Export–import	95	445	(20)	9	180	625	2.4
Domestic commerce	9	222	4 067	2.5	10 168	10 390	39.7
Industry	31	1 442	313	10	3 130	4 572	17.5
Artisal	3	712	77	2.5	193	905	3.5
Transport	3	150	1 552	1.2	1 862	2 012	7.7
Construction	10	347	126	8	1 008	1 355	5.2
Services	28	507	2 173	2.5	5 433	5 940	22.7
Hotels, guesthouses	2	228	24	6	144	372	1.4
Total	181	4 053	8 352	2.6	22 117	26 170	100

Note: State-owned establishments refer to those under Vientiane Municipality only.
Source: Own and municipality estimates.

Table 12.10   Numbers employed in industrial establishments under the Ministries of Industry, Culture and Public Health, 1989

Ministry responsible	No. of estabs	Mean no. employed	Numbers employed
Ministry of Industry	18	192	3 452
Ministry of Culture	2	134	267
Ministry of Public Health	2	87	173
Total	22	177	3 892

Source: Government of Lao PDR.

by the results (see Table 12.11) of a rural survey carried out in 1987 in Vientiane Province, covering 135 households (out of 372) in three villages (Maroczy, 1987). A list extracted from this might include small agricultural tools (axes, sickles, spades), ploughs and harrows, weaving mats and looms, fishing boats and gear, wheelbarrows and ox-carts. The backward linkages into agriculture here can be supplemented by forward linkages into agricultural processing, as will be discussed below. With respect to backward linkages, the expansion of mechanized irrigation can be expected to provide employment for

Table 12.11   Household ownership, tools and equipment in three villages,
Vientiane Province, rural survey 1987

Item	No. of items owned by 135 households	Households owning items No.	Per cent	Average number owned
Agricultural implements				
Plough	152	101	75	1.1
Harrow	111	98	73	0.8
Mattock	202	124	92	1.5
Axe	116	100	74	0.9
Sickle	513	119	88	3.8
Knife	493	134	99	3.7
Spade	138	107	79	
Sprayer	54	54	40	1.0
Motor pump	2	2	1.5	0.4
Tractor	1	1	0.7	–
Foot threshers	7	6	4	–
Handicrafts				
Weaving loom	17	17	13	0.1
Weaving mat	70	68	50	0.5
Pottery	7	1	0.7	–
Bellows	3	3	2	–
Construction and repair tools				
Sawing motor	16	13	10	0.1
Repairing tools	11	10	7	0.1
Construction tools	11	11	8	0.1
Transportation				
Wheelbarrow	113	107	79	0.8
Ox-cart	6	6	4	–
Bicycle	185	116	86	1.4
Motorcycle	10	9	7	0.1
Car	1	1	0.7	–
Pirogue canoe	27	27	20	0.2
Fishing				
Cast-net	42	35	26	0.3
Square net	177	63	43	1.3
Fishing net	95	84	52	0.7

Source: Maroczy, 1987.

rural workshops producing and repairing pumps and other equipment, as has occurred in other Asian countries such as Pakistan and Bangladesh.

With respect to forward linkages, rice-mills are easily the most important in Laos. Although there appears to be plenty of milling capacity in Vientiane Municipality, the 1988 ADB Report (ADB, 1988, vol. 2) referred to lack of adequate milling facilities in all provinces, with demand nationally for a further 1300 small village-level mills and 100 medium-scale mills. It is noted further that in Champassak and Saravane, for instance, 75 per cent of rice is still hand-pounded – and one would expect more remote provinces to be even worse off – compared with 20 per cent in Vientiane Province.

Vegetable oil processing represents another opportunity, in conjunction with increased production of oilseeds. It is reported (ADB, 1988, vol. 2) that only one oil-mill exists in Vientiane Province. More coffee processing will be associated with expanding coffee production, while tobacco-curing can constitute further manufacturing value added at village levels.

These agriculture-linked activities are often related to either wood-or metal-working industries. These are also linked closely to rural housing and construction. In addition to joinery and carpentry associated with often quite substantial wooden housing, there is a quite remarkable development of brickmaking in the Vientiane Plain at least, with labour-intensive methods giving employment to women and children as well as to men, and providing an apparently good rate of return on rural loan capital. There is, similarly, scope for the production of roof tiles.

There is potential, but less current activity, in the area of metal-working, in part because of the competition from cheap metal products made in Thailand. Associated with rural and low-income urban housing, however, there is a demand for metal window-frames; this demand will expand with rising levels of income. A more active search for appropriate metal products is needed. More generally, if linkages between agriculture and small-scale industry are to be developed to achieve a dynamic progression in rural development, it will be necessary to identify opportunities for introducing appropriate technology which can be applied in an economic and effective way in the rural sector and offer scope simultaneously for small enterprises to produce some of the relevant equipment.

If one prong of industrial strategy is to be based on the domestic market, one inevitable constraint is the low level of agricultural incomes and rural purchasing power. There has been major neglect of agriculture, unfortunately, and this needs to be given priority, for the sake also of expanding non-agricultural incomes. There appears to be much greater scope for import substitution and export promotion of agricultural and livestock commodities, in fact, than of industrial goods, in the present situation. There should be great scope for integrated rural development projects of a participatory type, including the participation of NGOs, given also the need for health care and education in the provinces.

THE STATE OF THE STATE-OWNED ENTERPRISE SECTOR

However, the most immediate issue refers to the existing large-scale industrial sector and new large-scale development. A review in the late 1980s (Girard and Correa, 1989) found much of the existing machinery and equipment to be obsolete, and a large proportion of it to be over twenty years old. Maintenance costs are high, there is substantial excess capacity, accounting systems are deficient or non-existent, with arbitrary determination of sales prices, and there is a lack of basic information on stocks, quality control and marketing effort.

As noted previously, state ownership in Laos extends downwards in the most comprehensive way to encompass quite small establishments. Those grouped under the Ministry of Industry include some of the largest enterprises (see Table 12.12) but most are small or medium in size. A large number of state-owned enterprises are under the jurisdiction of Vientiane

Table 12.12   Size distribution of industrial establishments under the authority of the Ministries of Industry, Education and Culture, 1989

Industry	Size of establishment (nos employed)						Total nos employed
	20–49	50–99	100–199	200–499	500–999	1000+	
Drinks and tobacco	–	1	–	3	–	–	1 051
Publishing and cultural products	1	2	1	–	–	–	380
Machinery, metal products	–	1	1	–	–	–	246
Chemical/medical products	1	1	2	–	–	–	322
Cement/concrete products	–	–	1	–	–	–	111
Electricity supply	–	–	–	–	–	1	1 020
Industrial services	1	2	–	–	–	–	141
Mining and quarrying	1	2	–	2	–	–	724
Total	4	9	5	5	–	1	4 005

Source: Ministry of Industry.

Municipality (see Table 12.9): in 1990 the mean numbers employed in state-owned manufacturing enterprises under the municipality was about forty-six and for all establishments, about twenty-two. Those in the provinces can be expected to be even smaller. The case for state ownership of comparatively small enterprises such as these appears weak, and it would be sensible to adopt scale as one criterion for divestment of enterprises.

THE NEW ECONOMIC MECHANISM AND REFORM PROPOSALS

Reappraisal of the Laotian economy began with the initiation of the NEM in 1985, this being carried forward in a number of subsequent decrees covering privatization and other matters. As far as industrial organization is concerned, one can discuss separately mechanisms for divestiture of existing state-owned enterprises (SOEs) and measures to encourage new local and foreign ventures; measures taken in respect of the macroeconomy; and the switch to market prices for products. Many specific market-orientated measures are likely to be incorporated into the new Plan.

The impact of the macroeconomic measures that have been taken since 1984 can be seen by examining the exchange rate (see Table 12.13). Thus the degree of currency over-valuation was reduced from 623 per cent to nil in just three years over the period 1984–87, especially as a result of the major devaluation in September 1987, since when official rates have been maintained near to the parallel market rate. Along with this, the switch to market prices for products, (which left only prices for minerals, electricity, water, ports and air transport controlled), will allow cost-revenue calcula-

Table 12.13   Official and market exchange rates, 1984–90

Date (month/year)	Official rate (average of buy and sell rates)	Market exchange rate (average of buy and sell rates)	Percentage of over-valuation
12/84	35	253	623
12/85	95	424	346
12/86	95	400	321
12/87	388	388	0
12/88	453	480	6
12/89	714	723	1
9/90	699	714	2

Source: State Bank of Lao PDR.

tions at the enterprise level to relate even more closely to real economic values.

Following a sluggish response by the private sector and overseas investors to the opportunities offered under the divestiture programme, this programme has been accelerated and a wholesale approach adopted, with a large proportion of the existing SOEs on offer. This has led to acceptance of rental agreements under which the factory or enterprise can simply be leased to the incoming entrepreneur for five to fifteen years, with expectations of renewal. The approach has been *ad hoc* rather than in line with agreed criteria, the government generally reacting to enquiries by private entrepreneurs in respect of specific enterprises rather than taking a pro-active line in deciding which enterprises are most suitable for transfer. One effect is that time is not always available to permit proper evaluation of the net worth of the enterprise being privatized. A small specialist team, which has been working on the establishment of a national programme based on appropriate priorities has, in fact, found it difficult merely to obtain a list of SOEs, let alone the required statistical and accounting information.

A number of policy observations may be made here. First, rental agreements should be considered very much a second-best policy, compared with outright sale of assets and full transfer of ownership. It does not provide the entrepreneur with the same incentive to build up the net worth of the enterprise through reinvestment or injection of additional capital through loans or new share participation and may, indeed, encourage them to maximize short-term profits at the expense of running down the enterprise. It also retains state or provincial government ownership of large numbers of SOEs, and the associated administrative burden.

Second, the fact that existing establishments possess equipment which is in many cases in need of complete replacement, in addition to the replacement of management which privatization implies, and that the enterprises exist as a result of historical decisions taken years before, suggests that project appraisal should very often be carried out *ab initio*. Is rehabilitation 'across the board' desirable? Should it be selective, concentrating on establishments offering genuine prospects, with closure of others?

A danger of the reactive policy being pursued, of course, is that only the best and most remunerative enterprises are transferred from public ownership, leaving a large residue of the weakest and least-effective ones as a burden to the national or provincial exchequer.

The emphasis on divestiture, and on wholesale across-the-board transfers where takers can be found, may divert attention from measures to establish new industries and enterprises. Privatization of existing SOEs should not be seen as a substitute for a new industrial development policy, though it may be a component part.

What is clearly needed, in the light of the foregoing discussion, and of Laos's history, is the establishment of an 'enabling environment' designed to cater for the needs of enterprises both large and small. It is not necessary to go into details here. Of fundamental importance, however, for foreign investors especially, is the fact that recent enactments, including the Foreign Investment Law of 1989, appear to have left unclarified under domestic enterprise law the concept of limited liability (ADB, 1989), and there remain a number of legal uncertainties affecting foreign investors which require that the legal position be spelled out in more detail than at present.

The issue of shares involves a number of questions. In relation to privatization, first of all, leasing arrangements leave ownership 100 per cent with the state. Participation between the entrepreneur and the state on the basis of shares would be more flexible, give the entrepreneur a more permanent stake in the enterprise (which could be expanded progressively or added to), and allow other partners to come in. More immediately, participation in the ownership of existing enterprises by insurance companies, social security funds, villages or employees, as appropriate, would be possible.

As stated above, it is important to look beyond transfer to ownership among establishments which already exist, to the establishment of new enterprises based on new domestic or foreign investment. This might still require some state participation in a subsidiary or catalytic role. At present, plans for transfer of ownership under divestiture are sent to the NEM Conversion Supervision Board, and to the Ministry of Economic Planning and Finance. Moreover, industrial and other establishments are supervised (effectively owned) by a number of different ministries, in which decisions are taken by civil servants rather than technical or financial experts. If these were brought together under a holding company incorporating this kind of expertise, this could facilitate evaluation of economic potential, assessment of net worth, and issue of share certificates, and thus transfer of ownership according to established criteria and priorities. Equivalent mini holding companies could be established at provincial level, providing also a mechanism for the injection of advice and expertise from outside at the national level. For major new developing industries, tourism for example, the establishment of a holding company at the national level with the expertise described would facilitate the establishment of joint ventures where appropriate, with state subsidiaries of the holding company as partners. All these possibilities depend on a legal and institutional system for share issue, in the context of a mixed economy.

Note

The section 'Historical Background' draws heavily on Stuart Fox (1986) and Zasloff and Unger (1991).

Part V

Sub-Saharan Africa

13 Mozambique: The Market and Transition
John Weiss

INTRODUCTION

A few years ago, sympathetic commentators could write with credibility of the respectable comparative performance of socialist developing economies, particularly in relation to industrialization (White, 1984; Jameson and Wilber, 1981; and Gurley, 1979). However, since the revolutions of 1989 in Eastern Europe and the change in the Soviet Union and some developing economies, the socialist path to development has looked particularly uncertain. In Africa, the economic performance of economies that have been described as socialist has often been weak, but not particularly so by the standards of the region. Table 13.1 brings together some basic macroeconomic data on several of these economies.

There are relatively few guidelines in the development literature on economic policy for socialist developing economies. The Soviet heavy-industry model is now seen as inappropriate for resource-poor, low-income economies. Clive Thomas's revised version (Thomas, 1974) focuses on basic as opposed to heavy industry, so that investment priority should be given to a range of industrial inputs that utilize local resources to meet local needs. Critics have pointed to the possible heavy investment and foreign-exchange costs of the strategy, and the neglect of the question of sequencing the establishment of the basic industries (Weiss, 1990). Further, disappointing results with a version of the strategy in Tanzania have given it a poor reputation in donor circles.

A more outward model of socialist development is articulated by Fitzgerald (1988) for low-income economies for whom local production of capital goods is not feasible even in the medium term. For these economies, department I – the capital goods sector – becomes the traditional export sector that can earn the foreign exchange to finance capital-goods imports. To some extent this model provides a rationalization of Cuban strategy since the 1960s, with sugar revenues remaining the dominant source of foreign equipment.

However, none of this literature provides guidance to economies undergoing a major macro-reform yet remaining at least nominally socialist. At

Table 13.1   Some socialist African economies; comparative performance,
percentage annual growth, 1980–8

Country	GDP	Industry	Agriculture	Exports	Aid/GDP ratio, 1988
Benin	2.4	5.8	4.2	2.4	9.0
Ethiopia	1.4	3.5	−1.1	−0.7	17.4
Somalia	3.2	2.3	3.9	−9.7	42.9
Madagascar	0.6	−1.0	2.2	−3.5	16.2
Tanzania	2.0	−2.0	4.0	−5.4	31.2
Zimbabwe	2.7	1.7	2.5	1.5	4.3
Yemen	n.a.	n.a.	n.a.	1.9	7.2
Zambia	0.7	0.3	4.1	−3.7	12.0
Mozambique	−2.8	−7.1	−0.8	−13.1	70.6
Sub-Saharan Africa	0.8	−0.8	1.8	−0.7	8.8

Source: World Bank (1990d).

a practical level, there is a series of questions relating, for example, to the
role of price incentives compared with direct controls; the objectives set
for public enterprises; the scope for private ownership; the sustainable
degree of external financial dependence; and the distributional effects of
economic reform. At a conceptual level, there is the wider question of to
where these economies are in transition: are they 'intermediate regimes'
(Kalecki, 1976) which because of their poverty and lack of a clearly-
defined class structure, are neither socialist nor capitalist? If this is the
case, will closer links with the international market, coupled with internal
reforms in terms of ownership and markets, lead to a weakening of the
position of the state bureaucracy and the emergence of a dominant capitalist class? These are fundamental issues of both theory and practice and
they are not resolved here. They need to be borne in mind, however, in
considering the recent experience of Mozambique, detailed in this chapter.

MOZAMBIQUE PRIOR TO THE ECONOMIC REHABILITATION PROGRAMME

Mozambique is an extreme case of an economy in transition. At independence in 1975, FRELIMO took over an economy severely disrupted by the
war of independence and the exodus of the settler community. The colonial economy had functioned in part as a transit trade centre, principally

for South Africa, an exporter of primary products, chiefly cashews, prawns and tea, and as an exporter of labour to South African mines. The level of educational and social development for the African population was very low, and the departure of the vast majority of settlers meant that factories and estates were abandoned, often with significant destruction of assets (Hanlon, 1984).

After 1975, the economy experienced a series of shocks. Climatic and terms-of-trade problems were similar to those suffered by other countries in the region. Specific to Mozambique were losses of foreign exchange because of the diversion of South African freight to other ports, and the drop in remittances as a result of a decrease in the number of migrant workers in South Africa. Most significant, however, was the insurgency campaign by the 'armed bandits', RENAMO, financed by South African and Portuguese groups. This became a serious problem in the late 1970s and has been the dominant constraint on economic progress since that time.[1]

In the years immediately after independence, with the departure of the previous owners, the government took over abandoned enterprises in agriculture, industry and services. These were given the legal status of 'intervened enterprises', as they were not nationalized formally. The exact degree of state participation in the economy in terms of ownership is not clear. Estimates for the early 1980s suggest that in industry, of the 575 larger nationally-registered enterprises, 114 were state-owned; 140 were intervened and part of the state sector; and the remaining 321 in the private sector including some co-operatives (UNIDO, 1987). Small-scale industry was mainly in private ownership. In agriculture, the abandoned settler farms were usually merged into state farms or taken over by co-operatives. Abandoned plantations of tea, sisal, sugar and copra also became state farms. Official policy was for the 'socialization of the countryside', with peasants living in communal villages and working on state farms or co-operatives. At the height of this policy, in 1981, it is estimated that there were 1266 communal villages covering about 17 per cent of the rural population (EIU, 1990).

Despite a non-dominant state sector in terms of ownership, economic policy moved towards considerably greater central direction. The third FRELIMO Congress in 1977 rationalized an active role for the state by adopting Marxism–Leninism as the official ideology of the party. This was associated with central planning on Soviet lines and in 1978 a National Planning Commission was established to set up and run a national plan. The planning system began to function at the end of the 1970s, with all larger enterprises subject to plan targets. The approach was of command, not indicative planning, since input allocations to enterprises were determined by output targets and their production was allocated to users within the plan distribution system. Prices for transactions between enterprises and between traders and users were fixed by the government. Small-scale informal-sector producers and peasant farmers were largely outside the scope of the plan.[2]

In terms of strategy, the government considered briefly a 'large project approach' with large-scale state farms and capital-intensive industrial projects. These activities were included in the ambitious Ten-Year Development Plan drawn up in 1981. However, this strategy was reversed at the fourth FRELIMO Congress in 1983, with the recognition that financial and managerial resources were not available for this approach. The new emphasis was on utilizing and rehabilitating existing capacity, and encouraging the small-scale sector with some division of unmanageable state farms and greater encouragement to peasant farming. Formally, the system of planning and controls remained in place until the beginning of the reform programme in 1987. However, with the deteriorating security situation and growing scarcity, the government had increasingly few resources to allocate and less control over the economy.

Economic performance during the period 1957–87 showed an alarming deterioration from pre-independence levels. How far this was because of shocks outside the government's control and how far it was as a result of the appropriateness of the planning system is difficult to establish.[3] What is clear is that under any set of policies there would have been a major economic decline as a result of the insurgency and loss of foreign exchange, noted above. From the weak statistics available, there is only a rough indication of the magnitude of the decline in activity. Economic activity recovered partially in the second half of the 1970s; however, with the worsening security situation, there was a major downturn. World Bank estimates imply that by 1985, real GDP was around two-thirds of its 1973 level, and only 50 per cent in per capita terms (World Bank, 1990g).

In large areas of the country where security could not be guaranteed, normal economic activity ceased. Industrial statistics for larger enterprises, which are relatively more reliable than other indicators, imply a halving of production between 1980 and 1985 (Weiss, 1992). Severe scarcities of both local and foreign goods emerged, leading to barter exchange in some parts of the country as money ceased to be acceptable. Scarcity led to the emergence of parallel markets for goods and foreign currency, with prices very much above official levels.

There is a rough indication of macroeconomic imbalance at this time from recent government estimates, which imply that in 1980 the investment/savings gap was 18 per cent of GDP, with foreign savings financing the bulk of domestic investment (World Bank, 1991b). The economy was already heavily dependent on external concessional finance, even before the reform programme launched in 1987. Although, as we shall see, this dependence has increased, not diminished, over time.

In this economic environment the government began to rethink the key elements of its economic policy. How far this was a genuine conversion based on perceived failings of the earlier strategy and how far a shift imposed by donor conditionality is difficult to determine. Ottoway (1988) suggests that the initial impetus for reform was internal, but even if this is accepted, the detailed implementation of the reform programmes was heavily influenced by the IMF and World Bank.

ECONOMIC REFORM IN MOZAMBIQUE

Prior to the Economic Rehabilitation Programme (ERP) launched in January 1987, there had been only limited changes to the system described above. An export-retention scheme, giving exporters access to a portion of their foreign-exchange earnings, was introduced in 1984. In 1985 the first removal of price controls – for fruit and vegetables – was introduced, and in the same year labour legislation was changed to allow enterprises greater use of performance bonuses and to make it easier to dismiss workers. These were minor changes, however, compared with the very major shift in policy implied by the ERP.

The central features of the ERP were:

(i) reduction of what was seen as the major macro-imbalance, the government-sector deficit;
(ii) liberalization of prices, with particular emphasis on a realignment of the exchange rate; and
(iii) alteration of the institutional framework of the economy with a dismantling of the central planning system.

These reforms were introduced in two stages after 1987. The first three years 1987–9 were the period of the ERP itself. This was replaced in 1990 by another three-year programme renamed the Economic and Social Rehabilitation Programme (ERSP).

Taking the three central features of the ERP in turn, the government deficit has been cut sharply through a combination of higher tax revenue and reduced expenditure. Budgetary revenues, for example, rose from 13 per cent of GDP in 1987 to 22 per cent in 1990. Particular attention was given to reducing the operating deficits of public and intervened enterprises and to cutting wage bills in the public sector. The current budget deficit was reduced substantially from 12 per cent of GDP in 1986 to 3 per cent in 1990 (World Bank, 1991b).

In terms of price controls, the ERP removed most goods from direct control. Most industrial products became subject to only *ex post* review, and in practice enterprises could set their own prices with little official check (Weiss, 1992). For agricultural goods, a major objective was to bring producer prices closer to world levels. Most agricultural prices are now in the form of minimum producer prices, at which the government trading corporation will purchase if private traders are not able or willing to do so. By 1990 the only goods subject to direct price controls were those distributed to refugees under the emergency programme; those basics sold through ration shops; those making a major contribution to government tax revenue; and energy products marketed by state enterprises.

Exchange-rate adjustment was seen as a central feature of the reform. Prior to the ERP, the official rate for the metical was only a fraction of its price on the unofficial parallel market. Exchange-rate realignment was seen as essential, both to bring foreign exchange out of the parallel market and to price foreign resources realistically. A number of step-wise devaluations were introduced, which appear to have led to a significant real depreciation of the metical by around 45 per cent between 1986 and 1990.[4] Most foreign exchange remains allocated centrally, but there have been modifications to the system. In 1989 a relatively small amount was set aside in a non-administered fund where any eligible importer was allowed to apply for a range of approved products. Subsequently, in 1990, a legal secondary market for small quantities of foreign exchange was established, with a rate determined by demand and supply. There were therefore three separate foreign-exchange markets by 1990 – the official controlled market, a small market-based secondary market, and the illegal parallel market. The stated objective is to unify the official and secondary markets by 1992 with a single rate of exchange that would vary with demand and supply conditions. In that year, it was hoped that a non-administrative licensing system would begin to operate, so that most imports could be brought into the country under an open general licence.

The dismantling of the central planning system occurred very rapidly after the beginning of the ERP. The broad objective was to give enterprises, both public and private, autonomy to operate on commercial terms in the new liberalized environment. Entrepreneurs and state managers, used to having decisions made for them, would now have to set their own prices and take their own production decisions.

In terms of ownership, the government has stated its willingness to encourage the private sector. Even prior to the ERP, legislation had been passed offering generous fiscal incentives to foreign investors, and in 1987 a similar law was passed for the local private sector. Symbolically, protection of private property is now enshrined in the constitution, with changes introduced in late 1990.[5] Policy towards public enterprises seems to be aiming at smaller, largely autonomous, sectors run on commercial lines. There have been some moves to transfer assets to private owners. In agriculture, the number of state farms has been reduced, with assets broken up and redistributed to the peasant-family sector or sold to private commercial estates. Estimates suggest that the fall in area managed by state farms has been substantial, from 150 000 hectares to around 90 000, with further reductions planned (EIU, 1990). In industry, there has been rehabilitation, some involving joint ventures and some with public enterprises. So far, most privatization has involved small and medium-sized enterprises. In the next few years, probably more significant than conventional privatization will be the change in the legal status of the intervened enterprises, with the expectation that most will revert to private ownership.

SOCIALISM AND TRANSITION

If this account of the major reforms post-1987 sounds familiar from experience elsewhere, it is appropriate to ask what, if any, is the socialist content of this reform? Is a form of socialism compatible with a transition to a new liberalized economic environment? The answer to the latter question is probably yes, since, as is well known but worth repeating, markets and socialism are not incompatible. It was the Stalinist command-economy model applied in the Soviet Union in the late 1920s that provided the blueprint for central planning systems in socialist developing economies. Its relevance to their conditions was always open to considerable doubt, particularly as large peasant sectors are extremely difficult to plan for and to control. Other parts of the socialist tradition, whether the New Economic Policy (NEP) of the early 1920s in the Soviet Union or the Lange–Lerner literature of the 1930s, allow for market relations between public enterprises. The rationality of market allocation can only be ignored at potentially high cost in terms of forgone real income. Some controls on prices can be justified, but their consequences and potential costs need to be assessed. The extent of government bureaucratic intervention – for example, in terms of the difficulty in getting an import licence, or the length of time for which a price is frozen – is no indication of socialist intent. Also, a socialist strategy cannot ignore basic macroeconomic relationships. Macro imbalances such as those in Mozambique in the early 1980s have to be corrected if growth is not to be constrained in the longer term. For example, the policy of funding the operating deficits of public enterprises by the Central Bank was unsustainable, and created both macro imbalance, in terms of excess credit, and micro inefficiency, in terms of high-cost production.

If a pragmatic set of socialist policies is not necessarily in contradiction with a market environment, what might such policies be based on? There is considerable difficulty in providing an acceptable definition of a socialist development strategy for an economy such as Mozambique. However, somewhat tentatively, three broad criteria can be suggested:

(i)   an active role for the state in terms of economic policy, primarily supporting rather than suppressing market signals, and including a significant, but not necessarily dominant, public ownership of activities;
(ii) a commitment to poverty alleviation and income distribution as policy objectives; and
(iii) an independence from external pressure, to allow strategic issues to be resolved by internal decisions that reflect national, democratically expressed concerns.

In terms of these criteria, what can be said of current policy? Although the instability of the country and the seriousness of the economic crises make it difficult to distinguish longer-term trends from short-run responses, on balance the answer must be that the country is moving away from what can be seen as a socialist path. First, in terms of the degree of state ownership, we have noted already that public ownership was never dominant even at the height of the central-planning period. Official statements imply that the government reserves the right to continue with selective ownership of productive activities in industry and agriculture as well as in public utilities. However, the 'commanding heights' view of public ownership is not envisaged, with only what are referred to as 'strategic enterprises' to remain in the public sector.[6] In agriculture, the clear trend is away from state farms and towards either peasant-household units or private commercial estates. In industry, the capacity of the state sector to retain the 'state entrepreneurs' necessary to run a commercially orientated public industrial sector is in serious doubt, particularly if foreign investors can offer significant salary differentials to recruit the most capable managers.

An active state economic policy need not imply major ownership of productive assets and there is a range of possible mechanisms for intervention that either support market-based solutions (tax-subsidy schemes, for example) or supplement them where the market does function adequately (see Cody *et al.*, 1990). In Mozambique, in the short run, an activist role for the state is likely to be required because of the situation of the country. For example, the emergency programme in response to the insurgency and climatic conditions requires an active government to oversee and channel resources for relief purposes. However, there are also likely to be forces working to weaken this interventionist role. The government's genuine attempts to attract foreign investors, for example, seem incompatible with a highly restrictive environment, given the well-known predilection of foreign investors for the minimum of restrictions on their activities.

By the criteria of distribution, what is the judgement on policy? Social issues have been given greater prominence in policy statements in recent years, as exemplified by the use of the word 'social' in the title of the second stage of the economic rehabilitation programme for 1990–92. How far this is due to the government and how far to donor concern it is not possible to assess. In the early stage of the reform, the government made some moves to shelter the more vulnerable groups from price adjustments. Many households that are net purchasers of food will probably have had a fall in real income with the relative rise in agricultural prices instituted by the ERP. Initial attempts to limit this effect were based on consumer subsidies for basic foodstuffs through a ration system. Subsidies were increased significantly in 1987, so that as a proportion of GDP they were considerably higher than before the reforms. However, with the objective of reducing the government deficit taking priority, the size of these subsidies was cut substantially in 1988 and 1989. Since then, the ration system has continued for urban consumers, though at prices that are much closer to market-clearing levels on the parallel market.

Access to health and education facilities is an important aspect of living standards that has been threatened, initially by the disruptions caused by the insurgency and more recently by the requirement to limit public expenditure. In health, for example, plans for increasing user fees were dropped, because of their probable distributional consequences. The proportion of public expenditure directed towards health declined significantly after 1980, when there was a need for greater military expenditure. Since 1987 it has started to rise again, but only moderately (World Bank, 1991b).

The main element of poverty alleviation in the Economic and Social Rehabilitation Programme (ESRP) is a new set of measures to assist peasant farmers in districts where the security situation allows the revival of agricultural activity. The argument is that as the vast majority of the poor are in rural areas, any poverty-alleviation programme must have a rural focus. Significantly, this can be seen as the culmination of the move away from state farms which began in the early 1980s, and if it succeeds, it should re-establish a viable peasant agricultural sector linked with the market economy.

There is nothing particularly socialist about these distributional policies. Essentially, the government has gone along with a programme that places restructuring above other objectives and has been constrained in its use of consumer subsidies. There has been concern over the distributional effects of the reforms; however, little is known about their precise impact on living standards, or on how changes in landholding have affected rural equality.

Finally, we turn to the question of government independence from external pressure. The concept of delinking from the world economy, as a central feature of a socialist strategy, was popular in the 1970s (Seers, 1981). For many, this has been replaced by an awareness of the potential gains from foreign trade (Fitzgerald, 1988). However, even for an economy participating in the world trading system, there is still the question of whether key decisions can be taken locally by appropriate local groups. In Mozambique the impending shift to a multiparty political system should convey a democratic legitimacy on a new government. None the less, the situation *vis-à-vis* the donor community is one of extreme dependence. The weakness in the balance of payments, arising essentially from an unbalanced economic structure, has not been improved significantly by the reform programme. In 1990, exports of goods and services financed only 25 per cent of imports, compared with 29 per cent in 1985 and 47 per cent in 1980. As a result, debt and aid dependence has grown substantially, with debt stock reaching over 320 per cent of GDP in 1990; however, with debt rescheduling, the debt-service ratio (long-term debt service to exports) has fallen significantly since 1987 (World Bank, 1991b). This reliance on concessional foreign finance is much heavier than for other countries in the region (see Table 13.1), and has left the government with little scope for disagreement over the detailed policy prescriptions of the international agencies. How far they would have wished to disagree is unclear, but for whatever reason, there has been less public conflict between the government and the IMF and World Bank than, for example, in Zambia, Tanzania or

Zimbabwe. Given this extreme financial dependence, it is difficult to envisage how the government could resist pressure to alter policies in favour of the private sector and to accept what have been a very ortho-dox set of economic reforms.

TRANSITION TO WHAT?

In economic terms, the initial outcome of the reforms is positive, if modest. Table 13.2 summarizes some macroeconomic indicators. The initial improvement faltered somewhat in 1990 and it is clear that any sustained recovery will have to await the resolution of the security problem.

Any answer to the question of where the economy is in transition *to* must be speculative. A renewed emphasis on socialist policies will require a new political constituency. The link between the nationalist movement and socialism that sustained FRELIMO in the early years of independence is now much less potent. A long-term economic recovery led by conces-sional-aid flows would no doubt see a resurgence in private investment, with foreign capital, particularly from South Africa, playing a leading role. In this scenario the transition would be to what can be termed convention-ally a 'mixed economy', with a relatively small state sector and a welcom-ing (low tax–low controls) environment for private capital. Failure of the reform programme to deliver long-term recovery, for example, because of significant debt-service problems, would call into question this path to development.[7] The continuing weakness of the economy would probably necessitate a stronger state involvement. None the less, what is highly

Table 13.2   Performance: macroeconomic indicators (per cent)

Real annual growth of:	*1980–8*	*1988*	*1989*	*1990*
GDP	–2.8	5.6	5.3	1.5
Agriculture	–0.8	7.2	4.0	1.2
Industry	–7.1	5.0	5.4	–3.3
Services	–7.6	–1.2	6.2	6.4
Exports	–13.1	7.8	8.4	11.5
Imports	–2.1	6.0	8.3	0.5
Inflation[1]	32.4	46.0	39.4	36.5

Note: [1]GDP deflator.
Source: World Bank, 1990d, 1990g and 1991.

unlikely is that the central planning model of the early independence period will re-emerge. Any future socialist policies will almost certainly have to be based on a pragmatic awareness of the constraints on development and the need to come to terms with both internal and external market forces.

Notes

1.   Recent estimates suggest that the insurgency has cost the country US$15 billion since 1981, and caused the deaths of 600 000 people; cited in EIU (1990).
2.   Weiss (1992) gives more details of the system as it affected industry.
3.   From a sympathetic perspective, the dangers of ignoring price signals in a socialist strategy have been commented on; see, for example, Mackintosh (1985).
4.   This is a government estimate, but it must be treated with caution because of the difficulty of deriving an accurate domestic price index.
5.   It is stated that the new economic order will be based on 'appreciation of labour, market forces, initiative of economic agents, participation of all types of ownership and action by the state as a regulator and promoter of economic and social growth and development', quoted in *Financial Times*, 23 October 1990.
6.   Policy on privatization is based on a law passed in August 1991. State enterprises are classified into three categories – commercially orientated enterprises, strategic enterprises, and non-strategic activities. The first are the main candidates for privatization, while the latter will be liquidated where they are not potentially viable.
7.   As a guide to what might happen, it is worth noting the emergence of significant labour unrest in urban areas, with a wave of strikes in 1990.

14   Trade and Industry in Zimbabwe
Tidings Ndhlovu

INTRODUCTION

When Zimbabwe gained independence in 1980, hopes were raised about the possibility of harnessing industrialization in such a way as to eliminate mass poverty and distribute income 'fairly and justly'. Frustrated expectations were too great (in terms of consumption and access to resources, especially land) to be met quickly, but they could not be ignored if the government was to ward off a generation of discontent. Yet addressing consumption at the expense of investment would arouse white people's fears of economic insecurity. In these circumstances, the leadership saw a 'balance' being necessary to enable economic growth to continue, while partially (and gradually) meeting black people's heightened expectations.

Inequalities had been exacerbated during the period of the Unilateral Declaration of Independence (UDI) (1965–79). International economic sanctions had forced the Smith regime to adopt an import-substitution strategy of establishing domestic industries behind protective barriers of tariffs and quotas. Exchange controls and general rather than selective import controls were seen as a way of replacing imports and expanding the domestic industrial base. This strategy succeeded in making Zimbabwe self-sufficient in the manufacture of basic consumer goods and some intermediate goods. It produced results in the form of increases in industrial output and the creation of employment.

However, the domestic market was too small to ensure the viability of industries which could compete in the world market. Exporting firms had to purchase inputs from protected domestic firms or via the relatively costly and illegal South African route (with additional foreign currency and brokerage fees accorded to business people who could arrange 'oil swapping' deals to circumvent the oil embargo). This discouraged exports and resulted in a deteriorating balance of payments. In the first months of 1975 alone, 220 firms went under, a figure only surpassed by the record 280 bankruptcies in 1963. Urban unemployment rose, and was further exacerbated by rapid rural–urban migration as the conditions of peasants worsened. They were denied access to credit and subsidies which were available to white commercial farmers, and they were dispossessed of land. By 1979, an estimated 500 000 peasants were already in squatter camps in Salisbury (now Harare) and Bulawayo. Having been enticed to the urban areas by the prospect of higher wages and better conditions, they found themselves living precariously within the informal sector. Income inequalities continued to widen, and it was from the informal sector that the bulk of the recruits for the guerrilla movement were drawn.

It is against this background that the newly independent state of Zimbabwe had to address popular demands for a higher standard of living, while also advocating a gradualist approach to the changing pattern of 'control' (that is, changing the pattern of control in a way that did not threaten growth in the intervening period with minimal 'indicative planning'). In other words, there were contradictory tendencies between 'pragmatism' (protection of private property, 'efficiency', and so on) and 'radicalism' (state control, national planning, redistribution of wealth along egalitarian lines and so on). As the balance between growth and distributional equity has become more difficult to maintain, the government has now begun to take heed of World Bank/IMF calls for liberalization which, however, will be introduced in 'a cautious and orderly' fashion to avoid 'disruption' in the economy. This still entails a high degree of government intervention, but one which is balanced by an export subsidy, an export revolving fund, a relaxation of the import licensing system and a 'realistic' exchange rate to promote manufactured exports.

This chapter will examine the contention that export promotion (as distinct from export-led growth) will require the extension of the market in the form of a free trade agreement, and that this will lead to industrialization along the lines of newly industrializing countries (NICs). It is often argued that a free trade agreement will solve the problem of unemployment and absorb new recruits to the labour market. In other words, that such an agreement will encourage a pattern of development that involves the creation of jobs through higher productivity, leading to higher wages and gradually leading to a socially acceptable distribution of income.

It is in this regard that we will examine Zimbabwe's apparent move away from a 'socialist' model of development: that is, from the emphasis on social policy primarily concerned with redistribution, towards liberalization and privatization encapsulated in the structural adjustment programme. It is to this end that we will analyse the problems of industrialization in a sparsely populated country such as Zimbabwe (about 10 million people in an area of 390 245 sq. km – about three times the area of England), whose government has 'socialist' ambitions. Concern here is with the attempt to widen Zimbabwe's small market through economic integration on the basis of the Southern African Development Co-ordination Conference (SADCC), in order to attract foreign investment in production. SADCC consists of Zimbabwe, Zambia, Malawi, Angola, Botswana, Lesotho, Mozambique, Swaziland, Tanzania and Namibia – a regional grouping initially designed to reduce 'dependence' on South Africa. Apart from Zimbabwe's responsibility for the region's food security, SADCC is expected to provide an increasingly important market for Zimbabwe's exports.

We will start by sketching briefly the events which have led to the adoption of the Zimbabwe government's present position. We will then examine the possible incompatibility between the concept and consequences of a free trade area and the nationalistic perspectives of some of the states, particularly Zimbabwe, which at the time of writing dominates SADCC. We also pose the question about the likely role of a democratic post-apartheid South Africa in Zimbabwe's development strategy. Will South Africa, assuming that it is admitted to SADCC, dominate the group, thus directly competing with Zimbabwe for markets and undermining the latter's plans for economic expansion accompanied by gradual redistribution?

FROM 'GROWTH WITH EQUITY' TO EXPORT PROMOTION

On the whole, the Zimbabwean government had come to office on a platform of reflation (expansionism), redistribution and the control of the balance of payments. There were subsidies, especially on food, and social services and infrastructure were developed to 'redress the injustices of the earlier time'. Expansion of aggregate demand, deficit financing and protectionism through import and exchange controls were, for some time, the cornerstones of the government's policy. An incomes policy was also incorporated into this strategy. Efficiency (minimum cost technical efficiency) was balanced carefully with distributional equity (the manner in which the output produced was to be distributed). Minimum 'indicative planning', rather than wholesale nationalization, was designed to discourage the withdrawal of capital and white 'expertise', while rural development and resettlement schemes would go towards meeting the expectations of the black population.

The first two years of independence produced spectacular results. Real domestic product (GDP) grew by 10.7 per cent in 1980, the first positive real growth since 1974, and by 13 per cent in 1981. With the utilization of unutilized capacity of up to 24 per cent of the total installed, the lifting of economic sanctions, and favourable conditions in the world market, manufacturing contributed around 25 per cent of GDP; while a good rainy season, buoyant world prices and the policy of subsidizing farmers led to a bumper harvest, with agriculture's contribution of 13 per cent to GDP in 1980 being the first such material growth of 30 per cent since 1974 (see Table 14.1). Investment increased by 19.2 per cent in 1980, and subsequently by 36.7 per cent in 1981.

Employment rose from 984 000 in 1979 to 1.01 million in 1980 and 1.04 million in 1981. Indeed, in 1982, employment was almost back to the 1.05 million figure recorded in 1975. Out of a total of 162 000 peasant families (about 1 million people) whom the government planned to resettle, 1 500 families (10 000 people) had been resettled in 1980, a figure which rose to a total of 4000 families in 1981.

This is the background against which the government's 1982–85 Transitional Development Plan (TNDP) was designed to consolidate its policy of 'growth with equity'. However, the growth target of 8 per cent for 1982–3 was not met as GDP grew by 1.5 per cent in 1982 and fell to -3.6 per cent in 1983, and then rose to 2.3 per cent in 1984. Agriculture and manufacturing sectors were also badly hit. In 1982, exports in volume terms were the lowest in twelve years. The balance of trade deteriorated from +Z$68 million in 1980 to –Z$115 million in 1982, while the current account position worsened from a deficit of Z$74 million in 1979 to Z$530 million in 1982, then gradually improved to deficits of Z$458 million in 1983 and Z$100 million in 1984. Employment fell from approximately 1.05 million in 1982 to 1.03 million in 1983, and then rose to about 1.04 million in 1984. A total of only 25 000 families had been resettled by 1983, a figure which rose to 35 000 families in total in 1985.

Table 14.1   Sectoral contribution to GDP, selected activities 1980–8

Sector	1980	1981	1982	1983	1984	1985	1986	1987	1988
Agriculture, forestry and fishing	14.0	14.6	13.2	11.6	14.0	16.2	14.9	12.3	14.3
Mining and quarrying	8.8	7.9	7.9	8.1	8.2	7.6	7.6	7.8	7.2
Manufacturing	24.9	25.0	24.4	24.6	22.9	23.7	24.1	24.7	24.5
Construction	2.8	3.0	2.8	2.7	2.4	1.7	1.8	2.2	1.9
Transport and communications	6.5	6.2	6.3	6.5	6.4	6.2	6.3	6.1	5.9
Public administration	9.0	9.6	9.3	9.8	10.3	9.8	9.6	10.0	9.8
Education	5.2	6.7	7.1	9.0	9.5	9.4	9.7	10.1	9.5
Health	2.2	2.1	2.5	2.6	2.6	2.6	2.6	2.5	2.5

Source: *The Southern African Economist*, April/May 1990, p. iii.

A number of factors contributed to the 1982–4 economic crisis. The world recession – particularly the slump in world prices – affected the manufacturing and mining sectors. In this atmosphere, investment from external sources fell short of that envisaged by the national plan. In fact, the boom had been due mainly to increases in capacity utilization and capital consumption. Shortages of foreign exchange meant that outdated plant and equipment could not be replaced, and manufacturers relied increasingly on protection to maintain their markets. The economic crisis led to plant closures, short-time working and redundancies. The severe drought of the 1982/3 and 1983/4 seasons also affected agricultural production.

It is against this gloomy picture that the government adopted austerity measures. In 1983, cuts were introduced in the Public Sector Investment Programme (PSIP). There were cuts in subsidies, particularly on food. While import and exchange controls were maintained, the Zimbabwean dollar was depreciated and interest rates were increased in an attempt to curb speculative activities in relation to transactions (current expenditure). Thus demand management and the manipulation of interest rates were seen as the surest ways of arresting the worsening balance of payments. Public sector recruitment for 1984/5 was frozen in order to keep the wages and salaries bill down and curb the rise in recurrent expenditure. The consumer price index for the urban lower income groups rose by 85 per cent from 1980 to 1985, thus confirming that even though the workers' money wages had risen, their living standards had been drastically reduced. White-owned and resettlement farms were given less protection and increasingly were required to adopt more competitive methods of production. Emphasis shifted from resettling the poorest to resettling 'progressive' or 'promising' farmers – the so-called 'master farmers'. In other words, government policy shifted from redistribution of income and wealth, justified on the basis of the equity objective or the notion of distributive justice, to commercial criteria in which the price mechanism was regarded as being capable of achieving allocative efficiency.

The IMF-inspired programme was temporarily abandoned in 1984, when the government introduced a 'cautious and modest' reflation to 'revive output'. The IMF had insisted on the budget deficit as a percentage of GDP coming down to 5 per cent. In line with this directive, the actual deficit was reduced from 8.0 per cent of GDP in 1982/3 to 5.7 per cent in 1983/4, but it rose again to 10.6 per cent in 1984/5.

The 1986–90 Five-Year Plan projected a much more modest real growth rate of 5 per cent per annum and the creation of 28–30 000 jobs per year. However, the foreign investment necessary to carry out this plan was not forthcoming. This necessitated an increase in the budget deficit (as a percentage of GDP) to 12.3 per cent in 1986/7. Business people blamed the government's 'socialist' rhetoric for discouraging investment. Coupled with this, drought and an epidemic of foot-and-mouth disease affected the agricultural sector. Continuing foreign exchange shortages affected the performance of the manufacturing sector. Because of these factors, including high debt servicing, GDP grew by only 2.2 per cent in 1986, falling to –0.5 per cent in 1987, and then rising to 7.3 per cent in 1988. With emphasis having switched to wealthier households – those with access to capital, who could buy title deeds which could be paid over twenty years and who were committed to private efficiency – the resettlement programme slowed down considerably. Indeed, only 52 000 families had been resettled in the period 1980/90. Opposition to speeding up the resettlement programme had come from the powerful agrarian bourgeoisie, mainly white commercial farmers who were increasingly augmented by black civil servants and ministers (the so-called 'telephone farmers' who own 8 per cent of commercial farmland).

It was the increasingly 'outward-orientation' of government policy, particularly from 1988 onwards, which led to some firms receiving import allocations from the Export Revolving Fund (ERF), or participating in barter arrangements, aid and export promotion programmes, and a supplementary allowance in foreign exchange for companies whose production was increasingly geared towards exports.

The gap between the public rhetoric of planning and economic reality was beginning to lead to disenchantment with the former. As we have already noted, the policy objectives were not only vague, they were also inconsistent. While, with the passing of time, investment was given priority over social services, the government – mindful of the social and political costs, as well as the economic ones, of rising unemployment and disappointed expectations of improvement – became increasingly reactive rather than pro-active. Its policies were formulated in response to crises (economic and social), the shift from a redistributive policy to one emphasizing allocative efficiency in response to the 1982–4 economic crisis being a case in point. Moreover, the targets set in the plans were not met, raising questions about the planning process itself, concerning the inadequate and unreliable data, bureaucratic inertia, and corruption.

Set against this background of perceived 'failures' of planning and the associated events in Eastern Europe, market liberalization ('get the prices right') had been proposed by the World Bank and the IMF. But because of the politically generated suspicion of IMF 'demands' – for example, the effects of sudden price rises, cuts in public-sector expenditure, and so on, and the consequent social problems – negotiations had dragged on since 1985. It was not until May 1989 that the government unveiled the stabilization and structural adjustment programme or the 'investment code' as it was named.

The stabilization policies involved:

(i)   further devaluation of the Zimbabwe dollar in relation to 'hard' currencies; that is, a 'realistic' exchange-rate policy based on Zimbabwe's inflation rate in relation to its main trading partners;

(ii)   a reduction in levels of protection over a period of five years; and

(iii)   fiscal reform involving the reduction of the budget deficit from 10 per cent of GDP to 5 per cent by 1994/5, incentives to local and, especially, foreign investors and reduction of rates of taxation.

The structural adjustment policies, for their part, required:

(i)   further cuts in subsidies and expenditure on social services, reductions in the civil service and the relaxation of wages and price control;

(ii)   pricing policies that enabled subsidies to parastatals to be targeted;

(iii)   the continuation of the high-interest-rate policy that was designed to encourage savings and, in turn, stimulate growth; and

(iv)   while privatisation of public-sector activities was not mentioned explicitly, the emphasis on parastatals working along 'productionist and business-orientated lines' seemed to point in that direction.

Not only are these policies expected to eliminate 'distortions' in the market so that prices reflect their relative scarcities, they are also seen as promoting export industries and improving Zimbabwe's comparative advantage. While there is no evidence of these policies having worked in any country (even Ghana, which the World Bank proudly refers to as the model of success for such policies, has had an average growth rate of 5 per cent which is attributable mainly to capital inflows rather than to policy measures – see Abbey, 1990; Stoneman, 1990; and Toye, 1990), Zimbabwe is now moving cautiously along this road. There is still protection for some industries which might otherwise be forced out of business if exposed to international competition. Mindful of social and political problems arising from the IMF policies, the government also continues to intervene in the economy 'to ease the pain of adjustment'.

Nevertheless, Zimbabwe is now geared up to finding markets for its manufactured and agricultural exports – a strategy which, by its very emphasis on export industries, may discriminate against those industries which produce for the local market. Nevertheless, Zimbabwe is looking to SADCC and Preferential Trade Area (PTA) countries to remove trade barriers and to provide an enlarged market which will encourage investment, allow it to take advantage of economies of scale, and thus enable its economy to industrialize further. Reference to NICs, and particularly to South Korea, seems to be misplaced in this respect as the latter's economic (industrial) growth was largely attributable to strong government intervention rather than to 'rolling back the state' to liberate private market forces (see Amsden, 1989).

IMPLICATIONS OF SADCC AND PTA FOR ZIMBABWE'S EXPORT PROMOTION STRATEGY

A number of problems spring to mind when considering Zimbabwe's export promotion strategy with regard to SADCC and the PTA. Unlike the PTA of Eastern and Southern Africa (which was formed in 1981), SADCC (which came into existence on 1 April, 1980) is concerned with indicative co-ordinated sectoral planning for priority projects in transport and communications rather than with trade. These projects are, however, carried out by individual states with their own resources and those from outside which are secured on the basis of their being members of SADCC. There is no formal mechanism by which 'gains' (and 'losses') can be distributed among members, except for linkages between different industries in different countries. Even though Zimbabwe has increased its exports to the SADCC region, export promotion is mainly confined to trade fairs and the exchange of information between governments and their chambers of commerce. Intra-SADCC trade has not been liberalized, and most trade is between individual SADCC states and countries such as the UK, South Africa, Germany and the USA.

For its part, the PTA is a common market along the lines of the EC. Its secretariat makes the important decisions, thus appearing as if it can circumvent member states, while in reality it does not have the ability to go against governments' wishes. Zimbabwe and a number of SADCC states are members of the PTA, but not all the members of the former are members of the latter. Even though membership of the PTA was originally determined by whether a country had a capitalist or 'socialist' orientation, eligibility is now based on whether the potential member has its borders next to a current member. Theoretically, this means that practically every country in Africa can conceivably become a member of the PTA. Its aims are to facilitate trade via (i) preferential tariffs, leading to a common market; (ii) acting as a clearing house (established in 1984) and moving towards a common, hard currency; (iii) relaxing or even subsequently removing preferential tariffs and import licensing; and (iv) establishing a development bank (this was done in 1986). While some tariff preferences have been put into place there is still very little trade between PTA members.

There has been suspicion between PTA and SADCC members, particularly voiced against Zimbabwe by the former who allege that 'Zimbabwe . . . behaved as though other countries had nothing to offer it and therefore that trade in its sense meant exports to them and no imports to it' (*The Southern African Economist*, 1990b, p. 33).

There are even more difficult problems for Zimbabwe to reconcile at a theoretical level. The PTA takes a phase-by-phase approach to eliminating preferential tariffs. In other words, it contends that, while tariff preferences may initially be the norm, a free market will ultimately dominate trade. Although Zimbabwe still maintains some forms of protection, this is the position which seems to be implied by following the IMF's structural adjustment policies. This is the so-called 'second best' neo-classical scenario.

In practice, however, Zimbabwe seems to be more in favour of managed markets and protection of their domestic market while insisting on other member states liberalizing barriers to trade. Zimbabwean officials rationalize this contradictory position, so the critics' argument goes, on the basis of the presumed irrelevance of imports from its neighbours and the apparent critical importance of its exports to its trading partners. To the extent that different states are not at comparable levels of development, this stance is likely to exasperate neo-classicists, who may feel that opportunities for free enterprise are being missed and that the exchange of information would be preferable to protectionism. In other words, that firms will be aware of conditions in the world market and will therefore network into the international situation, moving rapidly to take advantage of information on inputs – that is, global or regional sourcing. And to the extent that the PTA may also become a protectionist bloc – a view which Zimbabwe is often alleged to hold – against non-PTA members, then the neo-classicists would prefer a widening (more members) rather than a 'deepening' of the common market.

This last view becomes more crucial if we examine Zimbabwe's strategy in relation to SADCC. In so far as Zimbabwe subscribes to the latter's objectives, its position seems contradictory. Unlike the PTA, SADCC focuses on projects in each country which are co-ordinated through indicative planning, with targets, sectoral prioritization and greater state involvement. Indeed, member states such as Zimbabwe are concerned with production as a vehicle for creation of jobs at home – the 'growth with equity' objective. Export promotion is seen as a way of consolidating this strategy, albeit with the emphasis on growth rather than distributional equity. Perhaps this is why there has been a reluctance to move quickly towards eliminating tariffs, since this may have social and political costs in terms of rising unemployment. The position in SADCC also seems to be one of advocating a protectionist bloc, with increasing calls for an internal market, but one which discriminates against non-members. It is on this basis that the regional grouping was formed to reduce 'dependence' on South Africa, even though most members, including Zimbabwe, have a significant trade with South Africa. In fact, official statistics underestimate the amount of trade between South Africa and SADCC states, since unrecorded imports by visitors (in reality 'shoppers') to South Africa, especially from Zimbabwe, Swaziland and Botswana, are not included. Thus a 'parallel' economy has developed in order to circumvent import restrictions.

Finally, the prospect of a democratic post-apartheid South Africa joining SADCC may indeed affect Zimbabwe's export promotion strategy. In other words, the fact that South Africa's level of development is not comparable to its neighbours (see Table 14.2) means that its joining

Table 14.2 Whale among minnows

Country	GDP (US$ billions)	Population (millions)
Angola	5.1	9.2
Botswana	1.2	1.2
Lesotho	0.7	1.7
Malawi	1.3	8.3
Mozambique	1.6	14.7
Namibia	1.7	1.3
Swaziland	0.6	0.7
Tanzania	3.8	24.7
Zambia	2.2	7.5
Zimbabwe	6.1	9.3
Total (rounded)	24.8	78.5
South Africa	76.2	39.0
Income per head – US		
SADCC	315	
South Africa	2 310	

Source: Hawkins (1990).

of SADCC is likely to be disruptive to Zimbabwe's development model. While SADCC states will no doubt benefit through more convenient transport routes, an expanded market for their exports and regional co-operation, it is South Africa's dominance, if anything, which will mean that a free trade area will probably be impossible to develop. While regional co-ordination may permit industrial advance to occur, Zimbabwe (ironically) will have to compete more aggressively with South Africa for a share of the SADCC market. Even greater protection may follow as nationalistic interests become prominent.

CONCLUSION

Throughout this chapter we have attempted to analyse the inconsistencies of Zimbabwe's industrialization strategy, from 'growth with equity' to export promotion. This latter strategy seems to have led the Zimbabwean government to adopt contradictory positions. As investment decisions have become more prominent, the pledge of redistribution of income seems to have been played down. While this was always a social-democratic rather than 'socialist' objective (as the government claimed), Zimbabwe's relationship with the PTA and SADCC has meant that growth rather than equity will be emphasized. In justifying the implementation of the structural adjustment programme, government officials argue increasingly that industrial growth will eventually lead to redistribution.

Part VI

Conclusion

15 Is the Market the Answer?
Philip F. Leeson

The chapters in this volume document a range of responses to what is by now almost a world-wide trend, sometimes in countries where one might least expect it, towards reducing state economic activity, liberalizing economic decision-making, privatizing state economic property, and encouraging the private sector relative to the state sector. The process is most dramatic in the former socialist states of Eastern Europe and the erstwhile Soviet Union. But it is also happening in various ways in the Asian states which still call themselves socialist. It has been proceeding under IMF/IBRD influence in the Third World, including the African countries of 'socialist orientation', for the past decade and more. It has gone quite a long way in some of the countries of the Western Industrial Heartland.

What is happening is a reversal of the state economic interventionism which characterized a good deal of this century up to the 1980s. The state was already a significant economic actor in parts of the world in the nineteenth century. But, at different starting points and with differing degrees of intensity, the phenomenon has affected countries of all kinds during the twentieth century. It reached its most complete expression in the USSR after the Revolution (with a brief intermission during the NEP period), and in China and the other socialist countries after the Second World War. But 'development planning' became almost universal in the Third World in the post-war period, and a high level of economic interventionism survived the war in industrial 'capitalist' countries, where state spending as a share of GNP remained well above pre-war levels. There was also in the post-war period the beginnings of a new international interstate economic institutional structure.

The process involved macroeconomic control, indicative and other forms of planning, and regulation of many aspects of production. It also entailed state-organized social reform accompanied by massive redistributive expenditure. State purchases of public goods from private-sector producers were often exceeded by direct state production, both of pure public goods and of goods which could be purchased and consumed privately. State ownership and control over parts of the production process constituted a twentieth-century 'statist' form of production which grew up and interacted with the private capitalist economy.

There were many and varied reasons for the expansion of the economic role of the state in the twentieth century. Some of these will ensure a permanent economic role for government. Among them, relevant to the present discussion, there was earlier in the century a widespread antipathy towards the untrammelled operation of the private capitalist system. It was perceived by many to be ineradicably exploitative, generating inequality, and as being incapable of curing poverty. It was felt to be unable to resolve the crises which beset it, resulting in waste, poverty and unemployment. The experience of two world wars, the inter-war slumps and the rise of fascism all seemed related to the dynamics of the system. The atmosphere was one which created fertile ground for the acceptance of Keynesian economic analysis and policy, and in general for the analysis of 'market failure'. In the case of the LDCs, and earlier in the case of the capitalist latecomers, there was a sense of relative backwardness which, it was felt, could not be overcome by simply leaving capitalism to develop, but which necessitated state action in the fields of infrastructure, education, health, science, military preparedness, trade protection, and, increasingly, the planning and effecting of industrial production.

The intensity of these perceptions varied from country to country, as did the policy responses. These varied from demands for social reform and economic regulation in existing capitalist countries to the 'skipping of a stage' and the progression to a socialist form of society in those countries where capitalism had not fully developed.

Some of the arguments used to justify state intervention to correct market failure – that private investors were unable to deal with the problems of investment decisions which, in the face of uncertainties, indivisibilities, externalities, complementarities and information problems, required co-ordination, or the assertion of the wastefulness of the system for instance, – parallel the arguments currently being put forward to justify market solutions to 'state failure'. And the symmetry extends further. Arguments for state action were often put forward under the banner of the aim of a socialist utopia. This dream bore little relationship to the reality of 'actually existing socialism', or of LDC development planning, or of welfare statism, or indeed of what the working class actually wanted when they voted for 'socialist' parties. Similarly in the present period the case for the market is often based on a utopian ideology which holds out a vision of efficiency, freedom, prosperity, even equality, which is far removed from the reality of existing market regimes in the world in the 1990s.

As one step towards clarity it is better to refer to 'capitalism' than to 'the market', since the former term conveys more fully the reality of unequal power and unequal rewards in the labour market, to correct what might otherwise conjure up a harmonious world of transactions between equal participants. However, this amendment is not adequate to define the system under which most of the Western world has been living in the twentieth century. Just as what was called socialism was not the socialism of the pioneers of socialist thought, so, because of the role the state has played, what has been called capitalism in the West has not, over the past fifty years and more, been the capitalism of the textbooks either.

The model of the minimal state, mainly enforcing law and order and contractual obligations; maintaining property rights; carrying out minimal regulatory activities and macro-economic control; and producing, or purchasing, minimal public goods; is something which its supporters are attempting to create in the West as well as (apparently at one fell swoop) in the East. It is not something that exists. The reality has been an intricate interaction of capitalism and statism.

This powerful mixture led, in fact, to the longest period of sustained growth, rising living standards, and social reform of 'capitalism's' history. Both by comparing the situation before and after the advance of state action, and by comparing the respective records of 'capitalist' countries with minimal state action with those where state tutelage is prominent, it is clear that it was the latter which best met the needs of the post-war industrial world, at least among the systems on offer – better than pure statism or unregulated capitalism.

Just as two world wars (in addition to the arguments of academics and socialists) led to the growth of state spending, employment and control, so also the Cold War gave cohesion and legitimacy to national and international measures of intervention. It is paradoxical that the world-wide communist movement which ultimately failed in its aim of raising living standards and curing crises directly in the countries where it gained power, helped to do so via the 'threat' it posed to Western regimes, in countries where it was of marginal political significance and was indeed sometimes outlawed.

However, powerful though the mixture of capitalism and statism was, after the initial period of post-war recovery and reformist enthusiasm, statism began to manifest signs of crisis just as, in its own way, capitalism had earlier appeared to be moving into non-self-correcting anarchy. Signs of deep malaise – lack of motivation, corruption, dependency, patronage, paternalism, coercion, irrational investment decision-making, fiscal crises, inflation, undisciplined expenditure on armies, police and bureaucracy – appeared, more acute in some countries than in others. The failings of government in socialist, Third-World and Western countries alike, have been an easy target for New Right critics.

With the wheel turning against statism and in favour of a purer form of capitalism, the question arises whether appropriate lessons have been learnt from the gigantic experiment in different modes of conducting economic affairs that the world has seen in the twentieth century. Academic theory may have only a small part to play in a drama that depends more on the wisdom, or lack of wisdom, of statesmen; on whether even given wisdom, collective action by statesmen is at all possible; or on the possibility that events might move beyond the control of even a united set of leaders. Economists have (for example, during the Keynesian period) been deluded as to the extent of their influence. Nevertheless it seems that recently economists have been playing a very prominent role in the policy upheavals taking place. It would be reassuring to think that economic theory had absorbed the lessons of the post-war era.

Of the various specialisms, development economics ought to be the most relevant. It has throughout its life been concerned with countries that have attempted statist policies in what were predominantly private economies. It very much addressed itself to state action via development planning. In recent times it has been the branch of the subject most concerned with the impact of the IMF/IBRD stabilization and structural adjustment programmes in the Third World.

Development economics sought to consider the problems of a changing society, to get to grips with structural rigidities, with problems of growth and structural change. It recognized that the circumstances of less-developed countries were such as to deny the universal validity of static neo-classical economics.[1] But it did not apply the same healthy scepticism to state action. In its concentration on the role of the state, it could be said to have been a child of the statist era, unable to cope with the new situation. Certainly, its critics, many of whom objected to its departures from the neo-classical paradigm,[2] complained vigorously of its faith in state intervention. But perhaps more relevant is that it failed crucially to make any worthwhile progress towards a theory of the developmental state. The state remained an object of normative, prescriptive advice rather than a subject for analysis. Realism crept in on particular topics (urban bias, for instance), but by and large the picture was one of the benevolent state devoted to the welfare of the citizenry, with a worthy set of goals, deferring to the judgement of economists as to the planning techniques and strategies appropriate to the achievement of those goals.

This picture was, of course, violently at odds with the reality of most Third-World states, and clearly flew in the face of the direct experience available to development economists in their capacities as visitors and advisers. Some recognition of the problems was apparent in the recurrent but ineffectual call by developers for the pursuit of interdisciplinary study in co-operation with other social scientists. The more common manifestation of unease expressed itself in the plethora of breast-beating articles in the early 1980s bemoaning the fact that the subdiscipline was in deep crisis.[3]

The failure to develop a theory of the state to mesh with the progress being made on the workings of markets left development economics defenceless against the attack from the New Right when it arrived in the 1980s. A more balanced assessment of the aims and impact of state economic activity would have enabled it better to refute the current widespread nihilism in this area. But development economics did at least pose questions about social change, the meaning of development, the distribution of income and socio-economic structure. Its assumption of the vital role to be played by governments in the development process can by no means be said to have been refuted successfully by the New Right, and it might, given more self-confidence, have argued the point more tenaciously.[4]

The mainstream neo-classical theory from which development economics sprang was at least as innocent of any theory of the state and had no guidance to offer. It too was overly prescriptive. It said little about the role of institutions, spawned a not very successful theory of growth, found dynamic change difficult to handle, and was mesmerized by the limited notion of progress as consisting simply of the spreading to wider areas of the ramifications of the market (of equilibrium as the end of history?).

Its theoretical approach plus a somewhat arrogant attitude towards the other social sciences prevented economics from deriving much insight from the corpus of writings on the state that stemmed from political science. And the other long-standing body of thought which *did* spring from a base in economic theorising – Marxism – was *terra incognita* to most economists. Marxism did have several variants of a state theory, some of which sought in the name of realism to lessen the over-close link between capitalism and the state, posited in Marx's most prominent original formulation – without sacrificing the basic relationship that was felt to be the defining feature of a Marxist approach. The move towards realism did not go far enough. Moreover, in the field of development the brand of neo-Marxism – dependency theory – which was most prominent was one which was least likely to break through towards a realistic study of the workings of the state structure.[5]

In the circumstances, the field was left clear for the New Right which certainly did have very definite theoretical approaches to the activities of the state.[6] The influence of this blizzard is clearly seen in the plethora of recent theoretical offerings, coming from various specialisms within economics, which are certainly relevant to the workings of the state and to the interaction between market and state. The discussion of transaction costs, imperfect information, bounded rationality, firm structure, firm decision-making, principal – agent relationships, property rights, interest group formation, collective action, the 'prisoner's dilemma', free-riding, the 'tragedy of the commons', bureaucracy theory, rent-seeking, public goods and voting theory all concern themselves with matters going beyond the pure institutionless world of basic neo-classical economics. In most cases this did not reflect the absorption of insights from other social sciences, but on the contrary involved the extension of neo-classical methodology to new spheres.

Some of these, grouped loosely under the name of 'neo-classical political economy'[7] and claiming to be developments of the basic model, utilizing the methodology of individual optimization, have contributed in a powerful way to the critique of the over-large state, with the policy implication that its activities should be curtailed. Some, however, grouped loosely under the heading of the 'new institutional economics',[8] have contributed to the critique of the pure market model, stressing especially the institutional context within which markets operate. Some work falls into both categories. Development economics cannot claim credit for these innovations, which have originated elsewhere in economics, but some of them have spread into development studies where, of course, institutional questions are, or ought to be, paramount.[9]

It would be wrong to assert that this literature has led to a consensus on the role of the state, and it would also be rash to claim a consensus as to the relationship between markets and institutions. But it might at least be reasonable to conclude from the new institutional economics that how the market works depends on the institutional setting. This is certainly a different emphasis from the timeless, universal, contextless world of the original neo-classical propositions. Slightly less certain of universal assent would be the propositions that institutional development (in the sense of 'institution' as including customs, habits and laws, as well as formal organizations) takes time, that existing institutions even if already in market economies and even if they have developed 'organically', are not necessarily optimal, and that caution is needed in the application of sweeping policy changes.

In any case, common sense suggests that a reasonable level of stability and predictability in the socio-political setting is needed if the investment and growth process is to be encouraged. This caution would seem to be justified also by the ambiguous nature of the results of a decade or more of IMF/IBRD stabilization and adjustment policies world-wide – an ambiguity in which the propensity of different observers to concentrate on different indicators of success or failure (macroeconomic versus welfare indicators, for instance) is very much apparent.[10]

Just as each chapter in this book reveals different experiences in the liberalization process in the world at large, so it would be wrong to lump the whole of Eastern Europe and the erstwhile USSR together. But the cataclysmic events of recent years in that area have not been propitious for advocates of caution. Policies do differ from one country to another, but there has been a general tendency to lurch from one crisis to another with, therefore, short-term solutions being inevitable, or what is even more dubious, the attempt to arrive at long-term solutions in an exceedingly short time period.

The desirability of stability of administration clashes with the urgency of the impulse to get the 'old gang' out, especially when it is clear that the old gang includes most of the administratively competent personnel available. The replacements for the old gang have in any case their own interests and do not necessarily have a disinterested approach to societal needs. New institutions are fragile and old ones are hidebound.

In this situation, strident advice from those proposing radical solutions has secured a ready hearing, especially perhaps if the advice comes from overseas countries which might be the source of foreign aid. The dialogue will be complicated by overseas uncertainty over whether the promised policy changes are sincerely intended, and by local worries over whether the aid will really be forthcoming. The tendency will be to see the aid as the solution, regardless of the policy that attracts it. In this respect at least there is continuity between the statist era in LDCs and the present period.

When outcomes are of necessity unclear, advisers, whether home-grown or foreign, develop messianic zeal – 'if it can't be privatized immediately, it should be liquidated completely'. They seek to speed up and change the course of historical events, much as did the Bolsheviks at the onset of the statist era. The impulse to root out the old gang and the old structures mirrors the urge to root out the kulaks during the collectivization period of the early 1930's, lest capitalism reassert itself in the countryside. The immediate result is a drop in output and failure to maintain the capital stock (as with the animal stock in 1932). It must all be done at great speed (the Five-Year Plan accomplished in four years?). Will, in due course, some new Stalin come along, deflecting blame from himself, and rebuke the new 'Bolsheviki' as being 'dizzy with success'?[11]

During and since the stabilization and structural adjustment programmes in LDCs, there was, of course, discussion of the best ordering of liberalization and privatization measures, and of the various degrees and types of privatization.[12] Undoubtedly, similar discussion is going on in Eastern Europe, but the policy variations one observes seem to constitute lunges into the new order followed by partial drawings back caused by either old-guard resistance or public horror at the consequences of radical action, or both. In so far as any theory informs these dramatic lunges, it seems not to be one sustained by any experience elsewhere. It seems to say that not only is the market the optimal mode of conducting economic transactions, but that the market can in fact create much of the institutional background necessary for its successful operation. The government's main task is to set up the basic legal framework, to create and enforce private property rights, to unload its assets, and to let the market do the rest.

It is not uncommon for economists to ignore the economic suffering caused by their preferred policies, on the grounds that those policies will bring future benefits. It is even more common for economists to ignore the unfortunate non-economic impacts of their policies on the target society. The, possibly unconscious, presumption is that the economies and societies are two quite separable entities and, if allowed to do so by the state, one will function irrespective of the characteristics of the other. But we have in current policy-making the more heroic belief that the institutions of the market will mould society into an appropriate form. Again, there are echoes of the innocent enthusiasm of the earlier revolutionaries, for whom the creation of public property would result, in a more or less brief period, in socially conscious behaviour, work for the community and the elimination of the capitalist mentality.

Historians would agree that, given time, economic factors will bring about appropriate changes in the institutional setting. One modern school of historians asserts that economic factors – population change, technological change and the growth of trade – generate the supply and demand for institutional change, resulting in appropriate (Western) institutions which lower transaction costs, maintain property rights, and facilitate the further growth of the market. Marxist historians also see changes in the economic base as leading to changes in the political, legal and social superstructure. They would, or ought, however, to caution that there are interactions between base and superstructure, and that in any case the economic base includes the production relations and the class structure, as well as the productive forces. The institutional and power apparatus that goes with the existing class structure might mean that institutions resist change, or might cause perverse changes. For instance, the impact of market pressures from the fourteenth to the seventeenth centuries, which facilitated the growth of capitalism in parts of Europe, led in other parts to the strengthening rather than to the dissolution of feudalism.[13]

Above all, these historians, whether Marxist or anti-Marxist, are talking of lengthy historical time periods. To expect to accomplish institutional change by political decree would be an assertion of 'voluntarism' which the experience of communist politicians, who forgot their Marxist theory, ought to caution against. Of course, it can be argued that to create capitalism is going with the historical grain and is in line with world-wide trends, whereas the attempt to create communism was to try to change the course of history, and hence the two cases are not comparable. But then it is not being suggested here that the transition from statism to capitalism will take 400 years, merely that we cannot impose change at will.

It might also be argued that in times of cataclysmic change, the lessons of history cease to be useful. No steady evolution is possible, and those who urge caution are crying in the wind. Further, it might be objected that the plea for caution is tantamount to a plot to keep the 'old guard' in control. However, the essays in this book suggest the possibility that those countries which retain the old guard in political control may in fact move just as fast by orderly progress to the market as those attempting transition simultaneously on both economic and political fronts.

There seems little to suggest that in today's atmosphere, a statist ruling group may not in fact be very willing to embrace the market, or at least a measure of privatization. In fact, the complaint in Eastern Europe is often that the beneficiaries from privatization are the old guard in any case. If in this way members of an old ruling class reappear in dominant positions in a new class structure (as did feudal landlords when they became capitalist farmers), then this should cause no surprise except to those who have not allowed class categories into their mode of thinking, and have an idealized, classless concept of the market in mind. Capitalism is a class-structured system. Where do we imagine the members of the capitalist class will come from? The inequalities of the income distribution which may arise could dwarf the privileges of the old *nomenklatura* which, quite understandably, had become intolerable to the *have-nots*.

The prospect of a new class-stratified society certainly does not cause Western advocates of the market to lie awake at nights. The poignancy of the situation is that the political reformers who courageously struggled for change are often elbowed out in the process, just as during the statist era many thousands of communists and socialists suffered for their beliefs at the hands of Hitler, Stalin and many more respectable regimes.

One can certainly assert that economic change is unlikely to be successful without legal and social stability, preferably translated into an adequate supply of food and clothing. It certainly seems myopic or insensitive to assert that the market will in a short while relieve the sufferings of the not-so-fortunate, whatever may be claimed for it in the long run. Those who rush to embrace the dream world of Adam Smith may find themselves in the nightmare world of Thomas Hobbes.

However, notwithstanding one's fears concerning the present period of flux, it is clear that in spite of statist interference with, and in some cases attempts to abolish capitalism, capitalism has continued to grow in the twentieth century. This may have been temporarily obscured by the rhetoric of socialism in the Eastern bloc and in the Third World during the post-war boom years. But capitalism has continued to expand at the expense of pre-capitalist systems and currently at the expense of statist systems and statist regualtion.

Will the next period be one of capitalism, unregulated and uncontrolled, nationally and internationally, because statism has become so discredited that governments are unable or unwilling to exert the necessary degree of control over the market's naked tendencies? And will there be in due course a reaction to a statism of a more or less ugly kind – nationalistic, chauvinistic, xenophobic, racist or fascist?

On the other hand, is it conceivable that the necessary lessons – concerning state relationships with capitalism plus the necessary reforms of the operations of government – may have been learnt? The two are inseparable – a discredited state can hardly exercise effective regulation over the economy.

But the dialogue between state and market ought not to obscure the existence of the third actor in the drama, the institutions of 'civil society' – democracy at all levels, participation, voluntary, cultural, charitable, religious activities, pressure groups for reform, professional and trade union organisations, political parties, and survivals of traditional society. Many of these institutions bring pressure to bear on the government, and many bring pressure to bear on fellow citizens, seeking changes in social mores – sexual equality, anti-racism and its opposite, consumer taste, environmental issues, animal rights, abortion, for and against, and charitable concerns. This is a world of ideology, altruism, community, esteem, reputation and conceptions of the public good, as well as of self-interest, special pleading, status, class, family, professional monopoly. It is a complex of activities and influences which affect the context within which the market works, as well as the context within which government operates.

It is healthy that economists should recognize the non-economic institutional and historical context of their subject of study. The question is: how do they deal with that insight? The advance of markets and the reduction of transaction costs generates many benefits. The process also invades and tends to destroy areas of non-economic relationships, some of which might be impediments to human welfare and others which might generate welfare more effectively than do market transactions. In the latter case the reduction of transaction costs might not be a benefit. If the 'creative destruction' proceeds far enough it could destroy the context in which transactions take place. It would be sad if economists were to conclude that their recognition of non-economic phenomena is merely an opportunity to exercise their economics methodology on new material: that is, that they could continue self-sufficiently to avoid interdisciplinary co-operation with other social scientists – a conceit which impeded them from attaining a theory of the state during the earlier years of statism.

The dialogue cannot continue to be one simply of state versus market. Just as the over-powerful state might frustrate the market, it can also suffocate the autonomy of civil society. The market creates pressures to cut down the state but it also infiltrates and destroys elements of civil society. On the other hand, it is from civil society that the forces come to check the excesses of the state and market, and keep the market from absorbing too big a part of people's lives. When the rush to commercialize every aspect of life has spent its force, civil society will be the source of alternatives to both state and market, whilst also ensuring their proper relationship with one another.

Notes

1. The concern, continuous from its early days, shown by development economics over the relevance of orthodox economic analysis was well displayed, for example, in the reports of two conferences held in the 1960s. See Knapp and Martin (eds.) (1967) and Livingstone *et al.* (1973).
2. Perhaps development economics' most vociferous critic has been Lal (1983).
3. See, for instance, Seers (1979) or Hirschman (1981).
4. Some development economists however have made cool assessments of the new orthodoxy. See, for instance, Killick (1989).
5. Among the many surveys of state theory are Alford and Friedland (1985), Carnoy (1984), Dunleavy and O'Leary (1987), Held (1989), King (1986). For essays in which economists have interacted with political science over state theory, see, for example, Stiglitz (1989) or Brittan (1983). On dependency theory, a useful survey is Kay (1989).
6. Brief introductions to New Right thinking are in King (1987) or McLean (1987). Tomlinson (1990) is a brief assessment of Hayek.
7. See, for example, Collander (ed.) (1984). Much of the literature under this heading might, of course, also be listed under the New Right.
8. See, for example, Langlois (1986) or Putterman (1988), also *World Development* (1989b).
9. E.g. Stiglitz (1986).
10. For example, Cornia *et al.* (1987), Taylor (1988), World Bank (1988a), World Bank (1990e and 1990f), UNDP (1990), *World Development* (1991).
11. *Pravda*, 2 March 1930, reprinted in Stalin (1947).
12. See, for example, Cook and Kirkpatrick (1988), Vickers and Yarrow (1988), *World Development* (1989a).
13. Marxist arguments, for and against, are covered in Aston and Philpin (eds.) (1985). See also, for example, Brenner's chapter in Roemer (ed.) (1986). Earlier Marxist controversies are covered in Hilton (ed.) (1976). For non-Marxist arguments, see, for example, Postan (1973), North and Thomas (1973) and North (1981). Also of interest is Olson (1982).

Bibliography

Abbey, J. L. S. (1990) 'Ghana's Experience with Structural Adjustment: Some Lessons', in J. Pickett and H. Singer (eds) *Towards Economic Recovery in Sub-Saharan Africa: Essays in Honour of Robert Gardiner* (London and New York: Routledge).

ADB (Asian Development Bank) (1988) *Economic Report on the Lao People's Democratic Republic* , LAO: EC. 6 (November) (2 vols).

ADB (Asian Development Bank) (1989) *Final Report: Restructuring the Monetary and Banking System* (under TA-1115-LAO) (November).

ADB (Asian Development Bank) (1993) *Asian Development Outlook* (New York: Oxford University Press).

Akerlof, G. (1970) 'The Market for "Lemons": Quality Uncertainty and the Market Mechanism', *Quarterly Journal of Economics*, pp. 488–500.

Alford, R. R. and Friedland, R. (1985) *Powers of Theory: Capitalism, the State and Democracy* (Cambridge: Cambridge University Press).

Amsden, A. (1989) *Asia's Next Giant: South Korea and Late Industrialisation* (Oxford: Oxford University Press).

Anon (1991) 'Hungary – The Economic Programme of National Renewal', *East European Reporter*, 43, p. 39.

Aston, T. H. and Philpin, C. H. E. (eds) (1985) *The Brenner Debate* (Cambridge: Cambridge University Press).

Banister, J. (1987) *China's Changing Population* (Stanford: Stanford University Press)

Bannasch, H. (1990) 'The Role of Small Firms in East Germany', *Small Business Economics*, 2 (4), pp. 307–12.

Batbold, (1992) 'Main Issues in Mongolia's Transition to a Market Economy' in IAMD/UNDP Management Development Programme, *Mongolia's Transition to a Market Economy: Evaluation, Problems, Proposals* (Ulaan Baatar: UNDP).

Baumol, W. (1990) *Beyond Allocative Efficiency: How Perfect are 'Perfect' Markets?*, C. V. Starr Centre for Applied Economics, New York University.

Becker, G. (1981) *A Treatise on the Family* (Cambridge, MA: Harvard University Press).

Beresford, M. (1989) National Unification and Economic Development in Vietnam (London: Macmillan).

Ben-Ner, A. and Montias, J. (1991) 'The Introduction of Markets in a Hypercentralised Economy: The Case of Romania', *Journal of Economic Perspectives*, 5 (4).

Bettleheim, C. (1988) 'Economic Reform in China', *Journal of Development Studies* (Special Issue), 24 (4) (July).

Blanchard, O. and Layard, R. (1990) 'Economic change in Poland ', *Discussion Paper*, 3, Centre for Economic Performance, LSE (May).

Booth, A. and Vo Nhan Tri (1992) 'Recent Economic Developments in Vietnam', Working Paper, 7, School of Oriental and African Studies, University of London.

Borensztein, E. and Kumar, M. S. (1991) 'Proposals for Privatization in Eastern Europe', *IMF Staff Papers* (June)

Brittan, S. (1983) *The Role and Limits of Government* (London: Temple Smith).

Brus, W. and Laski, K. (1990) *From Marx to the Market: Socialism in Search of an Economic System* (Oxford: Clarendon Press).

Carnoy, M. (1984) *The State and Political Theory* (Princeton, N.J.: Princeton University Press).

Chan, T. M. H. (1988) 'The Development and Prospects of the Zhujiang Delta Open Zone', *China Economic Papers Series*, Friedrich Ebert Foundation, Shanghai.

Clague, C. and Rausser, G. C. (eds) (1992) *The Emergence of Market Economies in Eastern Europe* (Oxford: Basil Blackwell).

Coase, R. (1992) 'The Institutional Structure of Production', *American Economic Review* (September), pp. 713–19.

Cody, J., Kitchen, R. and Weiss, J. (1990) *Policy Design and Price Reform* (Hemel Hempstead: Harvester-Wheatsheaf).

Collander, D. C. (ed.) (1984) *Neo-classical Political Economy* (New York: Ballinger)

Collins, P. and Nixson, F. (1993a) 'Managing the Implementation of "Shock Therapy" in a Land Locked State: Mongolia's Transition from the Centrally-Planned Economy', *Public Administration and Development*, 13 (4) (October).

Collins, P. and Nixson, F. (1993b) 'Public Sector Management and the Transition to a More Open Economy: cautious reform in the Democratic People's Republic of Korea (DPRK)', *Public Administration and Development,* 13 (4) (October).

Collins, P. and Nixson, F. (eds) (1991) *Management Development and Economic Restructuring in the Mongolian People's Republic*, UNDP Management Development Programme (New York: UNDP).

Cook, P. (1993) 'External Savings and Domestic Resource Allocation: A Case Study of the Lao Peoples' Democratic Republic', paper prepared for UNCTAD, Geneva (December).

Cook, P. and Kirkpatrick, C. (eds) (1988) *Privatization in Less Developed Countries* (Hemel Hempstead: Harvester-Wheatsheaf).

Cook, P. and Kirkpatrick, C. (1994) 'Privatisation in Transitional Economies: A Comparison of European and Asian Experience', paper prepared for UK Academy of International Business Annual Conference, UMIST, Manchester (March).

Cook, P. and Minogue, M. (1991) 'Economic Reform in Myanmar', in R. Adhikari, J. Weiss and C. Kirkpatrick (eds), *Industry and Trade Policy Reform in Developing Countries* (Manchester: Manchester University Press).

Cook, P. and Minogue, M. (1993) 'Economic Reform and Political Change in Myanmar (Burma)', *World Development*, 21 (7).

Cornia, G. A., Jolly, R. and Stewart, F. (1987) *Adjustment with a Human Face* (Oxford: Oxford University Press).

CSO (Central Statistical Office) (1991) *Statistical Yearbook 1990* (Budapest: CSO).

Current Digest of the Soviet Press (1988) 'Gorbachev Defends Restructuring to Party', 11 (7), pp. 1–10.

Das Gupta, P. (1991) 'Nutrition, Non-convexities and Redistributive Policies', *Economic Journal*, 101 (404).

Davin, D. (1991) 'Women, WorFk and Property in the Chinese Peasant Household of the 1980s', in D. Elson (ed.), *Male Bias in the Development Process* (Manchester: Manchester University Press).

Demberel, L. and Ganzorig, Tch. (1992) 'Foreign Loans and Aid in the Transition Period' in IAMD/UNDP Management Development Programme, *Mongolia's Transition to a Market Economy: Evaluation, Problems, Proposals* (Ulaan Baatar: UNDP).

Devine, P. (1988) *Democracy and Economic Planning* (Cambridge: Polity Press).

Drèze, J. and Sen, A. K. (1989) *Hunger and Public Action* (Oxford: Clarendon Press).

Dunleavy, P. and O'Leary, B. (1987) *Theories of the State* (London: Macmillan).

EIU (Economist Intelligence Unit) (1990) *Mozambique: Country Profile* (London: Business International).

Ellman, M. (1989) *Socialist Planning*, 2nd edn (Cambridge: Cambridge University Press).

Elson, D. (1988) 'Market Socialism or Socialization of the Market?' *New Left Review*, 172.

Elson, D. (1991) 'Male Bias in the Development Process: An Overview', in D. Elson (ed.), *Male Bias in the Development Process* (Manchester: Manchester University Press).

Elson, D. (1992) 'Public Action, Poverty and Development', paper presented at seminar on Women in Extreme Poverty, UN Division for Advancement of Women, Vienna.

Estrin, S. (1983) *Self-Management: Economic Theory and Yugoslav Practice* (Cambridge: Cambridge University Press).

Estrin, S. (1991a) 'Yugoslavia: The Case of Self-Managing Market Socialism', *Journal of Economic Perspectives*, 5 (4).

Estrin, S. (1991b), *Privatization in Central and Eastern Europe: What Lessons Can Be Learnt from Western Experience?*, London School of Economics, *Working Paper*, 99.

Faber, M. (1990) 'Mongolia: Moves Towards Perestroika', *Development Policy Review*, 8.

Faber, M. (1991) *Myanmar: Difficulties in the Transition from Socialism to a Market-based Economy* (Geneva: UNCTAD).

Fenichel, A. and Khan, A. (1981) 'The Burmese Way to Socialism', *World Development*, 9 (10) (October).

Fforde, A. (1989) 'The Socialist Republic of Vietnam Since Mid-1988 – Major Policy Changes and Socio-Economic Developments', *Report for SIDA*, Hanoi (December)

Fitzgerald, E. (1988) 'State Accumulation and Market Equilibria', *Journal of Development Studies*, 24 (4).

Folbre, N. (1986) 'Hearts and Spades: Paradigms of Household Economics', *World Development*, 14 (2).

Fox, S. M. (1986) *Laos: Politics, Economics and Society* (London: Frances Pinter).

Fry, M. and Nuti, M. (1992) 'Monetary and Exchange-Rate Policies During Eastern Europe's Transition: Some Lessons from further East', *Oxford Review of Economic Policy*, 8 (1).

Frydman, R. and Rapaczynski, A. (1990) *Markets and Institutions in Large Scale Privatizations: An Approach to Economic and Social Transformations in*

Eastern Europe, Working Paper, C. V. Starr Center for Applied Economies, New York University.

Frydman, R. and Rapaczynski, A. (1993) 'Privatisation in Eastern Europe: Is the State Whitering Away?', *Finance and Development* (June).

Gamble, A. (1988) *The Free Economy and the Strong State* (London: Macmillan).

Gerelchuluun, T. (1992) 'The Implementation of the Privatisation Programme, Results and Further Tasks in IAMD/UNDP Management Development Programme, *Mongolia's Transition to a Market Economy: Evaluation, Problems, Proposals* (Ulaan Baatar: UNDP).

GGKY (The Editorial Group, *Guangdong Gaige Kaifang Yanjiu*) (1988) Studies of Guangdong's Reform and Openness: proceedings of the conference on Guangdong's reform and openness (Guangzhou: The People's Press, Guangdong branch).

Gibbons, G. (1992a) 'The Transition of Mongolia's Centrally Planned Economy in a Changing Global Economic Environment', paper presented to ODI/UNDP/MDP Seminar on 'Management Development of Centrally-Planned Economies in a New Global Environment' (London), mimeo.

Gibbons, G. (1992b) 'Civil Service Reform and Decentralisation', in IAMD/UNDP Management Development Programme, *Mongolia's Transition to a Market Economy: Evaluation, Problems, Proposals,* IAMD/UNDP/MDP (1992) Seminar, Ulaan Baatar, (Ulaan Baatar: UNDP).

Girard, G. and Correa, V. (1989) *Ebauche Stratégie de Développement Industriel, Horizon 2000*, UNDP Project, STAS-RAS/88/001 (April).

Gora, M. and Rutkowski, M. (1990) 'The Demand for Labour and the Disguised Unemployment in Poland in the 1980s', *Communist Economies*, 2 (3).

Gorbachev, M. (1991) 'The Law on the Principles of Entrepreneurship', reported in the *Current Digest of the Soviet Press,* 43 (16), p. 22.

Green, F. (1988) 'Neoclassical and Marxian Conceptions of Production', *Cambridge Journal of Economics*, 12 (3).

Green, R. H. (1990) 'Economic Integration/Co-ordination in Africa: The Dream Lives But How Can It Be Lived?', in J. Pickett and H. Singer (eds), *Towards Economic Recovery in Sub-Saharan Africa: Essays in Honour of Robert Gardiner* (London and New York: Routledge).

Greene, J. L. (1991) 'FIEs (Foreign Invested Enterprises) Face New Labor Obstacles', *China Business Review* (January–February).

Gurley, J. (1979), 'Economic Development, a Market View', in K. Jameson and C. Wilber (eds), *Directions in Economic Development* (New Jersey: Notre Dame Press).

Halliday, J. (1993) 'The North Korean Enigma', in G. White, R. Murray and C. White (eds) *Revolutionary Socialist Development in the Third World* (Brighton: Wheatsheaf).

Hanlon, J. (1984), *Mozambique: the Revolution Under Fire,* (London: Zed Books).

Hare, P. (1991) 'Eastern Europe: The Transition to a Market Economy', *The Royal Bank of Scotland Review*, 169 (March).

Hare, P. and Grosfeld, I. (1991) 'Privatisation in Hungary, Poland and Czechoslovakia', *Discussion Paper*, 544, Centre for Economic Policy Research (April).

Hare, P., Radice, H. and Swain, N. (1981) *Hungary, A Decade of Economic Reform* (London: Allen & Unwin).

Hawkins, A. W. (1986) 'Can Africa Industrialize?', in R. J. Berg and J. Seymour Whitaker (eds) *Strategies for African Development*, (University of California Press).

Hawkins, T. (1990) 'Hard-headed Realism', *The Southern African Economist* (October/November).

Hawkins, T. (n.d.) Extracts from paper presented to SADCC meeting, mimeo.

Held, D. (1989) *Political Theory and the Modern State* (Oxford: Polity Press).

Henderson, G. (1990) 'Increased Inequality in Health Care', in D. Davis and E. F. Vogel (eds), *Chinese Society on the Eve of Tiananmen* (Cambridge, MA: Harvard University Press)

Herrman-Pillath, C. (1991) 'Systemic Transformation as an Economic Problem', *Aussen Politik*, 42 (2), pp. 172–82.

Hewett, E. (1988) *Reforming the Soviet Economy* (Washington, DC: Brookings Institution).

Hill, H. (1984) 'Industrialisation in Burma in Historical Perspective', *Journal of Southeast Asian Studies*, 15 (1) (March).

Hilton, R. H. (1976) *The Transition from Feudalism to Capitalism* (London: New Left Books).

Hirschman, A. O. (1981) 'The Rise and Decline of Development Economics', in A. O. Hirschman, *Essays in Trespassing* (Cambridge: Cambridge University Press).

Hisrich, R. and Peters, M. (1992), *Entrepreneurship* (Tokyo: Toppan).

Hodgson, G. (1988) *Economics and Institutions* (Oxford: Polity Press).

Horsley, J. P. (1988) 'The Chinese Workforce', *China Business Review* (May–June).

Hricovsky, M. (1990), 'The Contribution of Small Business to the Demonopolisation of the Czecho-slovakian Economy', paper presented at a conference on The Role of Small Firms and Entrepreneurship: A Comparison of East and West Countries, Berlin (6–7 July).

Hsu, J. C. (1989) *China's Foreign Trade Reforms: Impact on Growth and Stability* (Cambridge: Cambridge University Press).

Hsueh, T. T. and Woo, T. O. (1989) 'The Changing Pattern of Hong Kong–China Economic Relations since 1979: Issues and Consequences', paper presented at conference on 'The Future of Industrial and Trade Development in Hong Kong', University of Hong Kong, Centre of Asian Studies (4–6 January).

Hussain, A. and Stern, N. (1991) 'Effective Demand, Enterprise Reforms and Public Finance in China', *Economic Policy*, 12 (April).

IIE (Institute of Industrial Economics, Social Science Academy of China) (1984) *Shan Zhong Quanhui Yi Lei Zhong Yao Wen Xian Xuan Bian* (A Selected Collection of the Important Documents Since the Third Plenary Session of the Eleventh Central Committee of the Chinese Communist Party) (Beijing: Economic Science Press).

International Monetary Fund (IMF) (1988) *Burma: Recent Economic Developments* (Washington, DC: IMF) (June).

International Monetary Fund (IMF) (1991a) *International Financial Statistics* (August).

International Monetary Fund (IMF) (1991b) *China: Economic Reform and Economic Management*, Occasional Paper 76 (Washington, DC: IMF) (January).

IMF (International Monetary Fund) (1991c) *The Mongolian People's Republic: Toward a Market Economy, Occasional Paper*, 79 (Washington, DC: IMF).

IMF (International Monetary Fund) (1992a) *Economic Outlook* (Washington, DC: IMF).

IMF (International Monetary Fund) (1992b) *International Financial Statistics* (Washington, DC: IMF) (June).

Jackson, M. (1991) 'The Rise and Decay of the Socialist Economy in Bulgaria', *Journal of Economic Perspectives*, 5 (4).

Jameson, K. and Wilber, C. (1981) 'Socialism and Development: Editors' Introduction', *World Development*, 9 (9/10).

Kabeer, N. (1991) 'Gender, Production and Well-Being: Rethinking the Household Economy', Institute of Development Studies, *Discussion Paper* 288, University of Sussex.

Kalecki, M. (1976), 'Observations on Social and Economic Aspects of Intermediate Regimes', in M. Kalecki, *Essays on Developing Economies* (Hassocks, Sussex: Harvester Press).

Kang, M.-K. and Lee, K. (1992) 'Industrial Systems and Reform in North Korea: A Comparison with China', *World Development*, 20 (7) (July).

Kaplinsky, R. (1991) 'Direct Foreign Investment in Third World Manufacturing: Is the Future an Extension of the Past?', *Institute of Development Studies Bulletin*, University of Sussex (April).

Kaser, M. (1990) 'The Technology of Decontrol: Some Macroeconomic Issues', *Economic Journal*, 100 (401).

Kaser, M. and Allsopp, C. (1992) 'The Assessment: Macroeconomic Transition in Eastern Europe, 1989–91', *Oxford Review of Economic Policy*, 8(1).

Kay, C. (1989) *Latin American Theories of Development and Underdevelopment* (London: Routledge).

Killick, T. (1989) *A Reaction Too Far* (London: Overseas Development Institute).

Killick, T. and Commander, S. (1988) 'State Divestiture as a Policy Instrument in Developing Countries', *World Development*, 16 (12).

King, D. S. (1987) *The New Right* (London: Macmillan).

King, R. (1986) *The State in Modern Society* (London: Macmillan).

Knapp, J. and Martin, K. (eds) (1967) *The Teaching of Development Economics* (London: Cass).

Knell, M. and Rider, C. (eds) (1992) *Socialist Economies in Transition: Appraisals of the Market Mechanism* (Aldershot: Edward Elgar).

Knight, J. and Song, L. (1991) 'The Length of Life and the Standard of Living: Economic Influences on Premature Death in China', Institute of Economics and Statistics, University of Oxford, mimeo.

Kolarska-Bobinska, L. (1990) 'Civil Society and Social Anomaly in Poland' *Acta Sociologica*, 33 (4), pp. 277–88.

Kornai, J. (1980) 'The Dilemmas of a Socialist Economy: The Hungarian Experience', *Cambridge Journal of Economics*, 4 (2).

Kornai, J. (1986a) 'The Hungarian Reform Process: visions, hopes and reality', *Journal of Economic Literature*, 24 (December).

Kornai, J. (1986b) *Contradictions and Dilemmas* (Cambridge, MA: MIT Press).

Lal, D. (1983) *The Poverty of Development Economics* (London: IEA).

Langlois, R. (ed.) (1986) *Economics as a Process: Essays in the New Institutional Economics* (Cambridge: Cambridge University Press).

Leipziger, D. M. (1992) 'Awakening the Market: Vietnam's Economic Transition', World Bank *Discussion Papers*, 157 (Washington, DC: World Bank).

Leung, H. M., Thoburn, J. T., Chau, E. and Tang, S. H. (1991) 'Contractual Relations, Foreign Direct Investment and Technology Transfer. The Case of China', *Journal of International Development* (June).

Lipton, D. and Sachs, J. (1990a) 'Creating a Market Economy in Eastern Europe: The Case of Poland', *Brookings Papers on Economic Activity*, 1.

Lipton, D. and Sachs, J. (1990b) 'Privatisation in Eastern Europe: the case of Poland', *Brookings Papers on Economic Activity*, 2, pp. 293–342.

Livingstone, I. (1986) 'International Transport Costs and Industrial Development in the Least Developed African Countries', *Industry and Development*, 19 (Vienna: UNIDO).

Livingstone, I. (1991) *Industry, Trade and Tourism in the Lao People's Democratic Republic: Issues and Recommendations*, Overseas Development Group, University of East Anglia.

Livingstone, I. *et al* (eds) (1973) *The Teaching of Economics in Africa* (London: Chatto & Windus).

Lowe, P. (1986) *The Origins of the Korean War* (London and New York: Longman).

Mackintosh, M. (1985) 'Economic Tactics: Commercial Policy and Socialization of African Agriculture', *World Development*, 13 (1).

Maroczy, M. (1987) *Report on Socio-Economic Survey of Three Villages in Vientiane Province, PDR, Lao* (Vientiane: FAO)

Matthews, R. C. O. (ed.) (1985) *Economy and Democracy* (London: Macmillan).

Marquand, D. (1988) *The Unprincipled Society* (London: Jonathan Cape).

Mayhew, K. and Seabright, P. (1992). 'Incentives and the Management of Enterprises in Economic Transition: Capital Markets Are Not Enough!', *Oxford Review of Economic Policy*, 8 (1).

McAuley, A. (1991) 'The Economic Transition in Eastern Europe: Employment Income Distribution and the Social Safety Net', *Oxford Review of Economic Policy*, 7 (4).

McLean, I. (1987) *Public Choice: An Introduction* (Oxford: Blackwell).

Meaney, C. S. (1991) 'Market Reform and Disintegrative Corruption in Urban China', in R. Baum (ed.), *Reform and Reaction in Post Mao China* (New York and London: Routledge).

Meyanathan, S. (1989) 'An Overview of the Recent Reform Movements in Socialist Economies', *Public Enterprise*, 9 (2).

Ministry of Economy Planning and Finance (1990) *Policy Framework for Public Investment Program, Lao, PDR* (Vientiane) (November).

Ministry of Economy Planning and Finance, State Statistical Centre (1990) *Basic Statistics about the Socio-Economic Development in the Lao PDR for 15 years (1975–90)* (Vientiane).

Nagy, A. (1992), 'Social Choice in Eastern Europe', *Journal of Comparative Economics*, 15 (2), pp. 266–83.

Naughton, B. (1989) 'The Pattern and Legacy of Economic Growth in the Mao Era', paper for the 'Four Anniversaries China Conference', Annapolis, Maryland (10–14 September).

Ndhlovu, T. P. (1990) 'Export Potential of a Democratic Post-apartheid South Africa to Zimbabwe', *Report to the Overseas Development Group (ODG)* 12 October (University of East Anglia).

Ndhlovu, T. P. (forthcoming), *Development Strategy in Zimbabwe: Rhetoric and Reality* (London: Zed Books).

Nellis, J. (1991) *Improving the Performance of Soviet Enterprises*, World Bank *Discussion Papers*, 118 (Washington, DC: World Bank).

Nixson, F. (1991) 'Economic Liberalisation and Alternative Industrialisation Strategies: The Case of the Mongolian People's Republic', in P. Collins and F. Nixson (eds), Management Development and Economic Restructuring in the Mongolian People's Republic, UNDP Management Development Programme (New York: UNDP).

Nixson, F. (1992) 'Economic Reform and Industrialisation in the Socialist Republic of Vietnam', in R. Adhikari, C. Kirkpatrick and J. Weiss (eds), *Industrial and Trade Policy Reform in Developing Countries* (Manchester: Manchester University Press).

Nixson, F. (1995) 'Enterprise Reform and Economic Restructuring in Transitional Economies: Mongolia, Vietnam and North Korea', in P. Cook and C. Kirkpatrick (eds), *Privatisation Policy and Performance: International Perspectives* (London: Harvester Wheatsheat).

Nolan, P. (1990) 'Introduction' in P. Nolan and D. Fureng (eds), *The Chinese Economy and its Future* (Oxford: Polity Press and Basil Blackwell).

Nolan, P. and Fureng, D. (eds) (1990) *The Chinese Economy and its Future: Achievements and Problems of Post-Mao Reform* (Oxford: Polity Press).

Nolan, P. and Sender, J. (1992) 'Death Rates, Life Expectancy and China's Economic Reforms: A Critique of A. K. Sen', *World Development*, 20 (9).

North, D. C. (1981) *Structure and Change in Economic History* (Aston: Aston University).

North, D. C. and Thomas, R. P. (1973) *The Rise of the Western World* (Cambridge: Cambridge University Press).

Nove, A. (1983) *The Economics of Feasible Socialism* (London: Allen & Unwin).

Nove, A. (1991) *The Economics of Feasible Socialism Revisited* (London: Harper-Collins).

Nuti, M. (1986) 'Economic Planning in Market Economies', in P. Nolan and S. Paine (eds), *Rethinking Socialist Economics* (Cambridge: Cambridge University Press).

OECD (Organisation for Economic Cooperation and Development) (1992) *Germany*, OECD Economic Surveys 1991/2 (Paris: OECD).

Olson, M. (1982) *The Rise and Decline of Nations* (New Haven: Yale University Press).

Ottoway, M. (1988) 'Mozambique: from Symbolic Socialism to Symbolic Reform', *Journal of Modern African Studies*, 26 (2).

Palmer, I. (1991) *Gender and Population in the Adjustment of African Economics: Planning for Change* (Geneva: ILO).

Peck, M. and Richardson, T. (eds) (1991) *What is to be Done? Proposals for the Soviet Transition to the Market* (New Haven: Yale University Press).

Perkins, D. (1969) *Agricultural Development in China, 1368–1968* (Edinburgh: Edinburgh University Press).

Pinchot, G., III (1985) *Intrapreneurship* (New York: Harper & Row).

Pomfret, R. (1990) *Investing in China, Ten Years of the Open Door Policy* (London: Harvester Wheatsheaf).

Post, K and Wright, P. (1989) *Socialism and Underdevelopment* (London: Routledge).

Postan, M. M. (1973) *Essays on Medieval Agriculture and General Problems of the Medieval Economy* (Cambridge: Cambridge University Press).

Putterman, L. (1988) *The Economic Nature of the Firm: A Reader* (Cambridge: Cambridge University Press).

Rashid, S. (1988) 'Quality in Contestable Markets: A Historical Problem?', *Quarterly Journal of Economics* (February), pp. 245–9.

Robson, P. (1990) 'Economic Integration in Africa: a New Phase?'. in J. Pickett and H. Singer (eds),

Roemer, J. (ed.) (1986) *Analytical Marxism* (Cambridge: Cambridge University Press).

Round Table Meeting (1989) *Report on the Economic and Social Situation, Development Strategy, and Assistance Needs of Lao PDR* (Geneva) (April).

Roy, D. J. (1990) 'Real Product and Income in China, Cuba, North Korea and Vietnam', *Development Policy Review,* 8 (1) (March).

Rybczynski, T. (1991) 'The Sequencing of Reform', *Oxford Review of Economic Policy,* 7 (4).

Sanders, A. J. K. (1987) *Mongolia: Politics, Economics and Society* (London: Frances Pinter).

Schwartz, G. (1955) 'Privatisation in Eastern Europe: Experience and Preliminary Policy Lessons', in P. Cook and C. Kirkpatrick (eds), *Privatisation Policy and Performance: International Perspectives* (London: Harvester Wheatsheat).

Seers, D. (1979) 'The Birth, Life and Death of Development Economics', *Development and Change,* 10.

Seers, D. (ed.) (1981) *Dependency Theory: A Critical Reassessment* (London: Frances Pinter).

Sen, A. K. (1984) *'Resources, Values and Development,* (Oxford: Basil Blackwell), Ch. 4.

Sen, A. K. (1990) 'Gender and Co-operative Conflicts', in I. Tinker (ed.), *Persistent Inequalities – Women and World Development* (Oxford: Oxford University Press).

Sen, A. K. (1992) 'Life and Death in China: A Reply', *World Development,* 20 (9).

Sen, G. (1992), 'Social Needs and Public Accountability: The Case of Kerala', in M. Wuyts, M. Mackintosh and T. Hewitt (eds), *Development Policy and Public Action* (Oxford: Oxford University Press).

SESRC (State Economic System Reform Commission) (1988) *Zhongguo Jingji Tizhi Gaige Guihuaji: 1979–87* (A Collection of Planning Works on China's Economic System Reform 1979–87), Academy of the Central Committee of the Chinese Communist Party Press.

Shackleton, J. (1987) *The Political Economy of Privatisation in Less Developed Countries,* paper presented to UK Development Studies Association Conference (September).

Shiozawa, Y. (1990) 'What Can we Learn from Marketization?', *Osaka City University Economic Review,* 25 (2), pp. 21–50.

Shirley, M. and Nellis, J. (1991) 'Public Enterprise Reform: The Lessons of Experience', *EDI Development Studies Series* (Washington, DC: World Bank).

Singh, A. (1993) 'The Plan, the Market and Evolutionary Economic Reform in China', *UNCTAD Discussion Paper*, 76, Geneva (December).

Smith, H. (1992) 'DPRK Foreign Policy in the 1990s: More Realist than Revolutionary?', paper presented to Conference on North Korea and the New World Order, City of London Polytechnic (October), mimeo.

Smith, M. (1991) *Burma: Insurgency and the Politics of Ethnicity* (London: Zed Books).

Solimano, A. (1993) 'The Post-Socialist Transitions in Comparative Perspective: Policy Issues and Recent Experience', *World Development*, 21 (11).

SPA (State Property Agency) (1991) *Annual Report*, 1991 (Budapest: SPA).

Spencer, G. and Cheasty, A. (1993) 'The Ruble Area: A Breaking of Old Ties', *Finance and Development* (June).

SSB (State Statistics Bureau) (1989) *Fengjin De Sishi Nian: 1949–89* (Forty Years' Progress: 1949–89) (Beijing: China Statistics Press).

Stalin, J. V. (1930) *Pravda* 2 March in J. V. Stalin *Problems of Leninism* (Moscow: FLPH, 1947).

State Statistical Office of the MPR (1991) *National Economy of the MPR for 70 Years, 1921–1991: Anniversary Statistical Yearbook* (Ulaan Baatar: SSOMPR).

Stiglitz, J. E. (1986) 'The New Development Economics', *World Development*, 14(2).

Stiglitz, J. E. (1989) *The Economic Role of the State* (Oxford: Blackwell).

Stoneman, C. (1990) 'Policy Reform or Industrialisation? The Choice in Zimbabwe', paper presented to the Conference on the Impact of Policy Reform on Trade and Industry Performance in Developing Countries, University of Bradford (21–22 June).

Swain, N. (1987) *Collectives that Work?* (Cambridge: Cambridge University Press).

Taylor, L. (1987) *Varieties of Stabilization Experience,* (Oxford: Clarendon Press).

Thanh-Dam, T. (1990) 'Human Resources, Training and Education: A Report on Quang Ninh Province' (The Hague: Institute of Social Studies).

The Economist (1991) Issue of June and Special Survey of 16 November.

The Far Eastern Economic Review (1991) Issues of 8 August, 22 August and 10 October.

The Southern African Economist (1990a) 'Zimbabwe's Up and Down Affair', *The Southern African Economist* (April/May).

The Southern African Economist (1990b) 'Looking for the Right Price', *The Southern African Economist* (June/July).

The Southern African Economist (1990c) 'Plunging Slowly', *The Southern African Economist* (August/September).

Thoburn, J., Leung, H., Chau, E. and Tang, S. (1990a), 'Foreign Investment and Economic Liberalisation in China', *Discussion Paper*, 9104, Economics Research Centre, University of East Anglia.

Thoburn, J., Leung, H. M., Chau, E. and Tang, S. H. (1990c) *Foreign Direct Investment in China under the Open Policy. The Experience of Hong Kong Companies* (Aldershot: Gower/Avebury).

Thoburn, J., Leung, H., Chau, E. and Tang, S. (1990b) 'Investment in China by Hong Kong Companies', *Institute of Development Studies Bulletin*, 22 (2).

Thomas, C. (1974) *Dependence and Transformation* (New York: Monthly Review).

Tomlinson, J. (1990) *Hayek and the Market* (London: Pluto).

Toye, J. (1990) 'Ghana's Economic Reforms 1983–7: Origins, Achievements and Limitations', in J. Pickett and H. Singer (eds),

UN (1991) *The World's Women*, 1970–1900, Social Statistics and Indicators, Series K. 8 (New York : UN).

UNDP (1990) *Human Development Report 1990* (Oxford: Oxford University Press).

UNDP (1992) *Human Development Report 1992* (Oxford: Oxford University Press).

UNECE (United Nations Economic Commission for Europe) (1992) *Economic Survey of Europe 1991–2* (New York: United Nations).

UNIDO (United Nations Industrial Development Organisation) (1987) *Industrial Situation in Mozambique* (Maputo: UN).

Utting, P. (1992) *Economic Reform and Third World Socialism: A Political Economy of Food Policy in Post-Revolutionary Societies* (London: Macmillan).

Vickers, J. and Yarrow, G. (1988) *Privatization: An Economic Analysis* (Cambridge, MA: MIT Press).

Vogel, E. F. (1989) *One Step Ahead in China, Guangdong under Reform* (Cambridge, MA: Harvard University Press).

Wang Dacheng (1985) 'Notes from the Editor: Coastal Open Economic Areas', *Beijing Review* (English edition), (April).

Weiner, C. (1990) 'Price Reform Stalled', *Journal of Asian Economics* (Fall).

Weiss, J. (1990) *Industry in Developing Countries* (London: Routledge).

Weiss, J. (1992) 'Industrial Policy Reform in Mozambique in the 1980s', in R. Adhikari, C. Kirkpatrick and J. Weiss (eds), *Industrial and Trade Policy Reform in Developing Countries* (Manchester: Manchester University Press).

WERI (World Economy Research Institute) (1991) *Poland: International Economic Report 1990/91* (Warsaw: Warsaw School of Economics).

White, G. (1984) 'Developmental States and Socialist Industrialization in the Third World', *Journal of Development Studies*, 21 (1).

White, G. (1991) 'Democracy and Economic Reform in China', IDS *Discussion Paper*, 286, Institute of Development Studies, University of Sussex.

Winiecki, J. (1990) 'Post-Soviet-type Economies in Transition: What Have We Learned from the Polish Transition Problem in its First Year?', *Weltwirtschaftliches Archiv*, 126 (4), pp. 765–90.

World Bank (1985) *China: Long Term Development Issues and Options, Annex 5: China: Economic Structure in International Perspective* (Washington, DC: World Bank).

World Bank (1988a) *Adjustment Lending, An Evaluation of Ten Years of Experience* (Washington, DC: IBRD).

World Bank (1988b) *Lao People's Democratic Republic, Country Economic Memorandum*, Country Operations Division (21 September) (Washington, DC: World Bank).

World Bank (1990a) China Country Study, *Between Plan and Market* (Washington, DC: World Bank).

World Bank (1990b) *Lao People's Democratic Republic: Issues in Public Economics*, Country Operations Division, Asia Region (10 August) (Washington, DC: World Bank).

World Bank (1990c) *Myanmar: Recent Economic Developments* (Washington, DC: World Bank).

World Bank (1990d) *World Development Report 1990* (Washington, DC: World Bank).

World Bank (1990e) *Adjustment Lending Policies for Sustainable Growth* (Washington, DC: IBRD).

World Bank (1990f) *World Development Report 1990* (New York: Oxford University Press).

World Bank (1990g) *Trends in Developing Economies 1990* (New York: Oxford University Press).

World Bank (1991a) *Mongolia: Country Economic Memorandum: Towards a Market Economy*, Report 10108–MON (Washington, DC: World Bank).

World Bank (1991b) *Trends in Developing Economies 1991* (New York: Oxford University Press).

World Bank, (1993) *Global Economic Prospects and the Developing Countries* (Washington, DC: World Bank).

World Development (1989a) Special Issue: Privatization, 17 (5) (May).

World Development (1989b) Special Issue: The Role of Institutions in Economic Development, 19 (9) (September).

World Development (1991) Special Issue: Adjustment with Growth and Equity, 19 (11) (November).

Wuyts, M., Mackintosh, M. and Hewitt, T. (eds) (1992) *Development Policy and Public Action* (Oxford: Oxford University Press).

Xiang Kongyan and Yu Zhiqing (1988) *Waixiang Xing Jingji Fanggui Wenjian Huipian: 1979–88* (Collected Laws and Documents on the Outward-looking Economy: 1979–88) (Hangzhou: Zhejian Provincial Library), p. 4. (Originally printed in *Guowuyuan Gongbao* (Communique of the State Council), 10 (1980).)

Yu Zhiqing and Xiang Kongyan (eds) (1985) *Jingji Tequ Yu Kaifang Yanjiu Gangkou Chengshi Zhiliao Xuanbian* (Selected Materials on Special Economic Zones and Open Coastal Port Cities) (Hangzhou: Zhejiang Provincial Library) (Originally published in Shijie Jingii (World Economy) (1984).)

Zasloff, J. J. and Unger, L. U. (eds) (1991) *Laos: Beyond the Revolution* (London: Macmillan).

Zimbalist, A. and Eckstein, S. (1987) 'Patterns of Cuban Development: The First Twenty Five Years', *World Development*, 5(1).

Zucker, L. (1986), 'Production of Trust: Institutional Sources of Economic Structure, 1840–1920', *Research in Organizational Behaviour*, 8, pp. 53–111.

Zysman, J. (1983) *Governments, Markets and Growth: Financial Systems and the Politics of Industrial Change* (Ithaca: Cornell University Press).

Index

270